The Library's Role in Supporting Financial Literacy for Patrons

The Library's Role in Supporting Financial Literacy for Patrons

Edited by Carol Smallwood

ROWMAN & LITTLEFIELD
Lanham • Boulder • New York • London

Published by Rowman & Littlefield
A wholly owned subsidiary of The Rowman & Littlefield Publishing Group, Inc.
4501 Forbes Boulevard, Suite 200, Lanham, Maryland 20706
www.rowman.com

Unit A, Whitacre Mews, 26-34 Stannary Street, London SE11 4AB

British Library Cataloguing in Publication Information Available

Library of Congress Cataloging-in-Publication Data Available

ISBN 978-1-4422-6591-2 (cloth : alk. paper)
ISBN 978-1-4422-6592-9 (paper : alk. paper)
ISBN 978-1-4422-6593-6 (ebook)

∞™ The paper used in this publication meets the minimum requirements of American National Standard for Information Sciences Permanence of Paper for Printed Library Materials, ANSI/NISO Z39.48-1992.

Printed in the United States of America

Contents

Foreword

Financial literacy is a broad, encompassing concept that includes—at a basic level—the critical, global need for mastering financial literacy competencies across all ages, all socioeconomic levels, and all disciplines. Included with this broader concept are a wide variety of terms or program branding phrases such as *financial wellness*, *smart investing*, *practical money skills*, and *money management*, to name just a few used to attract and convince people to look closely at their choices for earning, spending, saving, and investing dollars. These broad areas also include identifying opportunities as well as challenges that span from the basics of interest rates to recognizing and avoiding financial scams.

Delivering this content worldwide is not new and includes everything from children's television skits with beloved characters making both silly and wise financial choices to integrated curriculums with lessons and assignments in courses in all levels of education, individual courses in P–16 education, programs of study in higher education, as well as lifelong learning initiatives outside the structured educational arena but embedded in service association initiatives, social programs, and the banking industry itself. And although some may think that the myriad advertisers designing content to take people's money are unchallenged in delivering messages to consumers, there may be just as many entities delivering messages for how to spend, how to spend wisely, and—more importantly for many—why and how to save money.

So why is it important for all types of libraries to take a role in this critical initiative?

Public librarians play a critical role in the education of the community and play a major role in gathering, highlighting, and designing their own programs or delivering others' programs on how financial literacy contributes to overall literacy levels of constituents and the community's sound financial structure. Obviously, public librarians benefit immensely from partnerships and collaborations with any entities, but they absolutely benefit in both altruistic and self-serving ways from partnerships with the community's financial entities.

School librarians seek to support teachers, curriculum, and instruction but also to play a major role in inculcating students with information literacy as well as critical thinking across disciplines, which includes critical initiatives for understanding not only all areas of mathematical study but the application of mathematical study—such as calculus and algebra—to financial literacy. School librarians also play a major role in delivering messages throughout their programs on sound financial practices, which can include having story times on allowance and buying toys or purchasing and marketing materials on saving for a car or college.

Whether special libraries are supporting businesses such as lay firms, general businesses, banks, or specialized academic or public environments, the use of "special" implies a process of managing and delivering in-depth content on financial literacy as well as content on the application of information for personal needs or client information and needs.

Academic libraries—although broadly committed to and focused on the broadest definition of information literacy (IL)—include broad and multiple levels of literacy instruction, such as financial literacy through IL examples and exercises centering on financial issues and content as well as through partnerships with classroom faculty teaching financial literacy curriculum, designing pathways to financial literacy web content, and ongoing collection management issues on financial matters.

So why this book? It provides current content, a breadth of information, and not only a breadth of ideas but—when possible—specific ideas for making these important programs work. What do I like the most?

- Content with extensive area and departmental and discipline-specific financial literacy instruction and outreach ideas, instructional design suggestions, and inclusion and assessment of specific curriculum available in higher education today, along with good bibliographies that include a variety of higher education library programs and services
- Content with the uncomfortable but necessary focus on educating to create awareness of financial scams as well as avoiding and recovering from scams
- Content with extensive ideas on sharing information to assist specific and in many cases vulnerable target audiences such as children, teens, single parents, and seniors
- Content with advice for educating library employees on critical financial management issues

- Content with extensive resources for not only adding to collections but assisting in program planning
- Specific case method content to add in design and delivery of exemplary programs

And if you don't read anything else or *do* read but don't have time to implement or integrate the ideas, don't miss chapter 20, "Quick Tip Guides for the Reference Desk," by Jennifer Wright Joe. This unique look at our roles and responsibilities (as well as tips!) for delivering financial information should be required reading for every practicing reference librarian and library staff member in all types and sizes of libraries as well as for all those in library education in general as well as specific reference classes.

Finally, while there are many critics of the need for or success of financial literacy programs, one need only review a financial wellness quiz to realize the importance of the movement. And if you want to be personally humbled, *take* a financial wellness quiz. Note, I am *not* talking about mathematics knowledge quizzes or financial *management* quizzes, but rather a financial wellness or literacy quiz. Typically, it's fewer than ten questions designed to ascertain your knowledge about financial matters, matters we *should* be knowledgeable about, and your score (I'm not sharing mine) might amaze you.

Julie Todaro, PhD
Dean of Library Services, Austin Community College
2016–2017 President-Elect, American Library Association

Preface

The Library's Role in Supporting Financial Literacy for Patrons is an anthology of articles by practicing public, academic, school, and special librarians as well as LIS faculty in the United States that fills a gap in the literature on patron financial literacy. Financial literacy as a topic suitable for emphasis in libraries has always been an attractive idea, but turmoil in our economy has transformed the concept into a crucial need among library patrons of all types.

The thirty-one chapters are between three and four thousand words, and conciseness, sidebars, bullets, and headers make them easy to use. The contributors were selected for their creative potential in each topic—familiarity with various types of libraries, a command of financial literacy, and ability to communicate. The collection has three parts:

- Part 1 gives an overview of financial literacy: what it means, what needs exist among library patrons, and what approaches have been tried to date.
- Part 2 deals with resources available in libraries or which should be made available—such as collections, skill sets for librarians, and program opportunities.
- Part 3 provides case studies that demonstrate successes and best practices.

I'd like to thank Julie Todaro, the American Library Association president-elect, for writing the foreword, the librarians listed in the acknowledgments for writing blurbs, and Martin Dillon at Rowman & Littlefield for his editorial help.

Acknowledgments

Many thanks to the following people:

- Patti Gibbons, head of collection management, University of Chicago Library
- Andre Powe, coordinator of hospital storytelling, Brooklyn Public Library
- Carla Lehn, library programs consultant, California State Library
- Theresa McDevitt, government documents/outreach librarian, Indiana University of Pennsylvania Libraries
- Chelsie Harris, community relations manager, San Diego County Library
- Jane Gov, youth services librarian, Pasadena Public Library, Central Library
- Jeannine Berroteran, MLS, freelance writer and researcher
- Lindsey Smith, outreach services/volunteer coordinator, Worthington Libraries, Worthington, Ohio

Part One

Overview of Financial Literacy

Chapter One

Academic Libraries and Financial Literacy Programs

Lauren Reiter

Financial literacy matters at every age, as each life stage brings new money management challenges. For college students, these new challenges may include living independently on limited means, applying for and managing a credit card, borrowing loans for education, buying a first car, selecting a meal plan or buying groceries, negotiating a salary, or starting to save for the future. Overall, students are faced with the problem of budgeting the time and money needed for balancing school, work, extracurricular activities, and personal life. Even with financial experience and education, this can be a difficult problem to navigate, so it is understandable that many college students encountering these issues for the first time will struggle. This is especially true of today's college students, who confront typical individual money management challenges amid greater financial challenges at the state, national, and global levels. These students face skyrocketing college costs and rising student loan debt, as well as an uncertain future for their job and retirement prospects.

On campuses nationwide, these issues have ignited conversations among students, staff, faculty, and administration and spurred a search for solutions. Among other approaches, colleges and universities are looking to financial literacy as a means to alleviate the economic and financial challenges that students face. A focus on financial literacy for college students can raise awareness of major economic issues and improve student confidence and competence in managing their own personal financial decisions. Academic libraries are hubs for reliable information and student learning, and are well positioned to offer support for campus financial literacy initiatives. A review of the ways academic libraries are already involved in financial literacy and lessons from a case example at Penn State University Libraries will help a library at any college or university get started with supporting the financial literacy of college students through programming and events.

ACADEMIC LIBRARIES AND FINANCIAL LITERACY: THE WHO, WHAT, WHERE, AND WHY

Academic libraries can and do offer many types of support for campus financial literacy efforts. Some examples of academic library involvement in financial literacy include the following:

- Hosting programming and events
- Adding personal finance resources to the library collection
- Creating resource guides
- Reviewing financial information sources
- Teaching credit and noncredit personal finance courses
- Integrating financial literacy into information literacy instruction
- Collaborating with established financial literacy on campus

These types of support are in line with assignments that are typical for public services librarians in an academic setting, such as instruction, collection development, reference services, and outreach.

While academic libraries have been quietly supporting the financial literacy of college students through such instruction, collection development, reference services, and outreach activities for longer than anyone has on record, they have been taking on an increasingly active role in financial literacy and raising public awareness of their efforts in recent years. This development was spurred by the announcement of financial literacy as the presidential focus of the Association of College & Research Libraries (ACRL) division of the American Library Association (ALA) in 2013 (Dawes 2013). The presidential focus and its accompanying column series, "Libraries and Financial Literacy Education," in *College & Research Libraries News* shed light on numerous examples of academic libraries and their involvement in financial literacy, including a community college library's sessions on scholarships, financial strategies, and budgeting techniques as part of course-related instruction and one-shot workshops (Roggenkamp 2014) and a four-year university library's financial literacy partnerships with their first-year experience program, a career center, and a campus financial literacy program (Jagman et al. 2014). Other academic libraries have offered one-shot programs and program series as part of Money Smart Week @ Your Library, an initiative of ALA and the Federal Reserve Bank of Chicago. A record number of academic libraries participated in Money Smart Week @ Your Library in

2014 (Dawes 2014). Academic libraries also participate in campus financial literacy by creating online resource guides (Michigan State University 2015; Penn State University Libraries 2015; University of Denver 2015; University of Houston Downtown 2014; University of Illinois at Urbana-Champaign 2014; University of Maryland 2014; and Youngstown State University 2015) and partnering to create peer-to-peer financial education programs housed in library space (Reiter 2015).

ACADEMIC LIBRARIES AND FINANCIAL LITERACY: THE HOW

If an academic library has an interest in financial literacy and an individual or group willing to coordinate efforts, hosting a personal finance presentation is an excellent, low-stakes first step toward building an overall program and directly contributing to the financial literacy of students on campus. At Penn State University Libraries, MoneyCounts: A Financial Literacy Series began as a one-shot presentation about budgeting by the Commission for Adult Learners' financial literacy manager. After attendance at this initial presentation nearly breached fire code room capacity, Penn State University Libraries and the Commission for Adult Learners partnered for an ongoing relationship and officially established a monthly series held in the library.

Since April 2013, Penn State University Libraries has hosted twenty monthly workshops as part of MoneyCounts: A Financial Literacy Series, in addition to hosting other special, one-time-only financial literacy events. Over this time period, the academic library and its partner continually adjusted different aspects of the programs to address challenges, including accessibility for off-campus students, privacy, lackluster engagement, and low attendance. Each MoneyCounts workshop was an opportunity for experimental testing of new presenters, topics, locations, times, delivery, and marketing strategies, leading to discoveries that suggest the most and least effective approaches to financial literacy programming and events in the academic library. While there is no formula that results in consistently perfect programming, there are four key elements that contribute to a financial literacy learning experience that college students will seek out again and again:

- Trustworthy experts
- Careful topic selection
- Comfortable atmosphere
- Shameless marketing

Trustworthy Experts

A successful financial literacy program depends on a knowledgeable presenter who can speak candidly and accurately about money management. Librarians offer a great deal of expertise in a wide variety of areas; however, not all libraries have individuals on staff who feel qualified to instruct on financial literacy and personal finance topics. Identifying subject matter experts in-house or elsewhere is crucial to providing program attendees with accurate and applicable personal finance information.

In an academic setting, libraries need not look far for trustworthy financial educators. Financial literacy experts may potentially be found in a variety of college and university offices and units, including the following:

- Bursar's office
- Career services
- Financial aid
- Financial literacy or education
- First-year experience
- Student affairs
- Student services
- Student success
- Student wellness

Academic departments may also include faculty that already teach for-credit personal finance courses or that teach related content. The university's schedule of courses is a great tool for identifying the appropriate academic areas. While business schools and departments are likely places to find financial experts, it is useful to look beyond the usual suspects since personal finance and money management can cross many disciplines, including these:

- Accounting
- Agricultural economics
- Economics
- Education
- Family and consumer sciences
- Finance
- Human development
- Insurance
- Mathematics
- Personal financial planning

In the case of MoneyCounts, the primary presenter is the financial literacy manager, who is employed under the university's Commission for Adult

Learners, which focuses on the adult student population. The financial literacy manager has a passion for sharing financial education with the entire student body and views the library as ideally positioned to help with this goal. While serving as the face of MoneyCounts and conducting numerous other financial literacy efforts and initiatives on campus, the financial literacy manager is not the only financial literacy expert who participates in the program, which allows the series to avoid repetition and incorporate new ideas. A professor of consumer issues has been a ready collaborator and presenter at a number of programs as part of MoneyCounts and other financial literacy events at the library. This professor teaches a class on consumer and financial skills as part of the Department of Agricultural Economics, Sociology, and Education. Other MoneyCounts presenters have been drawn from the office of financial aid as well as the local credit union.

Banks, credit unions, certified public accountants, certified financial planners, and other financial professionals are eager to work with colleges and universities. Academic libraries will find knowledgeable partners in these communities but need to build the relationships with care. As trusted providers of information and education, libraries put their reputations at stake by hosting programs, making it essential to ensure that presenters have shared values and respect for providing accurate and impartial information. For the MoneyCounts programs that included outside presenters, this understanding was achieved by open conversations between the library and the potential partner about expectations and the need for educational, noncommercial content. For added assurance, the library can request a presenter's slides in advance to review for any indication of commercial, rather than educational, intent.

Careful Topic Selection

Selecting a topic for a financial literacy presentation can be daunting given the wide range of topics that could be covered, such as budgeting, credit cards, student loans, car loans, paying rent or a mortgage, retirement, salary negotiation, health insurance, and financial clutter and organization. Picking the topic of most relevance and appeal to the audience of college students makes selection all the more challenging. In the history of the MoneyCounts program, the most popular topics, based on in-person attendance and online views, were credit cards, getting student loans, repaying student loans, budgeting, and mortgages. MoneyCounts programs mainly attract undergraduate students, but certain programs, particularly those on student loans, budgeting, and mortgages, appeal to a graduate student audience. Once an audience is identified, different strategies can be used to select a topic, including the following:

- Asking the expert
- Gathering feedback via consultations and surveys
- Coordinating with calendar events

Letting the presenter take the lead on topic selection has the most potential as a successful strategy if the presenter has experience teaching college students about personal finance. For example, the aforementioned professor of consumer issues showed how well she knew her audience when she did a financial literacy presentation called "10 Things College Students Should Know about Money." The presentation content and style resonated with students as she counted down ten straightforward rules of thumb for money management. Similarly, a presenter from the local credit union had experience talking with college students about identity theft. During her MoneyCounts presentation, she used stories of hacked Facebook friends and references to the popular movie *Identity Theft* to connect with the audience and deliver key points about protecting one's identity.

Other strategies for topic selection include consulting with library student workers and deploying surveys of the student population. For MoneyCounts, the librarian gathered feedback from student interns on topic ideas and used an informal survey to reveal unexpected student interests on topics such as mortgages. A MoneyCounts session on mortgages was prepared in response to the survey results. Recognizing that the topic appealed more to graduate and adult students rather than traditional undergraduates, aged eighteen to twenty-four, the workshop was deliberately scheduled for late May, a quiet time on campus when the majority of undergraduates are on break and the session's target population would potentially have more availability. This session, "Mortgages: The Financial Process of Owning a House," remains the third most attended workshop.

Well-timed topics contribute to the success of a program. Even calendar events can be used to guide topic selection for financial literacy programs. For example, people receive W-2s and other tax documents in January, making January through April a prime time to hold a financial literacy session about taxes. Students who attended the MoneyCounts workshop "Tax and Wage Fundamentals" in January came with specific questions and needs to be addressed and left better prepared for the tax task at hand.

Comfortable Atmosphere

Money is something that people encounter every day, but very few people feel comfortable talking about it. This is especially true of students choosing to attend a financial education session. Their reasons for attending may include an embarrassing money mistake or total inexperience with personal finance. The vulnerabilities students carry into the session can lead to problems ranging from reticence to defensiveness if they are not considered and comforted with care. Developing a comfortable workshop setting is the first step to setting the right tone.

Early MoneyCounts programs were held in a large auditorium setting with over one hundred seats. The formal atmosphere was intended to underscore the incredible importance of financial education for college students. Additionally, the auditorium was equipped with recording equipment that made it possible to broadcast sessions live and record them for later viewing. While this was an essential means of connecting with remote users, the in-person audience was in a colder, formal setting that did not invite conversation and connection. Once a library of online content was developed, the program moved to a new location, a smaller room with tables and chairs that allowed for flexibility in arrangement of the room. With this new location and setup, the amount of discussion shifted dramatically. Audience members appeared more relaxed and comfortable responding to presenters and to each other. One session ran a half hour over time because of additional questions and conversations.

While a comfortable space is important, the role of the presenter in creating the right atmosphere cannot be ignored. Because of the sensitivity of the subject matter, a presenter who can project warmth, understanding, and openness is desirable. The MoneyCounts programs are fortunate to have the financial literacy manager involved in some way at each session, even when she is not the primary presenter. This individual is a highly competent and confident expert but is willing to admit money mistakes made and learned from, making jokes at her own expense but never at the expense of her audience. The list of characteristics that can make for a great financial literacy presenter is long and all individuals will have their own style, so the most important takeaway is to ensure that the presenter recognizes how *personal* personal finance can be and is willing to help develop a comfortable atmosphere for student learning.

Shameless Marketing

If you have a financial literacy expert present on a carefully selected topic in a comfortable atmosphere but there is no one there to hear it, does it make a sound? Financial literacy education is a difficult topic to market to college students, since it is far from the most attractive of the many options students have for spending their time. Marketing is key to getting students to attend financial literacy programs, and shameless approaches work best. From least to most shameless, here are a few ideas:

- Catching their eye
- Applying peer pressure

- Offering incentives

There are many things competing for students' attention, from classwork to independent research to involvement in student organizations to sporting events to parties to job searches. Eye-catching advertising is one way to help financial literacy stand out. The MoneyCounts program has a piggy bank mascot that appears on every poster, altered to reflect the month's topic. The mascot is used consistently to promote the programs, so students associate this friendly image with these opportunities to improve their financial literacy.

Peer pressure is another strategy to encourage students to attend financial literacy programs. Peers are students' source for a variety of information, from how to get started on a class project to what is going on during the weekend. Peers can also be a source for information about financial literacy and upcoming programs. Academic libraries can take advantage of the peer-to-peer effect by inviting student workers in the library to attend their financial literacy program and bring friends, making the experience both social and educational. Because the Penn State University Libraries house the Student Financial Education Center, a peer-to-peer financial education program, it is in a unique position to have peer educators attend the MoneyCounts programs and invite friends. All program attendees are also invited to bring friends the next month, creating a snowball effect with students sharing and spreading financial literacy among themselves.

The most shameless but effective financial literacy event marketing tactic of all is offering incentives to attend. These incentives can include food or giveaways, or extra credit for classes through partnerships with teaching faculty. For MoneyCounts, providing food and refreshments proved to be an easy and effective way to increase attendance, which doubled after the series began offering pizza at events. While some students may come just for the food and tune out the financial education, a majority enjoy a slice of pizza while participating in the experience. They listen to the talk, ask thoughtful questions, and return the next month to discuss a new financial literacy topic.

CONCLUSION

The bare minimum an academic library needs to get involved in campus financial literacy via programming or events is a presenter, a topic to talk about, a location, and marketing to build an audience. While these four elements will result in some kind of a program, the experiences of the MoneyCounts series indicate that finding an expert presenter, carefully selecting a topic, developing a comfortable atmosphere, and marketing shamelessly will result in a more successful program.

REFERENCES

Dawes, Trevor A. 2013. "Libraries, ACRL and Financial Literacy: Helping Students Make Sound Decisions." *College & Research Libraries News* 74 (9): 466–67.

———. 2014. "Academic Libraries' Impact on Financial Education: A Year of Programs and Projects." *College & Research Libraries News* 75 (6): 326–27.

Jagman, Heather, Krystal Lewis, Brent Nunn, and Scott Walter. 2014. "Financial Literacy across the Curriculum (and Beyond)." *College & Research Libraries News* 75 (5): 254–57.

Michigan State University. 2015. "Financial Literacy for College Students: MSU Financial Literacy Resources." http://libguides.lib.msu.edu/financialliteracy.

Penn State University Libraries. 2015. "Financial Literacy." http://psu.libguides.com/financial-literacy.

Reiter, Lauren. 2015. "Financial Literacy and the Academic Library: Exploring the Peer-to-Peer Approach." *Journal of Business and Finance Librarianship* (forthcoming).

Roggenkamp, John. 2014. "Financial Literacy and Community Colleges." *College & Research Libraries News* 75 (3): 142–43.

University of Denver. 2015. "Financial Literacy/Financial Education." http://libguides.du.edu/financial-literacy.

University of Houston Downtown. 2014. "Financial Literacy." http://library.uhd.edu/financial-literacy.

University of Illinois at Urbana-Champaign. 2014. "Financial Literacy." http://uiuc.libguides.com/financialliteracy.

University of Maryland. 2014. "Financial Literacy." http://lib.guides.umd.edu/financialliteracy.

Youngstown State University. 2015. "Financial Literacy Library Guide." http://maag.guides.ysu.edu/financialliteracy.

Chapter Two

Developing Services Based on Community Needs

Lisa Fraser

Today's libraries offer services and programs on financial and employment topics, but how do you know if you are providing the right mix? One way is to research the needs in your community before you start planning these services. King County Library System (KCLS) in the state of Washington started doing community discovery as part of a new service planning process. As a result, new services more closely meet the needs of local residents, and staff are more informed about and connected with residents and organizations in their communities. In this chapter we will explore some of the techniques that were used for gathering information about the community and about resources supporting community discovery. Exploring your community brings many benefits:

- Learning about residents who do not use the library
- Learning about other organizations providing services in your area
- Improving your ability to connect people to needed services
- Improving connections between service providers
- Presenting the library as an interested partner in providing services
- Identifying potential partnership opportunities

Community exploration need not consume vast resources; much can be done with only staff time and the same library information resources offered to the public. Deciding which staff should be involved will depend on the needs and organizational structure of the library. At KCLS, most of the community exploration work was done by librarians, with managers coordinating their activities and compiling the resulting information.

Once started, community exploration is likely to be an ongoing process. Having more information leads to more questions as often as it leads to answers. One key to success is to go into the process with an open mind as we each have a mental image of our community that is based on our own interactions and experiences. The longer we have lived and worked in a location, the more difficult it can be to set this mental picture aside; however, exploring your community will be most valuable if you are able to look at it as though you were a newcomer arriving for the first time.

DEFINING "COMMUNITY"

Public libraries strive to be inclusive and open to all, but most have an official service area or population that is defined by their governing documents. The service area can encompass a city, a county, a combination of areas, or a separately defined district. The residents in the service area usually provide the library's funding through some sort of taxing structure, either directly or indirectly. The population living in this service area is the focus of your community exploration.

Although the goal of this research is to learn about the community outside the library's walls, staff should be prepared to answer questions about the library. These may not be limited to services, collections, and programs. It is important that all staff understand the library's structure, mission, and funding stream, but it is essential that those involved in the community exploration process understand it well enough to explain it clearly to others.

Once the geography of the community has been defined, it is time to get started. There are two main categories of work: collecting data and talking to people. In the KCLS model, local managers developed their own plans for dividing up the tasks. Some matched the librarians with tasks depending on their skills and interests, so that those with an affinity for data did most of the research and those who preferred talking to people took on the more social tasks. Other managers required everyone to do a bit of each and paired librarians so that they had complementary skills. Both strategies resulted in high-quality end products.

At KCLS, we had a history of producing community profiles that were edited, branded, and published for public use. It was decided that the documentation of the community exploration would not be made public, so that staff could focus on the information rather than the format. This generally worked well, although some individuals who were contacted as part of the process expressed interest in knowing what was discovered. These requests were handled on a case-by-case basis.

EXPLORING DEMOGRAPHICS

One of the most fundamental sets of data for library planning is demographic information about the service area population. Defined by Oxford Dictionaries as "statistical data relating to the population and particular groups within it" (http://www.oxforddictionaries.com/us/definition/american_english/demographics), demographics commonly available include age, gender, race, ethnicity, income, educational attainment, citizenship, and housing status. A quick, free source for demographic information is American Factfinder (http://factfinder.census.gov), one of the information portals of the United States Bureau of the Census. Demographic information provides a broad, big-picture view of the community.

Current demographics are useful, but it is also important to understand how the population in the area has changed and will continue to change over time. These shifts usually happen over a matter of years, so start by comparing the changes between the 2000 and 2010 U.S. Census figures. Note whether any groups are on the rise or decline, and consider what factors may be impacting that change. It can be helpful to keep a list of questions that remain unanswered so that they can be addressed through other activities.

UNDERSTANDING STATISTICS

The volume of data available can be overwhelming, especially to those who are new to the topic. Disconnected statistics and vague descriptions will make it difficult to understand the story that the numbers show. These tips can help:

- Statistics don't have to be disconnected numbers. They tell a story about people. Try to figure out what the story is.
- Find a free online tutorial or course in understanding statistics. If you don't believe you are a "numbers person," take the course with someone who is.
- You don't have to know how to calculate the figures unless you intend to do your own original research. Focus on learning what you need in order to understand the numbers that you have.
- There are three different types of averages, each with its own pros and cons. Make sure that you understand the difference between the mean, median, and mode.
- Try to understand the background behind each statistic. Always find out who collected the data and why they wanted it.
- Examine the relationships expressed in the statistic. What units are being described? How do they fit together?

- Draw a picture.
- Sometimes looking at examples of badly described statistics or irrelevant correlations can make the higher-quality information stand out.

USING CENSUS GEOGRAPHY

Even if your library's service area is a city or county boundary, it can be helpful to look at data that is available for other geographic units. Many studies report data by one of three geographic units used by the U.S. Census Bureau to compile the information.

A *census tract* is "a small, relatively permanent statistical subdivision of a county delineated by a local committee of census data users for the purpose of presenting data. Census tracts nest within counties, and their boundaries normally follow visible features, but may follow legal geography boundaries and other nonvisible features in some instances. Census tracts ideally contain about 4,000 people and 1,600 housing units."

A census block is "a statistical area bounded by visible features, such as streets, roads, streams, and railroad tracks, and by nonvisible boundaries, such as selected property lines and city, township, school districts, and county boundaries. A block is the smallest geographic unit for which the Census Bureau tabulates decennial census data."

In between the census block and census tract is the census block group. This unit typically has about 1,500 people and is often the smallest unit at which data is reported due to the risk of personal identification at the census block level.

MARKET SEGMENTATION

Demographics provide one picture of your community; market segmentation lets you look at the population in a different way. Based on the concept that people who share specific characteristics will make similar choices, especially in purchasing goods and services, market segmentation assigns a profile to each household that predicts the behavior of its members. There are many companies that develop and provide market segmentation services and information, and each has its own system and underlying formulas. They are usually based on a combination of demographic and market research data, with characteristics like the stage of life of the head of household or the level of urbanization in the area being the basis for broad categories. A typical market segmentation product contains between sixty and eighty different segments that are developed for the United States as a whole, and most communities will be represented by some subset of those. While demographics seem clear-cut and trustworthy, market segmentation gives some library staff pause. Although it is a profile that is developed around aggregated data, the fact that it is applied at the household level brings up questions of privacy that are part of core library values. Although libraries are late to the game, companies are increasingly providing analytics and market segmentation products specifically for the library market.

USING PEST ANALYSIS AS A COMMUNITY RESEARCH FRAMEWORK

Even though the mission orientation of libraries is different from most businesses, the tools used for business planning can still be useful in our environment. For example, many businesses use a format called a PEST analysis as the framework to study the environment outside their organization. The goal of this exercise is to take a fresh, big-picture look at the things that might impact the success of the organization's products, services, or initiatives. PEST analysis provides a research structure that can also help library staff learn about the community they serve. For the PEST analysis to be most valuable, it is important to set aside one's assumptions and beliefs about the community and examine it as a newcomer might. This approach brings a new perspective and reduces the likelihood of limiting oneself to information that supports existing beliefs. Don't limit the research to areas that are related to financial programs; you will learn more by taking a more open view. This approach focuses on four areas: the political, economic, social/cultural, and technological environments.

For libraries, research into the political environment includes identifying the governmental structure, important projects and events, elected officials and other key governmental leaders and staff, and major legal issues that affect the community. It will often be most useful to start by focusing on the local political environment. However, depending on the library's service area and funding structure, there may be impacts from the county, state, or even national arenas. Examples include changes in tax laws and the incorporation of new areas into cities.

The economic environment includes major industries and businesses, as well as information about the workforce. Economic data that can be helpful for libraries includes unemployment rates, the cost of living and housing prices, poverty levels and distribution, and eligibility for free/reduced-price lunches. Economic issues can be particularly relevant to the need for financial services at the library. Is a large employer hiring or laying off workers? What are the growing industries in your area?

Information on the social and cultural environment includes structures that support the social fabric of the community, such as schools, religious institutions, recreational groups, and the arts. School information at the state and school district levels sometimes includes information that is difficult to locate elsewhere, such as language spoken at home. Keep in mind that this will apply only to households with school-age children and may over- or underrepresent the proportions in the population as a whole.

Technology can include infrastructure, such as access to high-speed Internet service, as well as usage of devices or access to services and training. Of the four areas examined in the PEST analysis, this can be the most difficult in which to find authoritative data. If your library offers a demographics product that includes some consumer behavior statistics, it may provide data such as an estimate of the number of households with Internet access.

The PEST analysis often results in questions that can't be answered by statistics. There are several ways to flesh out the picture of your community.

WALK OR DRIVE AROUND

If you live in your library's service area, you probably travel by habitual routes and visit favorite locations frequently, while spending little time in other areas. You may be unfamiliar with some areas or unaware of changes that are taking place outside your usual haunts. Walking or driving around your service area can provide valuable insight into the activities in your community.

Putting yourself into the role of a newcomer to the area, look for evidence that supports or disproves the data that you have gathered. Are you seeing many young children in an area that had a large retirement-age population in the 2000 Census? Those retirees may have downsized, selling their homes to young families. Since demographic data can take years to shift, an area that looks different than the profile can point to a change underway.

If your service area is small and walkable, that is the ideal way to explore. You can explore on a human scale and pace, and may even have a chance to talk to people. More often, though, at least some of your exploration will need to be made by car due to distance or safety issues. Either way, these suggestions can help you get the most out of your trip.

- Go out in pairs. This is especially necessary if you go by car, so that one person can drive while the other takes notes. It also helps to have a second person on hand to give a different point of view or to act as a reference source.
- Plan your route in advance. Use a print or online map to figure out where you will go and how long it will take. If you have limited time to devote to this task, you will need to prioritize your travels.

- Consider your PEST analysis or other data. You may have developed questions based on your research, so take advantage of this potential opportunity to answer them.
- Take recording tools. Make sure you will be able to capture important information by taking photos, recording audio, and writing notes. Using a product such as Evernote can help pull these into one place.
- Carry business cards. If you meet someone with whom you would like to have a follow-up conversation, providing a business card can be helpful.
- Look for connections. Like the research activities mentioned earlier, walking or driving around your service area is a more successful learning experience if you approach it with new eyes. However, it is also an opportunity to note findings that connect to your planned or existing offerings. Did you see a potential partner organization? Note it so that you can follow up later.

SURVEY COMMUNITY MEMBERS

A survey can provide valuable information, if it is well designed and reaches the intended audience. A community-wide survey can be a significant undertaking, and many libraries will contract this work to a consultant if the resources are available. Surveying a specific focus population can be easier, and it can provide more detailed information about that group. Here are some points to consider:

- Keep the survey short.
- Take advantage of any library-affiliated individuals with expertise who can help you develop the survey, administer it, or compile the results.
- Online tools such as Survey Monkey make it easier to create online instruments.
- Limiting your survey to online tools risks missing sections of your population that have limited Internet access.

GATEKEEPERS AND COMMUNITY LEADERS

In most communities, there are people who have a finger on the pulse of one or more groups, and they can help library staff to understand the needs of members of those groups. This can be particularly helpful if there are language or cultural differences separating the library staff from the group. Unlike a survey, where you are contacting many individuals in order to develop a picture of the group, talking to one community leader can provide information that is based on their knowledge of many individuals. When choosing community leaders for interviews, look for people whom others will go to for information and who are trusted in their communities. They may not be in formal positions of leadership. Here are a few possible community leaders to interview:

- Social service providers
- Clergy and spiritual leaders
- Business leaders
- Parent group leaders and members, such as homeschool groups or a PTA
- Groups indicated from your research or drive/walk around

Yolanda J. Cuesta, intercultural consultant to libraries, provides a guide for intercultural community leader interviews on her website, listed in the "Resources" section. It was developed for the Spanish-speaking community, but the framework can be adapted for other groups.

Because the purpose of community leader interviews is to learn about the group's needs, it is important that the conversation not be limited by either party to topics that are believed to be library related. Many people are unclear about the offerings of libraries today, so explain that you would like to hear about the important issues of the group regardless of whether they think the library would be interested. It may not be appropriate or possible for the library to address all of the needs, but we don't know until we learn about them. Tips for a successful interview:

- Ask open-ended questions.
- Avoid talking about the library or framing questions in terms of library services.
- Ask if you can record the interview, as it is hard to follow all of the details while taking notes.
- Ask for the names of others you should talk to.
- Arrange for an interpreter if needed.
- Meet on the community leader's home turf whenever possible.

BRINGING THE INFORMATION TOGETHER

At KCLS, we started with the concept of a "big, messy binder" that would hold all of the accumulated information. In reality, the information is stored on our intranet. As part of an annual planning process, a short summary of key points is prepared in early fall. This "fact sheet" includes a section on internal library issues that are impacting service planning, as well as key findings from the community exploration that support the goals for the coming year. The fact sheet serves as a tool for planning library services. Some questions that can be helpful when considering financial programming and services are the following:

- Did the community exploration uncover a need for financial programming in my service area?
- What groups need financial programming/services, and what do they need?
- Are there other organizations that are providing the programming/services? Do they fully meet the need?
- Is there a role for the library in meeting this need? What does that role look like? Does this idea align with the mission and values of the library?

The first community exploration process can require an investment of time, but the ongoing maintenance requires fewer resources. Research can be updated annually, while surveys and community leader interviews can happen at any time during the year.

SUCCESS STORY

During a weekday drive around their library service area, librarians at the Algona-Pacific branch of the King County Library System noticed a surprising number of cars in driveways. After reviewing their demographic data, which indicated that the area likely had two-earner families, they looked for additional information. An interview with a staff member at the local WorkSource office revealed that a large number of people in the area had lost their jobs in the economic decline. Additional interviews with community leaders supported this finding and suggested some gaps that were a good fit for library services. The librarians were able to partner with local organizations to provide job-search resources and related programming in the region.

DEMOGRAPHICS AND MARKET SEGMENTATION RESOURCES

Many libraries offer subscription resources for their patrons. Subscription resources for demographics and other statistics vary in content and price. Free trials may be available. Well-known products include PolicyMap, SimplyMap, DemographicsNow, Social Explorer, Business Decision, and ReferenceUSA.

RESOURCES

American Factfinder. http://factfinder.census.gov.

Cuesta, Yolanda. "Community Discovery Handbook." Cuesta MultiCultural Consulting. http://www.yolandacuesta.com/resources.htm.

Exline, Eleta. "Good, Bad, or Biased? Using Best Practices to Improve the Quality of Your Survey Questions." *University Library Scholarship* Paper 63, April 11, 2013. http://scholars.unh.edu/library_pub/63.

"PEST Analysis: Identifying 'Big Picture' Opportunities and Threats." Mind Tools. http://www.mindtools.com/pages/article/newTMC_09.htm.

"Statistics Intro: Mean, Median, and Mode." Khan Academy. https://www.khanacademy.org/math/probability/descriptive-statistics/central_tendency/v/statistics-intro-mean-median-and-mode.

United States Census Bureau. http://www.census.gov/.

Unites States Bureau of Labor Statistics. http://www.bls.gov/.

Usable Stats. "Tools, Tutorials, and Templates." https://www.usablestats.com/index.php.

WebJunction. "Library Surveys for Success Webinar." http://learn.webjunction.org/.

Chapter Three

Financial Literacy in Libraries

Free and Dependable Resources for Patrons of All Backgrounds

Sonnet Ireland

Everyone knows the phrase "It takes money to make money," but the people who need the most help with financial literacy are often the people who don't have a lot of money to spare and turn to their local libraries. This chapter will guide you with key websites for patrons of all ages and backgrounds.

THE BASICS FOR CHILDREN

There are many sites that can help patrons of all ages get started on the road to financial literacy. For children, there are fun sites, such as the Kids.gov site Money for Kids or the U.S. Mint's site H.I.P. Pocket Change. Both offer games and videos to help children learn more about money and how to use it responsibly. Kids.gov also links to AdMongo.gov, a site dedicated to teaching kids about advertising, and offers Money for Teachers and Money for Parents to aid adults in teaching kids about money. Another site that introduces kids to financial literacy is Biz Kid$, connected to the PBS show of the same name. This site offers games, lesson plans, and activities. Parents or teachers can use the site (and the show) to teach kids a variety of financial skills, including marketing and starting a business. Finally, Money as You Grow is a site recommended by the President's Advisory Council on Financial Capability. It helps kids learn about money as they get older. The activities are divided into age groups: three to five years, six to ten years, eleven to thirteen years, fourteen to eighteen years, and eighteen years and older. This site is easy to use and offers great information and activities. It was selected by the American Library Association as one of its Great Websites for Kids.

THE BASICS FOR TEENS

Money as You Grow is also great for teens, but there are many other resources just for them. Even Kids.gov offers Money for Teens, for grades six to eight, which includes information on credit cards and saving. The National Endowment for Financial Education also offers the High School Financial Planning Program, which has resources and materials for teachers and community organizations that want to help students become financially literate. It's completely free and great for teens. Project C.H.A.N.G.E. is another site for teens. Created by the U.S. Securities and Exchange Commission, it offers information for teens about saving, spending, and creating choices and includes a game, an interactive quiz, and a savings calculator. It's a good way to teach teens about the choices they have to make between saving for something they really want (like a car or new phone) and spending money on something ephemeral (like an extra slice of pizza at the mall). The IRS also offers a site for teens called Understanding Taxes. This site has a student section and a teacher section. The student section includes activities, tutorials, and simulations, while the teacher section offers lesson plans, downloads, and educational standards. It even allows teachers to order free tax forms for classroom. MoneySKILL is another site for teachers and students. MoneySKILL is a free online financial literacy course created by the AFSA Education Foundation. This site allows teachers, homeschool parents, employers, members of the military, and nonprofit organizations to register for an account. Once the account is approved, the instructor creates logins and passwords for his or her students. Like Money as You Grow, this site can be used by middle schoolers, high schoolers, and even college students.

THE BASICS FOR ADULTS

Of course, children and adolescents aren't the only ones who need help with financial literacy. In 2012, over 1.5 million people filed for bankruptcy in the United States. This only reflects the number of people who realized they were in over their heads with debt. There are many more out there struggling with debt and other financial issues. In fact, in 2011, 69 percent of households had some kind of debt, and that debt averaged seventy thousand dollars per household (Vornovytskyy, Gottschalck, and Smith). That's why we shouldn't assume an adult does not need financial literacy help—even if the adult has been working and living independently for decades.

Luckily, the government has quite a few sites to help adults learn how to manage their money. MyMoney.gov is a great place to start. This site, created by the Federal Financial Literacy and Education Commission, offers information and resources on topics such as earning money, borrowing money, saving and investing money, spending money, and protecting money. It even offers guidance on life events, such as having a baby or facing a death in the family. The site also offers quizzes and tools, such as calculators and budget worksheets. MyCreditUnion.gov also offers financial literacy tools and resources, as well as information about whether or not joining a credit union is right for you. While USA.gov offers information on a variety of topics, it has a few pages on the site that can direct patrons to the information they need. The Unclaimed Money, Taxes, and Credit Reports site offers information on consumer protection and identity theft prevention, as well as information on how to find out if the government owes you money. The Benefits, Grants, and Loans site, on the other hand, offers information on how to apply for financial assistance. It even directs you to Benefits.gov, a site designed specifically to connect people with the right government benefit and assistance programs for their needs. Another site that might be popular with adults is SBA.gov. The U.S. Small Business Administration offers a wealth of information on how to start or manage your small business. With blogs that offer advice on everything from taxes to how to survive on irregular income and articles on how different laws affect your business, this is a great site for the beginning or advanced entrepreneur. SBA.gov offers information on loans and grants, as well as local assistance.

PROTECTING YOURSELF AND YOUR MONEY

The number one issue most patrons are concerned about is protecting themselves from fraud. This can seem a monumental task with all the different scams that exist today. AnnualCreditReport.com can help. Don't let the .com fool you; this is the official site for free annual credit reports as guaranteed by law. The Fair Credit Reporting Act requires the three credit reporting agencies—Equifax, Experian, and TransUnion—to provide citizens with a free copy of their credit report once every twelve months. The reports must be requested through AnnualCreditReport.com: online, by phone, or by mail. Users can get all three at once in order to more easily spot errors, or they can request one report from one agency every four months in order to monitor their credit. Credit reports from different agencies can differ; sometimes fraudulent accounts will appear on one credit report but not on the other two. Credit Karma can also help you keep an eye on your credit reports and even your credit score. Credit Karma is a completely free service that you've probably seen advertised at some point while watching television or reading a magazine. It offers TransUnion and Equifax credit reports and credit scores for free. It also breaks down the credit score into various factors: credit card utilization, payment history, derogatory marks, age of credit history, and credit inquiries. The site then grades the user on each of these factors, showing where improvement is needed. It also offers different calculators for home affordability, debt repayment, simple loan, and amortization. A credit score simulator is forthcoming. The site also offers articles with tips on financial issues, such as saving for retirement or planning a wedding on a budget.

Two more sites that everyone should be aware of are the Federal Trade Commission's Consumer Information site and ConsumerFinance.gov. FTC Consumer Information is often overlooked, but it offers information on various consumer issues, including scams and background checks. This site is most popular for the Do Not Call Registry and for reporting violations of the Fair Debt Collection Practices Act. Now consumers can use the site to report identity theft or unwanted texts, telemarketing, or SPAM too. The site's Scam Alerts page allows consumers to check for the latest scams to beware of—they can even subscribe to Scam Alerts emails. The site also offers pages on money and credit, homes and mortgages, health and fitness, jobs and making money, and privacy and identity. ConsumerFinance.gov also offers information on similar topics, such as paying for college or owning a home. It, too, offers the option to submit complaints.

For patrons who are interested in knowing about the latest scam, there are other sites besides the two previously mentioned. USA.gov has a Money Scams page that divides the scams by type. The FBI Common Fraud Schemes site is also a great place to learn about common scams to avoid. Finally, when reporting an Internet scam, visit IC3.gov, the Internet Crime Complaint Center. This site offers prevention tips and information on the latest Internet crime schemes.

STUDENT LOANS

Many of the sites mentioned earlier have pages dedicated to paying for college. While all of these sites are useful to prospective or current students, there are some sites that every college student should be familiar with. The first is FAFSA.gov: the government site for the Free Application for Federal Student Aid. Students often confuse this site with FAFSA.com, a fee-based FAFSA preparation service. FAFSA.gov is the site that students must use to fill out their financial aid forms, and FAFSA.com benefits from people who mistakenly enter *.com* instead of *.gov*.

Every student should also know StudentAid.ed.gov, a Department of Education site dedicated to informing students on the types of aid available as well as what kinds of aid they are eligible for. The site even offers information on preparing for college, such as choosing a school, taking the required entrance exams, and applying to schools. It explains why students should consider going to school, including a graph that compares the salary and unemployment rates of various education levels (see fig. 3.1). #AskFAFSA Office Hours is a live Q&A session on Twitter every month; students can get their questions answered by an expert from the comfort of their smartphone, computer, or tablet.

StudentLoans.gov is another great site for students and new graduates alike. This site offers information on getting loans and managing repayment. It even offers information on various student loans and TEACH grants. Graduates can use this site to start the process of student loan consolidation and to learn about the Public Service Loan Forgiveness (PSLF) program. Students can also learn about the various repayment plans available upon graduation. Graduates can apply for one of the income-drive repayment plans: income-based repayment, pay as you earn, or income-contingent repayment. The site offers information on the differences between these three plans.

The Federal Direct Loan site is used for students who wish to apply for a student loan directly from the U.S. government. It is also used for loan consolidation, particularly for anyone interested in entering the PSLF program. Through the PSLF Program, "borrowers may qualify for forgiveness of the remaining balance of their Direct Loans after they have made 120 qualifying payments on those loans while employed full time by certain public service employers" ("Public Service Loan Forgiveness" 2015).

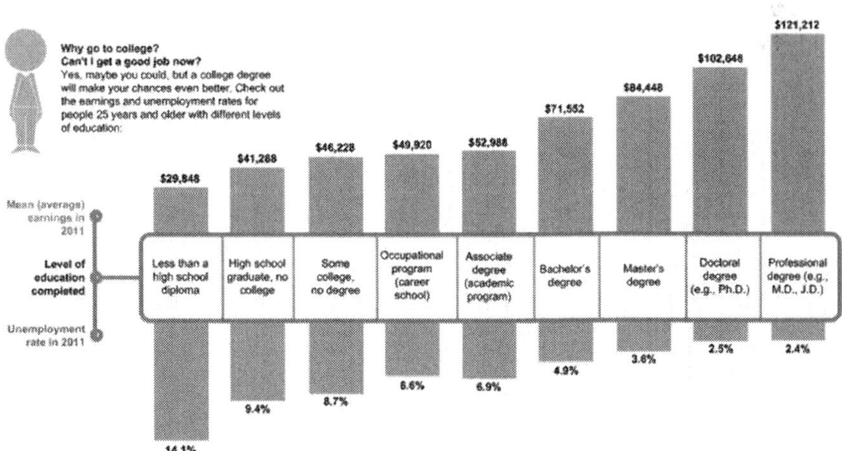

Figure 3.1. Why Go to College? Bureau of Labor Statistics, *Current Population Survey*, unpublished tables, 2012.

A great site on college spending is the Consumer Finance Protection Bureau's Paying for College site. It offers two student financial guides, one on student loans and one on student banking. It also offers a tool that allows students to compare the financial aid offers of up to three different schools, and provides information on repaying student debt.

SAVING AND INVESTING

All financial gurus agree that saving is the key to financial health. Of course, not all of them agree on the amount that you should be saving. Some say you need an eight-month income emergency fund, while others say three to six months will do. Some say to focus on paying off your credit cards first, while others say that saving should be the priority. Add to that the confusion of needing multiple savings accounts—an emergency fund, a 401(k), a Roth IRA, a college fund, a down payment for a house—and it's no wonder that most patrons don't know where to begin. These sites will help those patrons who want to start saving get on the right track.

Choose to Save, a site by the Employee Benefit Research Institute, offers free financial education on saving. It offers brochures with information on various savings issues, as well as savings tips on a wide range of topics. The site also provides calculators for just about everything from auto insurance to tax refunds, including the Ballpark E$timate interactive tool for retirement savings. It's the perfect place for any would-be saver to get started.

Feed the Pig is another great site. Created by the American Institute of CPAs, Feed the Pig offers steps to a secure financial future: budgeting, goal setting, spending, and taxes. Each section offers its own calculators and tips, as well as more information on each step within that section. There are also steps to manage money, master credit and debt, and plan ahead, making this a thorough tool that can be used by the novice and the advanced saver. The site provides an online toolbox that offers calculators, podcasts, tips, and other resources. The toolbox also has a tool called You Save that offers guidance on a variety of financial goals, from combining finances to improving a credit score. The user can select up to three goals and get a personalized plan to reach those goals.

Building Wealth is a site by the Federal Reserve Bank of Dallas that offers information on wealth-building strategies. With resources for consumers, community leaders, teachers, and students, this site serves a variety of needs. It offers a free guide entitled "Building Wealth: A Beginner's Guide to Securing Your Financial Future," both online and in print. This guide teaches users important skills and offers interactive tools to help you determine your own financial information. This is a great tool for all ages.

INVESTING

Investor.gov is a great starting point for anyone interested in investing money. With sections like Introduction to the Markets and Investing Basics, this site introduces investing in an easy-to-understand way. The site also offers information on researching investments and managing them once you've started. It even offers a section called Life Events, with guidance on how to handle events like marriage or caring for a loved one. Like other financial education sites, Investor.gov offers calculators, quizzes, and worksheets; it also has videos on issues that affect investors and links to other recommended resources.

SEC.gov's Get the Facts: The SEC's Roadmap to Savings and Investing offers information on both saving and investing. This site includes step-by-step guidance with worksheets for each step. It also connects to various tools and calculators. The tools and calculators, however, range from the simple (such as the College Savings Calculator) to the advanced (like the Mutual Fund Breakpoint Search Tool), which may intimidate a new user.

TreasuryDirect.gov's Ready.Save.Grow. offers information on saving and investing. TreasuryDirect is "the only financial services website that lets you buy and redeem securities directly from the U.S. Department of the Treasury in paperless electronic form" ("About TreasuryDirect" 2015). This means that the patrons don't have to worry that the site (or person) they are purchasing or redeeming securities from is actually scamming them. It also aims to educate users by connecting them to other resources on saving and investing.

RETIREMENT

While retirement is addressed by many of the saving and investing sites in the previous section, it is also a greater financial issue on its own. As a result, there are many sites dedicated to helping users navigate their way on the road to retirement.

The Social Security Retirement Benefits site is where patrons can apply for retirement benefits with Social Security, but many don't realize that this site also offers a retirement planner and a retirement estimator. It even offers calculators for retirement age and life expectancy. There is even a retirement income estimator for patrons to use. Though this site is focused on Social Security benefits, its calculators can be used by anyone.

The IRS also offers a site called Saving for Retirement. This site offers information on types of retirement contributions (and their limits), rollovers, vesting, and automatic enrollment with your employer. It also links to the Department of Labor's Lifetime Income Calculator to estimate your monthly income based on your account balance. Finally, it links to the Department of Labor's Retirement Savings Toolkit, which offers publications, videos, and calculators to help educate patrons about saving for retirement.

FREE WEB-BASED BUDGETING PROGRAMS

While all the sites mentioned in this chapter are helpful, they can't solve everything. Patrons need to bridge the gap between intention and action, and that begins with budgeting money and being aware not just of what they are spending but of how they are spending. Unfortunately, many people don't balance their checkbooks regularly or accurately. Some people use spreadsheets, but many others are intimidated by spreadsheet programs. That is why there is personal finance software. Of course, not everyone can afford Quicken, but that's okay. Free options are available.

One of the most popular is Mint.com, a site created by Intuit. Users can link their accounts (checking, savings, student loans, car loans, credit cards) to their Mint.com account, giving them a real-time picture of their financial situation. The user can even include asset information, such as the value of their home or car. Users can categorize their transactions to better track where their money goes. They can also create their own budgets and goals. The software will track spending, providing the user with alerts when they are going over budget. It also offers guidance on how users can meet their goals. With an intuitive design and useful tips, this is a great site to track money. And, since it is web based, users don't need to worry about installing software or losing information when a computer dies. It also means that they can access their information from anywhere. Of course, that leads to concerns about security. The site uses 128-bit SSL encryption and has the same physical security standards as banks. These are also verified and monitored by third-party experts such as TRUSTe and VeriSign. While this isn't foolproof, it's close—and it means that using Mint.com offers the same security as using a bank's site. For those who are still antsy about linking their accounts to Mint.com, there is the option to add information manually. Plus, Mint.com now offers a free credit score to its users.

But Mint.com isn't the only free site. Personal Capital is another. The main difference between this site and Mint.com appears to be that Personal Capital can be used to invest through their firm. In fact, the user's dashboard includes information from the day's holdings. Yodlee MoneyCenter is another site for personal finance. Like Mint.com and Personal Capital, users can either link their accounts or manually enter the information. Unlike the others, Yodlee will actually track reward points from hotels, airlines, and credit cards. All three of these programs have apps for smartphones.

These are only a few of the options available. There are numerous free and low-cost options for personal finance software. When helping a patron find one, try searching for articles on Forbes.com or Fortune.com. It is also very important that patrons understand the security of the program they choose. Most of these sites have a section dedicated to explaining their security. The section should detail information on the level of security used, as well as why that security works. If there is no section on security (or the information in that section is vague), then the patron might be better off finding another program. As with all financial issues, there are predators lurking behind misleading sites.

FINDING MORE RESOURCES

These are just a few of the many sites out there that can help patrons with a variety of financial literacy issues. It's important to remember, however, that not all sites are created equal. Sticking with government sites or even sites recommended by government sites is usually a safe bet. Using Google's advanced search options to limit to .gov domains can bring up a lot of great resources (Ireland 2015). For example, searching for "debt collection" with this limiter will find sites from the Federal Trade Commission and the Consumer Financial Protection Bureau, among others. It's important to also realize that search engines often have ads, so don't confuse those first few links with the actual search results.

Using this tip and the sites included in this chapter, patrons can find the exact information they need. Not only will this increase the patron's financial literacy skills, but it just might also create a new appreciation for government information—and for the librarians who connect those resources to patrons.

BIBLIOGRAPHY

"About TreasuryDirect." 2015. TreasuryDirect. http://www.treasurydirect.gov/about.htm.

"Benefits, Grants, and Loans." 2015. USA.gov. http://www.usa.gov/Citizen/Topics/Benefits.shtml.

Biz Kid$. 2015. http://bizkids.com/.

"Building Wealth: A Beginner's Guide to Securing Your Financial Future." 2015. Federal Reserve Bank of Dallas. http://www.dallasfed.org/microsites/cd/wealth.

"Calculators and Interest Rates." 2015. Direct Loan Program. http://www.direct.ed.gov/calc.html.

"Choose to Save." 2015. Employee Benefit Research Institute. http://www.choosetosave.org/.

"Common Fraud Schemes." 2015. Federal Bureau of Investigation. http://www.fbi.gov/scams-safety/fraud.

"Consumer Information: Free Credit Reports." 2015. Federal Trade Commission. http://www.consumer.ftc.gov/articles/0155-free-credit-reports.

Credit Karma. 2015. https://www.creditkarma.com/.

Direct Loan Program. 2015. http://www.direct.ed.gov/.

"Feed the Pig." 2015. American Institute of CPAs. http://www.feedthepig.org/.

"Financial Literacy & Savings Resources." 2015. TreasuryDirect. http://www.treasurydirect.gov/readysavegrow/start_saving/savings_resources.htm.
"Financial Literacy Tools & Resources." 2015. MyCreditUnion.gov. http://www.mycreditunion.gov/tools-resources/.
"Get the Facts: The SEC's Roadmap to Saving and Investing." 2015. U.S. Securities and Exchange Commission. http://www.sec.gov/investor/pubs/roadmap.htm.
"High School Financial Planning Program." 2015. National Endowment for Financial Education. http://www.hsfpp.org/.
"H.I.P. Pocket Change." 2015. U.S. Mint. http://www.usmint.gov/kids/.
Ireland, Sonnet. 2015. "Googling for Answers: The Ins and Outs of Using Google Effectively." Presentation at the 2015 Southeastern Library Association/Alabama Library Association Conference, Point Clear, AL, April 2. http://www.slideshare.net/SonnetIreland/selaalla-2015-conferencegoogling-for-answers.
Lawless, Robert M., and Elizabeth Warren. 2013. "The Bankruptcy Data Project at Harvard." Harvard Law School. http://bdp.law.harvard.edu/.
"Money as You Grow." 2015. President's Advisory Council on Financial Capability. http://moneyasyougrow.org.
"Money for Kids." 2015. Kids.gov. http://kids.usa.gov/money/.
"Money for Parents." 2015. Kids.gov. http://kids.usa.gov/parents/money.
"Money for Teachers." 2015. Kids.gov. http://kids.usa.gov/teachers/money.
"Money for Teens." 2015. Kids.gov. http://kids.usa.gov/teens/money.
"MoneySKILL." 2015. American Financial Services Association Education Foundation. http://www.moneyskill.org/.
"Paying for College." 2015. Consumer Financial Protection Bureau. http://www.consumerfinance.gov/paying-for-college.
"Prepare for College." 2015. Federal Student Aid. https://studentaid.ed.gov/prepare-for-college.
"Project C.H.A.N.G.E." 2015. U.S. Securities and Exchange Commission. http://project-change.sec.gov/.
"Public Service Loan Forgiveness." 2015. Federal Student Aid. https://studentaid.ed.gov/repay-loans/forgiveness-cancellation/public-service.
"Ready.Save.Grow." 2015. TreasuryDirect. http://www.treasurydirect.gov/readysavegrow/.
"Retirement Savings Toolkit." 2015. Employee Benefits Security Administration. http://www.dol.gov/ebsa/publications/fitoolkit.html.
"Saving for Retirement." 2015. Internal Revenue Service. http://www.irs.gov/Retirement-Plans/Plan-Participant,-Employee/Saving-for-Retirement.
"Scam Alerts." 2015. Federal Trade Commission. http://www.consumer.ftc.gov/scam-alerts.
"Scams and Frauds." 2015. USA.gov. https://www.usa.gov/scams-and-frauds.
"Social Security Retirement Benefits." 2015. Social Security Administration. http://www.ssa.gov/retire/.
"Unclaimed Money, Taxes, and Credit Reports." 2015. USA.gov. http://www.usa.gov/Citizen/Topics/Money-Taxes.shtml.
"Understanding Taxes." 2015. Internal Revenue Service. http://apps.irs.gov/app/understandingTaxes/index.jsp.
Vornovytskyy, Marina, Alfred Gottschalck, and Adam Smith. 2011. "Household Debt in the U.S.: 2000 to 2011." U.S. Census Bureau. https://www.census.gov/people/wealth/files/Debt%20Highlights%202011.pdf.

Chapter Four

Financial Literacy Is a Lifetime Skill

Joanne Kuster, with an introduction by Maryann Mori

WHY YOU SHOULD READ WHAT THIS AUTHOR SAYS

"This lady knows how to run a meeting and get things done!" That was my first impression of Joanne Kuster. I met her when I attended a meeting after being asked to represent the state library on a district committee for Iowa's Money Smart Week. The meeting consisted of diverse people who all had one thing in common: they were all associated with some kind of money-related field. They were bankers, business associates, and brokers; they were insurance executives and investment gurus. I was the odd duck on the committee as a librarian and as someone not wearing a business suit. As we went around the room and introduced ourselves along with our title and place of business, I could feel the questioning stares when I said I was a librarian for the state library. I could read the other committee members' minds: What is a librarian doing on this committee of knowledgeable, money-smart people? Did she mistakenly choose the wrong meeting room? After attending a few of these meetings, though, I saw just how I could fit in the committee. But Joanne Kuster saw the connection long before I did, which is likely why she extended the invitation for the state library to join the committee. My role on the committee would become one of advocate for Money Smart Week (MSW), promoter of financial literacy, and provider of publicity notices—all for libraries throughout the state.

Having served on the MSW committee for over three years now, I am convinced that Joanne not only knows a lot about financial literacy, but she also has a passion for sharing that knowledge with other people in a way that is fun, friendly, and not at all intimidating. Joanne has been the backbone not just of the committee in central Iowa but of statewide MSW activities. She has developed numerous ideas for MSW events that she often creates especially for library environments, for Joanne is not only an advocate of financial literacy but also a big proponent of libraries. She knows the value of librarians and their ability to provide unbiased, free, reliable information to the public. She understands the types of reference questions librarians field, the kinds of programs they present, and the variety of resources available from the library on the topic of financial literacy. Joanne incorporates libraries with her MSW activities not to exploit her own MSW agenda, but as a positive means of getting viable financial information into the hands of people who need it. She doesn't let lack of funding or deadlines or geographic challenges get in her way. Her favorite mantra is, "It's not a problem!" When faced with a challenge, Joanne simply applies a bit more of her endless supply of energy, makes a few more contacts, and soon her contagious enthusiasm for a project becomes a reality—everything from a kite festival to a bike ride—all in the name of financial literacy. Joanne is a friend of librarians, and the knowledge she has shared with Iowa libraries is now available for other librarians who read this chapter and a subsequent one in this book that Joanne and I co-authored.

When it comes to financial savvy, it seems most U.S. adult consumers have bare-bones skills. As they navigate the financial marketplace, consumers are forced either to build up money skills by making mistakes or to go searching for help and information as financial issues become front and center in their lives—a "just-in-time-of-need" philosophy.

So it shouldn't be shocking that most U.S. adults show low levels of financial literacy and cannot answer questions about basic concepts such as compound interest, as evidenced by the failure rate on a five-question quiz from the 2012 National Financial Capability study (FINRA Foundation 2013). The study was conducted by the Investor Education Foundation of FINRA—the Financial Industry Regulatory Authority. Similar tests given to students by organizations such as the Jump$tart Coalition for Personal Finance yield similar outcomes (Mandell 2008).

On the bright side, financial educators can attest to the fact that as little as ten hours of financial education can boost financial success (Sherraden and Boshara 2008). The need for financial education is great and keeps compounding as the financial landscape becomes more complex, and as more brokers and others try to sell financial products for profit. Libraries with well-stocked reference departments can offer a depth and breadth of materials for individuals seeking to boost their financial savvy. Plus, libraries provide educational tools to research answers in an unbiased environment, a counterbalance to high-pressure salespeople who may not share all the facts when trying to sell financial answers.

WHO IS FINANCIALLY LITERATE ANYWAY?

Even some really smart kids and well-educated adults are financially illiterate. This is understandable. Few parents help their kids build great money management skills, and many of these parents lack the confidence to delve into financially complex topics themselves. The 2014 Parents, Kids & Money Survey conducted by T. Rowe Price indicated that 74 percent of parents have some reluctance to discuss financial topics with their kids (T. Rowe Price 2014).

Plus, most Americans do not receive much financial education in school. A few take a budgeting or consumer math class, but true financial savvy extends far beyond budgets. According to the Council for Economic Education, only seventeen states require high school students to take classes that include personal finance, up from thirteen states in 2013 (Council for Economic Education 2014). Being financially literate entails having knowledge about how money works in order to make informed decisions regarding personal finances. This involves learning how to earn, spend, save, invest, borrow, protect, and share money wisely.

The national Jump$tart Coalition defines financial literacy as a "state of competency that enables each individual to respond effectively to ever-changing personal and economic circumstances" (Jump$tart Coalition for Personal Financial Literacy 2014). So being financially literate means staying financially agile and increasing in financial knowledge, evolving as the economy progresses through stages of expansion and contraction, highs and lows. Changing economic circumstances bring historically unseen financial dilemmas, new financial products that meet these changes, and, unfortunately, new financial scams to avoid. Having the latest knowledge and awareness is key.

FINANCIAL LITERACY LEADS TO CAPABILITY

In recent years, financial literacy has evolved to become financial capability—a relatively new buzzword that refers to *developing the ability* to use acquired financial knowledge to keep building on key skills in handling money wisely for a lifetime of financial security. It is not only about access to the information, but also about using that information to make wise decisions.

Financially capable consumers are the result of promoting financial literacy, something for which several librarians can take credit as they beef up resources, provide educational events, and increase financial awareness through programming such as Money Smart Week, the economic awareness campaign from the Federal Reserve Bank of Chicago.

As these librarians have come to understand, handling money effectively is a necessary lifetime skill. That is why community-minded librarians care about financial literacy and financial capability. Financial literacy impacts both a community's and its citizens' health and wellness, happiness, financial success, and relationships. Financial capability can be harder to achieve since it involves applying money skills and adapting behaviors.

Libraries are uniquely positioned to provide information to patrons about how to improve their lives, be productive citizens, and stay healthy. Libraries that provide resources to address personal finance topics fulfill their mission of being a go-to, informational warehouse that promotes literacy in general and personal wellness in particular. Being adept in handling personal finances is integral to a healthy lifestyle.

FINANCIAL FITNESS BOOSTS PERSONAL WELLNESS

Several recent studies indicate that a lack of money management skills often leads to other stresses in life, including undue mental, emotional, and relational strain. Such strains and stresses can manifest as a variety of physical and mental illnesses—from loss of appetite or overeating to depression and alcoholism.

The stress of debt can cause the body to fall apart, as evidenced by a study linking low credit scores to poor cardiovascular health. According to an article in the *International Business Times*, researchers "found that each 100-point increase in a person's credit score was associated to an almost one-year drop in heart age determined by cholesterol and blood pressure levels. . . . Lead researcher Terrie Moffitt from Duke University said the study suggested that people who don't take care of their money also don't manage their health" (Su 2014).

Moffitt led a long-term study of one thousand New Zealanders that linked heart health and credit scores (Israel et al. 2014). Part of that relationship—about 20 percent—was due to the participants' attitudes, behaviors and competencies when they were younger than age ten. One of the study's authors, Salomon Israel, said, "The factors contributing to poor health and low credit scores take root early in life" (Israel et al. 2014).

While consumers of any age may not immediately verbalize the cause-and-effect relationship of their money and health, they often intuitively see that the two are intertwined. It may be no coincidence that the top two resolutions adults typically make as a new year begins are to save money and get healthy (Ebiquity 2015).

Young adults who lack the financial knowledge to make informed decisions engage in behaviors detrimental to their financial health, according to a 2013 survey from the FINRA Education Foundation (Mottola 2014). Again, a bit of knowledge and understanding up front—as little as ten hours of education—can help young adults avoid a downward spiral of using credit cards, not paying monthly bills, and racking up interest charges. Once they understand how finance charges and interest can compound, they may try harder to pay off the monthly bill or not buy the item on credit. The study of New Zealanders mentioned earlier states, "Childhood self-control is of particular interest because of evidence that self-control is amenable to intervention early in life, and because economic models suggest that early investment may be more cost-effective than later remediation" (Israel et al. 2014). The researchers declared that their study suggested "that interventions successful at improving children's self-control may benefit their financial and physical well-being decades later in life" (Israel et al. 2014). Financial literacy education needs to begin earlier rather than later in life.

As testament to the benefit of education, consider the outcomes of similar awareness programs that promoted use of sunscreen, wearing seat belts, or cutting down on smoking. Dispensing the knowledge and information—a basic strategy for libraries—effects the biggest change. Libraries are in ideal positions to reach the public with these kinds of messages and with information related to these lifelong financial skills.

LIFELONG LEARNING, THE LIBRARY MISSION

Because libraries espouse "lifelong learning," it is important for both individuals and librarians to understand this "lifetime skill" component of financial literacy. Gaining financial competence is not a "once-and-done" deal. Rather, it is a skill that continues to morph throughout a lifetime, growing in depth as the financial landscape changes and as a consumer's own financial needs evolve.

Like any other literacy, financial literacy is an incremental skill to master. Consumers learn the basic building blocks first and construct strategies as they encounter life circumstances that make a topic more applicable. For example, a six-year-old learns how money adds up in a piggy bank, and it may be a few years before making deposits to an interest-bearing savings account makes sense. Likewise, accumulating enough to have an investment account and understanding risk versus reward are much more understandable by about age twelve, but both build on that initial six-year-old knowledge of accumulating coins.

Consumers are more apt to learn, listen to, and seek the appropriate financial knowledge when the topic applies to them, even though the resources should be available to them on a continuing basis. For example, a young adult has a better understanding of taxes after she or he receives a paycheck, sees the deductions, and files an income tax return. Student loans are at the top of the mind when college tuition looms, and mortgage rate fluctuations seem more important when buying a home.

Thus, it is crucial that a library reference department contain up-to-date resources and materials on personal finance and that librarians themselves stay abreast of the latest information to aid consumers in decision making. Several studies show a high correlation between financial literacy and poor decision making, with education improving financial behavior. Unbiased educational information—that found in a library rather than from a salesperson—is again key to capability.

Financial literacy can also be compared to a personal fitness program; it is never too late to learn and practice these skills. Practice brings competence and confidence!

When considering financial education programming and the patrons it benefits, many librarians find it difficult to attract the millennial demographic (ages eighteen to thirty-four), even though this group is one that most needs the education. One challenge in reaching this group is that persons between eighteen to thirty-four years old typically prefer to do research via their smartphones and other mobile devices rather than by actually visiting a brick-and-mortar library or attending a sit-down event. That is why the Investor Protection Trust and the Iowa Insurance Division developed a program called the DASH for the STASH, which debuted in Iowa in 2014. It was a tremendous success to reach this demographic, and 2015 promises to be even bigger. The program consisted of four posters with a variety of financial information on them. The posters were eye-catching and were part of a game that participants played by scanning the poster's QR code to answer questions about financial literacy—questions that had the answers contained within the posters. Younger patrons were attracted to the DASH program at libraries and enjoyed using their smartphones to enter the contest.

One of the "extras" that several libraries chose to offer along with the DASH for the STASH was an evening workshop focused on additional investment education topics. For the millennial age group, a beginner investment workshop was most appropriate and most attractive. Along with the workshop, attendees were typically interested in steps they should take to be financially successful. The information in textbox 4.1 was developed by the author for this purpose and is shared here for librarians to use with rightful credit given.

SUCCESS COMES IN "KNOWING YOUR NUMBERS"

Having access to financial resources and understanding that information helps consumers save and invest wisely, become better managers of credit, and avoid massive debt. In some cases, a simple mistake or lack of information can lead to bankruptcy, foreclosure, or other catastrophes. Consider what happened during the Great Recession of 2008, when thousands of mortgagees forfeited homes because they didn't understand (and perhaps didn't read) the financial terms of the mortgage contracts they willingly signed.

Textbox 4.1
Financial Checklist for Employed Young Adults

1. Sign up for auto-deposit of paycheck
2. Evaluate withholding amounts—W-4—annually
3. Sign up for and max out your 401(k) or 403(b) or 457
4. Evaluate health insurance plans/flexible spending plans annually
5. Contribute to an IRA or Roth IRA
6. Buy assets—like stocks or real estate
7. Plan for job advancement
8. Take advantage of education benefits
9. Update your net worth statement
10. Pay off loans quickly
11. Get a versatile credit card
12. Check your credit report
13. File income taxes—*annually*
14. Check into insurance to protect your assets
15. Keep your resume and network up to date
16. Brainstorm ways to add income—find your entrepreneurial side
17. Maintain a financial timeline, adding financial goals.

Live below your means and pay your bills on time!

Financially literate adults have increased capacity to invest and build wealth, start a business, be philanthropic, and make a variety of other financial decisions. From reading a spreadsheet to creating a budget or evaluating fees in an investment, financially capable adults understand the "numbers" related to their finances, putting them in a better position to make wise decisions.

People associate many different types of numbers with finances—salaries, investment fees, return on investment, profit and loss, net worth, interest rates, and more. Perhaps one of the most impactful and important is the credit score.

Credit scores used to be primarily a tool for lenders to assess a borrower's ability to repay. But today, many other individuals also use consumers' credit scores not only to determine risk related to repaying loans but also to assess character. These include insurers, utility companies, landlords, and even employers. Imagine the financially illiterate person who pays no attention to his or her credit history, not realizing the impact the resulting score has down the road.

Learning to understand financial concepts is a lifetime journey, not unlike a young student learning to read. Learning to interpret a financial report enables consumers to understand an investment and the prospects of risk versus rewards. Learning to invest leads to building a bigger nest egg and knowing how to protect it. Creating a sizable nest egg allows for a more comfortable retirement as well as financial independence.

FINANCIAL CAPABILITY IS A JOURNEY, NOT ONE TEST

Whether a consumer is ten, twenty, sixty, or more, the door of financial opportunity opens with the ability to understand the numbers. Gaining financial knowledge compounds as a consumer ages, and in turn elicits financial behaviors that are often repeated throughout a lifetime. As such, a librarian's role in relating financial concepts to everyday experiences improves financial capability at critical developmental stages for any age. For example, the librarian who reads at preschool story time can set the stage for the simplest financial concepts of saving, spending, sharing, or deciding on wants versus needs. A librarian for teen programming might focus on entrepreneurship or concepts about investing in stocks, whetting a teenager's appetite to make money and build wealth. The librarian who hosts a seminar about the latest tax rules on estate planning or Social Security changes offers crucial new knowledge to retirees whose decumulation strategies may be impacted beyond measure.

When it comes to helping consumers, quality, reliable financial information and programming is imperative. Because personal finances are much more complex than they were twenty-five years ago, it is important that information is constantly updated, accessible—and accurate. Sometimes, the Internet is not as accurate a resource as assumed. As more people from all walks of life see and hear financially related discussions in mainstream media and via social networking, they want a trusted, go-to resource to verify what they have heard or discovered. The library fulfills this role as well, since accurate information is perpetuated while unreliable or outlandish resources tend to disappear.

In summary, librarians are in a position to help their patrons build life skills in personal finance throughout their lifetimes. Librarians are trusted to reach out to consumers of all socioeconomic classes and all ages since they are promoters of equal access to information and places of education. And last, but not least, librarians themselves are typically lifelong learners and can personally offer patrons snippets of financial education that can be life changing. That's a challenging task that offers much satisfaction and opportunity for creative programming.

REFERENCES

Council for Economic Education. 2014. "Survey of States: Economic and Personal Finances Education in Our Nation's Schools." http://www.councilforeconed.org/wp/wp-content/uploads/2014/02/2014-Survey-of-the-States.pdf.

Ebiquity. 2015. "American Express Spending & Saving Tracker: Millennials Make 2015 the Year of the Milestone." American Express. http://about.americanexpress.com/news/sst/report/2015-01_Spend-and-Save-Tracker.pdf.

FINRA Foundation. 2013. "About the National Financial Capability Study." National Financial Capability Study. http://www.usfinancialcapability.org/about.php.

Israel, Salomon, Avshalom Caspi, Daniel W. Belsky, et al. 2014. "Credit Scores, Cardiovascular Disease Risk and Human Capital." *Proceedings of the National Academy of Sciences USA* 111(48):17087–92. http://www.ncbi.nlm.nih.gov/pubmed/25404329.

Jump$tart Coalition for Personal Financial Literacy. 2015. "Jump$tart Coalition Frequently Asked Questions." http://www.jumpstartcoalition.org/faq.html.

Mandell, Lewis. 2008. "The Financial Literacy of Young American Adults." Jump$tart Coalition for Personal Financial Literacy. http://www.jumpstartcoalition.org/assets/files/2008SurveyBook.pdf.

Mottola, Gary R. 2014. "The Financial Capability of Young Adults." *FINRA Foundation Financial Capability Insights*, March. http://www.usfinancialcapability.org/downloads/FinancialCapabilityofYoungAdults.pdf.

Sherraden, Michael, and Ray Boshara. 2008. "Learning from Individual Development Accounts." In *Overcoming the Savings Slump*, edited by Annamaria Lusardi, 280–296 . Chicago: University of Chicago Press.

Su, Reissa. 2014. "New Zealand Study Finds Link between Low Credit Scores and Poor Health." *International Business Times—AU Edition*, November 19. http://au.ibtimes.com/new-zealand-study-finds-link-between-low-credit-scores-poor-health-1390142.

T. Rowe Price. 2014. "6th Annual Parents, Kids & Money Survey." March. https://corporate.troweprice.com/Money-Confident-Kids/images/emk/2014-PKM-Report-V10_Supplemental-Data.pdf.

Chapter Five

Financial Literacy

Meeting the Need

Kit Keller and Mary Jo Ryan

A recent Pew Charitable Trust study of American families found a striking level of financial fragility: "Despite the national recovery, many families have experienced minimal wage growth, have few savings, and could not withstand a financial emergency" (Pew Charitable Trusts 2015, 2). While the economic downturn of 2008 has had a long-term impact on many families, a bigger problem is the lack of understanding of basic personal finance topics. According to the 2012 National Financial Capability Study, "Americans demonstrate relatively low levels of financial literacy and have difficulty applying financial decision-making skills to real life situations" (quoted in Palmer 2015, 1). The need for a better understanding of personal finances is clear, and libraries, traditionally accepted as sources of free, unbiased information resources, are the ideal community institution to meet the growing demand for financial literacy education services and programming.

MEETING THE NEED

The 2014 State of America's Libraries report focuses in part on this changing role of public libraries. "As libraries continue to transform in 2014, they deepen engagement with their communities in many ways, addressing current social, economic, and environmental issues, often through partnerships with governments and other organizations" (American Library Association 2014, 4). A 2014 report from the Institute of Museum and Library Services, "Public Libraries in the United States Survey," notes, "Public libraries support community improvement by providing programming that addresses the health, education, and workforce development needs of local residents" (quoted in American Library Association 2015). Academic libraries too are actively engaged in providing financial literacy guidance and reference services to their populations, as evidenced by many recent articles in *College & Research Libraries News* and other publications.

GETTING STARTED

In an effort to help libraries respond to community financial literacy needs, the Reference and User Services Association (RUSA) authorized the development of "Financial Literacy Education in Libraries: Guidelines and Best Practices for Service." This report covers broad content areas, and each content area lists program outcomes that can be applied to a variety of workshops and classes. The guidelines have suggested program topics, with a guide to relevant content and resources to facilitate the preparation and presentation of appropriate, successful financial literacy workshops, classes, and other programs.

Additionally, the successful Smart investing@your library grant program administered jointly by the American Library Association (ALA) and the FINRA Investor Education Foundation and started in 2007 has demonstrated successful implementation techniques that serve as models for effective financial literacy programming. Since its inception, this grant program has distributed 132 grants totaling more than ten million dollars to library facilities in thirty-nine states. Many lessons have been learned through the work of this expansive network of grants focused on financial literacy, and these are outlined below.

WHAT WORKS: LESSONS LEARNED

Start with Staff: First Target Audience

The webinar "Public Libraries as Financial Literacy Providers," provided by the University of Wisconsin–Madison's Center for Financial Security (CFS), describes this topic and accompanying challenges. These researchers noted that there are many challenges for library staff in their effort to meet the demand for financial information. One major challenge is the lack of formal training in financial education. For many librarians, this topic is not in their sphere of expertise, even for library staff who are professionally trained librarians.

As CFS Affiliate Kristin Eschenfelder notes in the comments section for this webinar, "As society's financial functions become more complex, information driven, and technology focused, public libraries and librarians may begin to play a more significant role in financial literacy—both providing trustworthy information and offering training to increase the public's capacity to navigate more complicated financial systems" (University of Wisconsin–Madison CFS 2012). In order to be a confident, authoritative resource for their constituents, library staff have to build their own financial literacy skills. Smart investing@your library grantees found that their staff members were underprepared to respond to questions about financial issues.

When this fact is coupled with the identified need in communities for unbiased financial information, it signals the need for financial literacy programming and resources for community members, as well as the need for skill building for library staff. One ALA/FINRA grant recipient noted, following the successful completion of grant activities, "Now that our library staff is more financially savvy and comfortable arranging and presenting financial workshops, festivals and events, we will pursue other grants that allow us to continue 'outside the box' financial programming." The Santa Clara County Library grant project in California emphasized staff training as a primary grant activity. Project leaders developed an online training course, "Smart Investing: Reference Strategies and Resources," which was offered in partnership with Infopeople, a statewide project that functions as the training arm of the California State Library. The training was led by faculty from nearby higher education institutions and was made available to all librarians throughout the region. Data indicate a substantial increase in participant knowledge and confidence in using resources and strategies for personal finance and investing reference transactions. The course has been adapted and used by other grantees, including a statewide project launched by the Nebraska Library Commission.

Resources for staff development—including training needs assessment, webinars and online courses, learning evaluation, and collection management—are available from the ALA/FINRA Smart investing@your library website (http://smartinvesting.ala.org/staff-training/).

Get Help: Partnerships Are Critical

Partnerships improve project sustainability and establish a library's position in its local community as a source of reliable, unbiased financial information. Collaboration with partners increased public awareness, expanded project reach and access, and influenced success. The most effective partners identified include education partners such as university extension offices, local school districts, and local colleges and universities; social service partners such as Head Start, veteran services agencies, and YMCA/YWCA organizations; and broader community organizations such as the United Way, chambers of commerce, and local churches. Project partners have built sustaining collaborative relationships with community groups, creating a supportive working team that, through a shared purpose, supports members of the community in a wide variety of ways. Partners proved essential in many cases by helping to tap into a ready audience and building on already existing trust and relationships. As more than one grantee noted, "We will continue to work together to promote and support each other's services through joint program development, marketing, and resource sharing."

Multnomah County Library in Portland, Oregon, reached at-risk parents by establishing partnerships with Head Start agencies and by leveraging the expertise of a local nonprofit organization, Innovative Changes, which assists low-income people with low-cost loans and financial literacy. In five ninety-minute workshops, eighty attendees learned how to model good financial habits and were introduced to the idea that children learn lessons about money from hearing and seeing what their parents say and do. Partnering with Head Start was crucial to the program's success. Head Start organizations are familiar and trusted service providers for parents, and this opened the door for the library to reach that target audience. The project director at the Georgetown County Library in South Carolina reported:

> We continue to value and get a great return on our grant partnerships, whether a group is providing space, instructors, dissemination of marketing materials, volunteers at job fairs or festivals, or input on the direction we are taking. We have reaped rewards when we remained flexible. Many of these events were born out of direct requests from residents and patrons, and demonstrate that the library is responsive and savvy, rather than institutional and rigid.

A key factor in developing a good working partnership is effective communication. Recommendations include the following:

- Establish an ongoing process for conversation to nurture the relationship.
- Schedule regular face-to-face meetings in addition to phone calls and email communications.
- Identify one contact person at each partnership agency, and clarify expectations from all participants.

Build on Success: Embed Financial Topics in Existing Programs

Building an audience for programs can be a challenge. So don't. Take the successful programs already in place and insert the financial content for the ready audience. A technique that proved effective—for both initial program attendance as well as sustained interest—is embedding financial literacy programs and activities into existing, already popular library activities. Many library programs have long-established reputations and steady attendees. Incorporating financial literacy activities into these programs helps to ensure good attendance and also improves the sustainability of these offerings.

The Ida Rupp Public Library in Port Clinton, Ohio, integrated children's financial literacy programming into the region's Summer Lunch Club, which serves low-income families at three locations in the county, including the library. Instruction focused on basic concepts, such as needs versus wants; earning, saving, and spending money; and banking. One library's existing Teen Club helped support and promote Money School workshops to their peers, which increased awareness and attendance of teens, a traditionally difficult audience to attract to the library. Georgetown County Library has demonstrated the technique of embedding financial literacy content into popular, well-established library programming. Its very successful project Powerful Investment Education (P.I.E.) engaged a broad target audience, but in particular those who are economically disadvantaged. Georgetown reports that, systemwide, its libraries have incorporated financial content into many long-standing youth activities. Such efforts have been deeply appreciated by residents. One participant commented, "I applaud what you are causing to happen in our community. Financial illiteracy is the civil rights issue of the twenty-first century and it is fulfilling to work with this program to empower our youth."

Libraries often struggle to respond to demands for new or expanded library services that compete for staff and monetary resources. One potential solution to this challenge is incorporating financial literacy into existing program areas such as adult literacy, teen programs, and summer reading.

Use the Wealth: Customize Existing Resources

The abundance of quality educational resources can be reviewed and customized to meet local community needs and programming preferences. For example, if we return to the families mentioned at the beginning of this chapter, the ALA/FINRA Smart investing@your library website lists seven ready-made financial education programs for families with young children (http://smartinvesting.ala.org/audiences/audiences/children/).

Materials are widely available for specific target audiences for use in library programs. Sources of free resources include the following:

- FINRA Investor Education Foundation (http://www.finrafoundation.org/): This site has an extensive list of educational materials, many of which can be downloaded from the site, and many in Spanish. Online tools and programs are also available.
- U.S. Securities and Exchange Commission (http://www.sec.gov/investor): The education portal of this site provides publications for seniors and investors and a link to Investor.gov, an educational tool for investors, from beginners to experts.

- AARP (http://www.aarp.org/aarp-foundation/our-work/income/): Many local affiliates offer both free workshops on financial topics, as well as providing speakers who can lead programs at local libraries.

Library collections need to be enhanced and managed to support financial education programs. Systematic assessment of existing resources—print, electronic, audiobook, ebook, DVD, online—and assessment of the needs of the target audience set the stage for adding to the collection. Tools to help librarians in this endeavor are found on the ALA/FINRA Smart investing@your library website (http://smartinvesting.ala.org/staff-training/staff-training-toolkit/).

Consider the Source: Don't Sell Anything!

Special care is required in providing reference services and programming in the area of personal finance and financial literacy. This is not a new consideration for librarians; for many years, librarians have distributed income tax forms and brochures, while carefully reminding patrons that they do not provide filing or tax advice. The same principle applies here. However, what differs is the need to ensure that speakers and other program participants in financial-related programming and workshops also provide unbiased, noncommercial content.

Aspects of ensuring that accurate, unbiased information is delivered to library customers include careful partner selection, developing a memorandum of understanding, and checking with an independent organization to verify credentials of speakers and other program presenters. Analysis of more than seven years of developing partnerships for the ALA/FINRA grants revealed that the following groups are, in general, the best choices for libraries to work with when developing personal finance, budgeting, and investing programs: public schools, other library organizations, cooperative extension educators, chambers of commerce, colleges and universities, government organizations, social service agencies, faith-based organizations, and museums and cultural organizations. As noted on the website of the Consumer Financial Protection Bureau (CFPB) (http://www.consumerfinance.gov/), "You have the right to free, unbiased financial information."

And speaking of the CFPB, this group has identified libraries as a viable partner for the delivery of reliable financial resources, and they offer free financial webinars and resources for specific target groups, such as veterans, students, and older Americans, as well as webinars focused on specific life events, such as owning a home, paying for college, and establishing credit.

Tell the Story: Pitch the Programs

It is important to plan and implement a communication and outreach strategy that markets library financial education programs to the target audience. The strategy has to reach the specific audience where they are located, at a teachable moment. It capitalizes on activities that amplify word-of-mouth marketing, outreach, social networking, and empowering trusted intermediaries. Informal activities and events held inside and outside the library to raise community awareness about the library as a source for financial education can be incorporated as part of the marketing plan. Library staff reach out to key local organizations and unbiased partners, asking them to assist in the marketing planning and engaging them as stakeholders to work as intermediaries, sharing information on library financial education activities and resources with their constituents.

Marketing planning does not have to be complicated or unduly time consuming. It simply has to be intentional and inclusive. Input from library staff, volunteers, and key partners can help narrow the focus onto the target audience and select from a wide menu of communication options.

Evaluate: What Good Did It Do?

Milton Friedman famously said, "One of the great mistakes is to judge policies and programs by their intentions rather than their results." Outcome-based evaluation focuses on results and is key to successful provision of library financial education programs. Successful techniques include:

- Pre- and post-surveys for assessing the efficacy of staff training and programs for library customers
- Anecdotal information gathered from focus groups and key informant interviews with staff and library customers
- Circulation tracking, starting with baseline data and systematic review throughout the implementation process
- Responses on customer comment cards to aid collection development, as well as future program planning
- Face-to-face interviewing, identified by ALA/FINRA Smart Investing grantees as the most effective technique, for valuable anecdotal stories that demonstrate impact
- Partner feedback for insight from people vested in the process and with strong community connections

Evaluation planning should start at the beginning of the process, not after the fact. Establishing baseline information about, for example, staff knowledge of the content, or circulation statistics in a specific content area, has to happen prior to the intervention of programming or training. Part of the plan should be a clear identification of intended outcomes—what difference will this program make?

Outcomes are the ways people benefit from the program and are identified as changes in skills, knowledge, attitude, condition, or life status. They can be short-term or long-term. They can also be difficult to assess, given the nature of the topic. But this information is worth planning for. One grantee noted, "Bringing people together at the end of a series of programs, in an informal focus group, helped to provide us with some really good information."

Short-term outcomes might include learning to balance a checkbook, finding out one's credit score, opening a savings account, or feeling in control of one's finances. Longer-term outcomes could include paying off a credit card or establishing a retirement account. But how will you know when these happen? You need a plan to capture that information.

This evaluation plan should include:

- Tracking inputs: staff, time, computers, facilities, materials, money, consultants, website, software, Internet, instructors
- Tracking activities: recruiting, coordinating, promoting, purchasing, scheduling, evaluation activities
- Tracking services: conducting workshops, mentoring, online offerings, following up with customers
- Tracking outputs: number of participants served, materials developed and used, workshops offered, website usage counts

Intended outcomes should be clearly identified. And be prepared to recognize unintended consequences. Many FINRA grantees have provided stories of unintended consequences resulting from this adaptation, but few quite as compelling as that reported by Pioneer Library System in Norman, Oklahoma, where the community was devastated by tornadoes in May 2013. When disaster struck, project coordinators for the grant brainstormed ways to assist in meeting the immediate financial issues that resulted. The libraries responded with a series of community disaster relief meetings held at library facilities and featuring speakers from the public school system, FEMA, the Red Cross, the Small Business Administration, and the area chambers of commerce. The libraries involved realized that they were in a unique position to fill the information gap at this critical time in their communities. The project principal from Pioneer Library System described their response as follows:

> It quickly became apparent that important financial information needs were not being addressed: the need to understand insurance settlements and to have specific tax-related questions answered; basic education on borrowing prac-

> tiecs and how to understand terms on mortgages and car loans for people who had not had car payments in a long time, or who had owned their homes for years. Stories emerged about settlements of large sums of money paid to people used to living paycheck-to-paycheck, with no real budget and no guidance on how to manage those funds to replace all their personal possessions, vehicles, businesses, and homes.

MAJOR CONTENT AREAS

There is no shortage of financial literacy content, standards, guidelines, and classes. A simple web search yields millions of results. In developing the RUSA guidelines for librarians, many of these sources were scrutinized carefully, with the result being the identification of five major content areas: earning, borrowing and credit, saving and investing, spending, and protecting against risk. Additionally, there are corresponding resources available from authoritative organizations whose major focus is developing financial capacity of Americans of all ages. Some of these include the Federal Reserve Education organization (https://www.federalreserveeducation.org/), which offers lesson plans, games, activities, and publications for all ages. Another is the National Endowment for Financial Education (http://www.nefe.org/), which offers training tools and youth and adult financial education resources. The RUSA guidelines include an extensive appendix listing many other recommended resources and organizations.

CONCLUSION

The establishment of the Consumer Financial Protection Bureau was part of a widespread response to the growing need for reliable financial information. The CFPB was established by the Dodd-Frank Wall Street Reform and Consumer Protection Act of 2010, with a mission "to make markets for consumer financial products and services work for Americans—whether they are applying for a mortgage, choosing among credit cards, or using any number of other consumer financial products" (CFPB 2015). A recent study conducted by the CFPB identified four elements that define personal financial well-being—feeling in control, having the capacity to absorb a financial shock, being on track to meet financial goals, and having flexibility to make choices (http://www.consumerfinance.gov/blog/four-elements-define-personal-financial-well-being/). Additional chapters in this book further examine the library role in helping Americans achieve financial well-being.

REFERENCES

American Library Association. 2014. *The State of America's Libraries*. Chicago: American Library Association.

———. 2015. "ALA Library Fact Sheet 26." http://www.ala.org/tools/libfactsheets/alalibrary-factsheet26.

CFPB. 2015. "About Us." http://www.consumerfinance.gov/the-bureau/.

Palmer, Kent. 2015. "Boost Financial Literacy during Money Smart Week, April 18–25." Naperville Public Library, April 15. http://www.naperville-lib.org/blog/Boost%20Your%20Financial%20Literacy.

Pew Charitable Trusts. 2015. "The Precarious State of Family Balance Sheets." January. http://www.pewtrusts.org/~/media/Assets/2015/01/FSM_Balance_Sheet_Report.pdf.

Ratcliffe, Janneke. 2015. "Four Elements Define Personal Financial Well-Being." Consumer Financial Protection Bureau, January 27. http://www.consumerfinance.gov/blog/four-elements-define-personal-financial-well-being/.

RUSA. 2014. "Financial Literacy Education in Libraries: Guidelines and Best Practices for Service." http://www.ala.org/rusa/sites/ala.org.rusa/files/content/FLEGuidelines_Final_September_2014.pdf.

University of Wisconsin–Madison CFS. 2012. "Public Libraries as Financial Literacy Providers." December 17. http://www.youtube.com/watch?v=AX6TilIaozM.

Chapter Six

Information Has Value

Financial Literacy Meets Information Literacy

Shana Gass and Joyce Garczynski

In October 2013, Association of College & Research Libraries (ACRL) President Trevor Dawes recognized an urgent need and timely outreach opportunity in promoting financial literacy among college students (Dawes 2013). These students—already an attractive market for financial services (*Financial Brand* 2015; Stratford 2015)—will be making key financial decisions on college debt, careers, spending, and savings, armed with a level of general financial knowledge that has been rated a "D" (Inceptia 2013, 5).

Given the steepness of the learning curve, academic library financial literacy programs have tended to focus on imparting the fundamentals of credit, budgeting, saving, and investing and recommending key sources of personal finance information. Meanwhile, an opportunity has been neglected: libraries should be equipping students not only with basic financial literacy content and sources but with the tools to continue to ask the right questions as they make financial decisions in the years after college. In other words, libraries should consider the relationship of financial literacy (FL) to information literacy (IL).

The Reference and User Services Association's (RUSA) "Financial Literacy Education in Libraries: Guidelines and Best Practices for Service" recommends that "principles of information literacy should be integrated at each level of the financial literacy guidelines," and advises that library FL programs should be teaching how to access, evaluate, and apply knowledge from a variety of financial information sources (RUSA 2014, 2). However, in the guidelines, IL outcomes are sparse. Ashley Faulkner, in her review of financial literacy's treatment in the library literature, found financial and information literacies often discussed together, but with no consensus on the relationship between the two: information literacy might include financial literacy, it might serve as a foundation, or financial literacy might be an offshoot (Faulkner 2015, 12). The case for applying information literacy instruction to the financial literacy domain is compelling: much of our financial lives have become disintermediated, with individuals shouldering the responsibility of selecting from the massive amount of relevant information in order to make personal finance decisions (Špiranec, Zorica, and Simončić 2012, 267–68).

This chapter will explore the intersections between financial literacy and information literacy by drawing on the world of investing, a particularly rich illustration of both concepts. Investing will be examined from the standpoint of the "Framework for Information Literacy for Higher Education" (ACRL 2015), and this chapter concludes with an outline for a workshop on investment with an emphasis on mutual development of IL and FL.

"INFORMATION LITERACY COMPETENCY STANDARDS" AND THE NEW "FRAMEWORK FOR INFORMATION LITERACY"

On February 2, 2015, the ACRL board voted to accept the "Framework for Information Literacy for Higher Education" as "one of the constellation of information literacy documents from the association" (ACRL 2015, 1). The adoption of the framework arrives fifteen years after the publication of the "Information Literacy Competency Standards for Higher Education" (ACRL 2000, 1), and with this new document comes a new, expanded conception of information literacy. One of the driving forces behind the new framework has been the sense that the earlier standards did not reflect the complexity of the learners' role in the current information landscape. The standards focus on how librarians can guide students through an "environment of rapid technological change and proliferating information resources," to accomplish a series of prescribed outcomes in order to become information literate (ACRL 2000, 5). Going beyond this, the framework recognizes students as content creators who "have a greater role and responsibility in creating new knowledge, in understanding the contours and the changing dynamics of the world of information, and in using information, data, and scholarship ethically" (ACRL 2015, 2). Thus the framework acknowledges not only that learners need to know how to properly use information, but that they also need to recognize and account for how the new information they have created will be used by others.

In addition, the framework transforms the process of becoming information literate from completing a series of consecutive tasks to gaining an understanding of the six intertwined core concepts that shape information literacy. These core concepts include the idea that "information has value," meaning that information has the power to serve as a commodity, as well as a means of education and persuasion, and the idea of "scholarship as conversation," meaning that there exist related sources, with competing perspectives and interpretations, on any given topic (ACRL 2015, 8, 10–11). With this shift comes the recognition that the journey of becoming information literate is not linear but involves a series of complicated twists and turns in which learners become increasingly comfortable with a nuanced understanding of the information landscape. For example, in order for learners to become information literate they will need to recognize that there is no formula to determining the value of a particular information source and that the value of a source depends on the context of the source itself as well as their use of that source in their own information creation. Thus, the intersection of financial literacy and the framework provides librarians with the opportunity to help learners move along their journey toward the understanding that both the information they use as well as the information they create have value (even when, on the surface, these are freely available) and that this value is tied, at least in part, to the role that the information plays in a larger conversation.

(MARKET) INFORMATION HAS VALUE

Considering IL in light of investing is apt. Information literally moves the market. In fact, a preeminent finance theory, the efficient market hypothesis, posits that the current and future value of a stock is perfectly reflected in its price, with any novel information being incorporated into a new price (*Financial Express* 2014). Company, industry, political, and economic news can all have an influence. Earnings surprises (when the actual earnings per share diverges from company guidance or analyst consensus estimates), especially negative ones, can inspire strong reactions, depending on the context as perceived by investors. Some companies "manage" their earnings to avoid a backlash (Lev 2012, 19–32).

Information does not have to be entirely new or even accurate to move stock prices significantly. For example, when a six-year-old article about United Airlines' bankruptcy surfaced on Google News, it got picked up by Bloomberg as a new story, leading to a precipitous drop in the company's stock price (Boulton 2008), with effects lingering up to four days later despite authoritative public denials (Marshall, Visaltanachoti, and Cooper 2014). In cases of subterfuge, unfounded rumor, and overreactions to bad news, prices eventually settle, but in the meantime, real losses have occurred. Investors should be conscious of these informational risks.

Though investors large and small execute thousands upon thousands of trades daily based on the information they receive, the specter of unequal access to market information remains. High-frequency traders depicted in Michael Lewis's 2014 book *Flash Boys* employ technology to gain an advantage measured in milliseconds, enabling them to profit by "front running" other investors whose information comes over the regular pipes. Some believe these traders will trigger the next economic crisis (Wirth 2014).

SOME PLAYERS IN INVESTING

Companies benefit from a healthy stock price via reduced cost of capital, C-level compensation tie-ins and tenure, relief from shareholder activism and class-action litigation, and prestige (Lev 2012, 4–6). Investors, naturally, like to see their holdings rise in value. Some investors choose to tilt their own odds: unscrupulous investors might spread rumors in so-called pump-and-dump schemes in which positive rumors juice a stock, upon which the perpetrators hasten to cash out. These schemes, particularly rife in penny/Pink Sheet stocks, range from amateurish message board postings and scam emails (Bullock and Scannell 2014) to the sophisticated. Recently, a fake merger announcement for Avon was somehow filed via the Securities and Exchange Commission–run EDGAR service, lifting Avon's stock fully 20 percent before the hoax was discovered (Hoffman, Tan, and Cimilluca 2015). Unaware investors face a disadvantage in the marketplace as they may not realize it is also possible to make money betting against a stock via a short sale, in which investors sell borrowed stock in anticipation of being able to buy it back later at a lower price.

To seek out investment picks, market news, and strategies, many individual investors spend substantial time consulting information and engaging in dialogue with other investors. In her study of investment message boards, Lisa O'Connor (2013) found that these environments are relatively information dense, but that investors tended to lack a critical stance on their information, especially problematic given a tendency to draw on less authoritative or noncorporate sources.

Investors also rely on the work of professional analysts who research and evaluate stocks, often specializing in a particular industry. Quintessential information workers (Kuhlthau 2004, 167), analysts rely on public disclosures, the business press, and primary research, such as their own observations and interviews with company and industry personnel. In any given earnings conference call, many of the questions asked of company leadership will be asked by analysts, who can be quite probing as they attempt to ferret out information about a company's health and prospects. Institutional investors, such as mutual funds, employ their own in-house, "buy-side" analysts. The general public is most likely to come across "sell-side" analyst reports put out by the brokerage division of an investment bank. Since investment banks depend on companies for IPO business, this might account for the overall positive tenor of analyst ratings. It has been reported that over 48 percent of analyst reports are "buys" and that nearly 45 percent are "holds" (Cox 2015). Investors can still benefit from consulting analyst research but may want to take the ratings themselves with a grain of salt. Standard & Poor's and Value Line are not associated with investment banks and are thus considered independent analyst firms. Though they are certainly not infallible, this is a distinction worth making.

While some believe they failed as watchdogs in the 2007–2009 recession (Tambini 2010, 158–59), investigative journalists remain a key independent information source. Examples of journalism must still be evaluated on their own merits and in the context of their publishing platform, however, as everything from multi-article investigative series to recycled press releases are in the offing.

EVALUATING INVESTING INFORMATION SOURCES: FIVE CONCEPTS

Disclosure

Companies that sell stock to the public must adhere to standards of disclosure. Companies listed on U.S. exchanges, for example, must by law file material financial and other information with the Securities and Exchange Commission, on both a routine and as-needed basis. Disclosure requirements have evolved through legislation and regulation. In the wake of the Enron and WorldCom bankruptcies, Regulation FD (for Fair Disclosure) democratized investment information by requiring that company disclosures become available to all investors, not just privileged parties such as analysts, simultaneously (Roush 2011, 25–26, 128–29). Since the Securities and Exchange Commission gave its blessing in 2014, social media has taken its place alongside the traditional press release blast. This new form of disclosure presents compliance challenges due to the sheer number of platforms, informal style, and character limits (Hudson 2014). In addition to required disclosures, it has become more common for companies to share certain information voluntarily, including earnings guidance, and, increasingly, corporate social responsibility information. Baruch Lev (2012) argues that strategic disclosures beyond the bare minimum are beneficial for both companies and investors in the long run. As of 2002, analysts and securities firms must disclose any financial interests (U.S. Securities and Exchange Commission 2010).

Avoiding Conflict of Interest versus Maintaining Transparency

Whenever journalists have a financial interest in entities on which they report (including illegal insider trading on information gained), this should be considered a conflict of interest (Roush 2011, 35–39). Journalistic ethics hold that such conflicts should ideally be avoided; if they cannot, they should be disclosed (Smith 2014). In contrast to traditional media's emphasis on avoidance of conflicts of interest, newer media have often relied on statements of transparency detailing conflicts of interest (Smith 2014). At times, glaring conflicts of interest have been taken as the price of entry for insight into hot new industries: the relationship between tech industry news sites and venture capital is often uncomfortably close (Carson 2015). Unfortunately, readers of traditional media may not be aware of conflict-of-interest policies until they're violated, as when it was reported that three journalists from Reuters' Breakingviews website had written dozens of stories about companies in which they owned stock (Peters 2010).

Fiduciary versus Suitability Standards

Individuals seeking personal finance help should understand how advisers' standards of fiduciary duty differ from suitability standards followed by those acting as brokers. Fiduciary duty entails acting in the client's best interests, while suitability standards are less stringent. Individuals should also take into account the potential influence of different compensation structures for financial industry professionals, and stay abreast of changing laws and regulations affecting such standards (Rieker 2015; Siegel Bernard 2014).

OUTLINE FOR A WORKSHOP ON INVESTING SOURCES

This interactive workshop is aligned to both ACRL's competency standards and the new framework. In introducing some key types of investing information, it helps participants locate, evaluate, and use information in an investing context. In emphasizing the connections between investment sources and the need to incorporate diverse information sources into decision making, it also accords with two of the IL frames: "information has value" and "scholarship as conversation." Participants not only learn about investing information but begin to crystallize their conclusions on a sample stock, in a span of seventy-five to ninety minutes.

A version of the workshop has been provided for "Business Cornerstone" classes, taken at the midpoint of business coursework, at the authors' home institution. This variation is suitable for an audience with some exposure to investing knowledge, such as beginning business students or those who follow business news. The instructor can be a financial professional or a librarian or library staff member with experience in business research. The emphasis is on the information sources themselves and the role they play, rather than on recommending a particular investment methodology.

To provide common ground for exploration and discussion, the instructor should choose a single public company as the focus of the lesson (ideally, a company currently faring neither dramatically poorly nor too well). In cases of preregistration, the company could even be voted on from a short list of possibilities in advance. It should be stated that no endorsement of the company discussed during the workshop is implied. Participants should be broken up into small groups to consider a set of varied information sources relating to the selected company. Possibilities include:

- A 10-Q, a designated portion of the 10-K/annual report (the letter to shareholders is accessible to novices), or an earnings call transcript posted to the company website
- An analyst report evaluating a stock (from databases such as Standard & Poor's NetAdvantage, Value Line, Morningstar, or Investext)
- Market share information (from sources such as *Market Share Reporter*, *Business Rankings Annual*, or the RDS Business Suite database's TableBase module)
- Company financial data (from the Mergent Online database, LexisNexis Academic's Company Dossier section, or Yahoo Finance website)
- A blog posting (from *Seeking Alpha*, *The Street*, etc., or less reputable cousins) or investment message board thread
- Articles from the general business press (*Wall Street Journal*, *Bloomberg BusinessWeek*, etc.), trade publications (*Wall Street Transcript*, *Chain Store Age*, etc.), and/or wire services (Dow Jones, Reuters, BusinessWire, PR Newswire—the latter two distribute company press releases)

Each group can work patchwork fashion, dividing up the resources among themselves. Pathways can be provided for accessing the relevant documents, or alternatively, the instructor can distribute copies, explaining how to find these and similar documents after the analysis and discussion. Participants should be given a set of relevant questions to consider for each source, to facilitate gathering of key data points as well as consideration of qualitative factors, to plant the seeds of a fruitful discussion. Key questions relate to the creators, audience, and relationship of each source: Who produced the source? What stake might the information producers have? For whom is the source intended? Might this source relate to other sources, and if so, how?

Once the sources have been examined individually, the instructor can convene the groups to discuss two questions: How have things been going for the company? And what are its future challenges and plans for addressing them? The instructor can then capture responses from the class as a whole on a whiteboard, soliciting a source for each insight. This activity provides opportunity to tease out differences among sources and to raise more obscure issues such as conflict-of-interest policies. Participants can be led to recognize the inherent biases of types of sources yet work beyond them. For example, financial journalists and investors are dependent on individual companies for much information. It isn't simply a matter of setting aside "biased" sources, but of learning how to balance the company view with other views—coming to see sources as part of an ongoing "conversation" rather than sources that are simply "good" or "bad."

Finally, after some additional time to search for information on the company on their own, teams submit their tentative recommendation of buy, sell, or hold, providing sourced support for their recommendation. (One option would be for teams to submit their rating via an online form or web polling site to create a "consensus" rating.) The instructor can invite two or three groups to share their recommendation, rationale, and key sources. This should serve to illustrate that different sources (or even different information drawn from a single source) may lead to varied conclusions. Asking participants to articulate their nascent conclusions accords with the investment research process as described by an analyst interviewed by Carol Kuhlthau: "He explained that he constructed his point of view in the process of information seeking by building his conclusions from the very beginning and changing his view according to the information he collected" (Kuhlthau 2004, 174)—very much in the spirit of a third concept of the new ACRL framework, "research as inquiry" (ACRL 2015). The session can close with some general disclaimers and ideas for next steps:

- Again, the selection of the company is not an investment endorsement.
- Serious stock research should extend beyond research on individual companies to competitor, industry, and general economic research and awareness. The instructor can provide a resource list; follow-up workshops are another option.
- Picking stocks is not an appropriate strategy for all investors. It takes knowledge, attention, self-discipline, and risk tolerance. Index funds and exchange traded funds involve fewer transaction costs and research requirements and allow investors to share in the broad gains of the market.

One session will not make a successful investor. However, the workshop described above will accomplish a number of goals for both libraries and learners. By offering a workshop such as this one, an academic library can broaden its repertoire of financial literacy programming and explore the connections between financial literacy and information literacy as defined in the new "Framework for Information Literacy for Higher Education." Thus libraries will be able to align their information literacy mission with the need for expanded financial literacy training and ultimately better prepare students for financial decision making over the course of their lifetimes.

WORKS CITED

ACRL. 2000. "Information Literacy Competency Standards for Higher Education." http://www.ala.org/acrl/standards/informationliteracycompetency.

———. 2015. "Framework for Information Literacy for Higher Education." http://www.ala.org/acrl/standards/ilframework.

Boulton, Clint. 2008. "Searching for a Better Process." *Eweek* 25 (26): 18.

Bullock, Nicole, and Kara Scannell. 2014. "Beware Jolly Roger Flag on Pink Sheet Stocks." *Financial Times*, August 27.

Carson, Biz. 2015. "Here's One Way to Become a Venture Capitalist: Be a Journalist." *Business Insider*, June 5. http://www.businessinsider.com/journalists-who-became-vcs-2015-6#ixzz3csqKzitd.

Cox, Jeff. 2015. "All Analysts Want You to Do Is Buy; Here's Proof." *CNBC*, February 26. http://www.cnbc.com/id/102459645.

Dawes, Trevor A. 2013. "Libraries, ACRL, and Financial Literacy: Helping Students Make Sound Decisions." *College & Research Libraries News* 74 (9): 466–67. http://crln.acrl.org/content/74/9/466.full.

Faulkner, Ashley E. 2015. "A Systematic Review of Financial Literacy as a Termed Concept: More Questions Than Answers." *Journal of Business & Finance Librarianship* 20 (1/2): 7–26.

Financial Brand. 2015. "Why Targeting Millennials Will Get Harder for Bank Marketers." May 15. http://thefinancialbrand.com/51857/millennial-college-students-bank-marketing/.

Financial Express. 2014. "Efficient Market Hypothesis: The Long and Short of It." June 10.

Hoffman, Liz, Gillian Tan, and Dana Cimilluca. 2015. "SEC Reviews Fishy Avon Bid—Purported Offer Came in a Government Filing, Sent Shares up over 20%; Company Sees It as Hoax." *Wall Street Journal*, May 15.

Hudson, Subrina. 2014. "Companies Not Sweet on Tweets: SEC's Change in Disclosure Regulations Sets Firms Atwitter." *Los Angeles Business Journal*, April 28.

Inceptia. 2013. "College Students are Put to the Test: The Attitudes, Behaviors and Knowledge Levels of Financial Education." January. https://www.inceptia.org/PDF/Inceptia_FinancialAptitudeAnalysis_researchbrief.pdf.

Kuhlthau, Carol Collier. 2004. *Seeking Meaning: A Process Approach to Library and Information Services*. 2nd ed. Westport, CT: Libraries Unlimited.

Lev, Baruch. 2012. *Winning Investors Over: Surprising Truths about Honesty, Earnings Guidance, and Other Ways to Boost Your Stock Price*. Boston, MA: Harvard Business Review Press.

Marshall, Ben R., Nuttawat Visaltanachoti, and Genevieve Cooper. 2014. "Sell the Rumour, Buy the Fact?" *Accounting & Finance* 54 (1): 237–49.

O'Connor, Lisa G. 2013. "Investors' Information Sharing and Use in Virtual Communities." *Journal of the American Society for Information Science & Technology* 64 (1): 36–47.

Peters, Jeremy W. 2010. "Reuters Writer Resigns over Ethics Policy Breach." *New York Times*, October 18. http://www.nytimes.com/2010/10/19/business/media/19ethics.html.

Rieker, Matthias. 2015. "Fiduciary or Broker? Many Financial Advisers Wear Both Hats." *Total Return*, February 25. http://blogs.wsj.com/totalreturn/2015/02/25/fiduciary-or-broker-many-financial-advisers-wear-both-hats/.

Roush, Chris. 2011. *Show Me the Money: Writing Business and Economics Stories for Mass Communication*. 2nd ed. New York: Routledge, 2011.

RUSA. 2014. "Financial Literacy Education in Libraries: Guidelines and Best Practices for Services." http://www.ala.org/rusa/sites/ala.org.rusa/files/content/FLEGuidelines_Final_September_2014.pdf.

Siegel Bernard, Tara. 2014. "Before the Advice, Check Out the Adviser." *New York Times*, October 10. http://www.nytimes.com/2014/10/12/business/mutfund/before-the-advice-check-out-the-adviser.html?_r=0.

Smith, Kevin Z. 2014. "Personal Disclosure: Transparency Isn't Enough." *Quill*, May/June. http://digitaleditions.walsworthprintgroup.com/article/ETHICS/1720256/0/article.html.

Špiranec, Sonja, Mihaela Banek Zorica, and Gordana Stokić Simončić. 2012. "Libraries and Financial Literacy: Perspectives from Emerging Markets." *Journal of Business & Finance Librarianship* 17 (3): 262–78.

Stratford, Michael. 2015. "Fight over Campus Banking." *Inside Higher Ed*, May 15. https://www.insidehighered.com/news/2015/05/15/obama-administration-propose-new-rules-campus-financial-products.

Tambini, Damian. 2010. "What Are Financial Journalists For?" *Journalism Studies* 11 (2): 158–74.

U.S. Securities and Exchange Commission. 2010. "Analyzing Analyst Recommendations." August 30. http://www.sec.gov/investor/pubs/analysts.htm.

Wirth, Gregg. 2014. "Reform from Outrage? As the Ashes Cool from the Raging *Flash Boys* Debate, Experts Ponder Changes That Could Fix What Many See as a Broken System." *Traders Magazine*, June 2.

Chapter Seven

Library Employee Education Programs

Jennifer Townes, Jacquelyn Daniel, and Tanji N. Gibson

This chapter will examine the outreach efforts of the Atlanta University Center's Robert W. Woodruff Library to raise awareness of financial literacy for library staff and Atlanta University Center faculty. The Robert W. Woodruff Library instituted a financial literacy taskforce that advises all library financial literacy outreach efforts. Among these efforts are *Money Smart Week* (sponsored by the American Library Association and the Federal Reserve) and internal training for library staff. Every April during *Money Smart Week*, the library provides programming and workshops about financial literacy, including the development of financial-literacy-targeted digital research guides and presentations. The library also provides library employee education programs on a variety of topics, and the taskforce recommended two for financial literacy: "Financial Fitness—Living with a Realistic Budget" and "What's Your Spending Personality?" The initiatives listed above have a positive impact on library personnel. This chapter will detail how librarians can support their library colleagues in developing sound relationships with finance.

The Atlanta University Center (AUC) is a unique organization in that it comprises four separate historically black colleges and universities: Clark Atlanta University, the Interdenominational Theological Center, Morehouse College, and Spelman College. Each institution is served by a single library, the Robert W. Woodruff Library (RWWL). RWWL supports the financial and entrepreneurial acumen of AUC students through its financial literacy taskforce, which advises all library financial literacy outreach efforts.

Financial literacy for library staff (and, indeed, all working persons, no matter the industry) is an incredibly important concept, recognized by human resources and financial professionals the world over. In 2014, the International Foundation of Employee Benefit Plans surveyed members representing multiple employers about the types of retirement and financial education offered by their organizations. The findings are published in "*Financial Education for Today's Workforce: 2014 Survey Results*." Key among these are the following:

- "Among organizations offering financial education, the three most common topics are retirement plan benefits, investments and savings."
- "Some of the most common methods of providing financial education are voluntary classes/workshops, retirement income calculators, online resources/courses, free personal consultation services and projected account balance statements and/or pension benefit statements."
- "The biggest obstacle to providing financial literacy is a lack of interest among participants." (International Foundation of Employee Benefit Plans 2014, 3–4)

The report goes on to state that "the two most common reasons for providing financial education are increasing participants' ability to manage money and improving retirement asset allocation/investment decisions" and that "one in ten organizations offering financial education makes the education mandatory."

In the context of libraries, a financially literate staff is a workforce able to meet the financial literacy needs of its patrons, be they public or academic. Adi Redzic, the executive director of iOme Challenge, a national think tank on financial literacy and empowerment for young people, points this out in his 2013 *College & Research Libraries News* article "Financial Literacy: Why Students Need Librarians to Get Involved." Redzic waxes philosophical on the government shutdown of 2013 and the financial problems to be faced by the Millennial generation. "We face a serious, and dangerous, gap in our financial literacy," he writes (Redzic 2013). Redzic posits that librarians are uniquely positioned to fill that gap, as they are trustworthy, unbiased, able to make important connections between campus and community stakeholders, and bring the power of research done well to bear on the situation.

Additionally, Trevor Dawes, former president of the Association of College & Research Libraries, made clear his opinion that librarians can assist college students to make financial decisions. Dawes describes the rising cost of higher education and the librarian's role in helping students navigate troubled financial waters: "Being embedded in the academic culture gives us a unique opportunity to provide access to the information, resources, education, and tools that our community members need to make good financial decisions" (Dawes 2013).

Clearly, a financially literate staff is important, and not just for their own benefit. Librarians of all kinds have a stake in the financial acumen of their patrons. The key to providing excellent financial literacy education is to be financially literate oneself.

FINANCIAL LITERACY TASKFORCE

The RWWL financial literacy taskforce (FLT) is an initiative sparked by the Financial Literacy and Education Commission, a national organization established under the Fair and Accurate Credit Transactions Act of 2003 (U.S. Department of the Treasury 2015). The commission developed a national strategy on financial education, initiating a national conversation on financial literacy. As a result of this conversation, the RWWL created the FLT to advise and plan the library's financial literacy outreach efforts.

The FLT was started in 2012. The taskforce is made up of the library's chief financial officer, senior accountant, business librarian, human resources director, and representatives from each department in the library. The charge of the FLT is to encourage financial literacy among its target audiences: library management, library staff, and Atlanta University Center students, faculty, and community. Integral to financial literacy initiatives at the RWWL are those efforts focusing on library staff.

As mentioned above, the findings of the International Foundation of Employee Benefit Plans indicate that "the biggest obstacle to providing financial literacy is a lack of interest among participants." This interest level among RWWL staff was gauged by surveying staff on potential topics for training. Potential topics were the following:

- Budgeting and saving: how to plan a level budget and stick to it; ways to simplify finances and save money.
- Credit 101: credit scoring, the relationship between a credit report and a credit score, what factors make up one's credit score, how one's score can change over time, and how to improve one's credit score.
- Home buying for first-time homebuyers: how to get prequalified for a loan, what one needs for a down payment, and an introduction to different home-buying programs.
- Identity theft: what identity theft is, how identity theft happens, and how to deter, detect, and defend against identity theft.
- Managing credit cards: how to get rid of credit card debt and use credit responsibly.
- Retirement planning and basic investing: know how much you need to retire; learn the difference between a Traditional IRA and a Roth IRA; transferring 401(k)s from previous employers.

The survey was sent to all RWWL staff and the results collated. Staff preferences were developed into programs delivered through the library's employee education program, discussed below.

LEEP—LIBRARY EMPLOYEE EDUCATION PROGRAM

The Robert W. Woodruff Library created a library employee education program (LEEP) for the purpose of keeping employees engaged, increasing their knowledge, and exposing them to different development opportunities. The official mission of the RWWL LEEP program is "to establish a means of ensuring that the skills, knowledge, abilities and performance of the workforce meet current and future organizational and individual needs." Typically, a "LEEP calendar" is created by the human resources department each quarter, and any department or unit in the library is welcome to submit a training session proposal. Past LEEP sessions included wellness (yoga, Chachersize, mindfulness), technical skills (Camtasia, Excel, Pinterest), and professional development (communication, time management, personal digital archiving). The LEEP program also focuses on financial literacy.

The financial literacy programs that the library employee education program has sponsored are the following:

- Drugstore Savings Class—Learn How to Effectively Use Coupons (March 2013)
- Stress-Free Debt Elimination (March 2013)
- Financial Wellness—Your Credit Report and Credit Score (February 2014)
- Building a Confident Retirement (April 2014)
- Financial Fitness—Living within a Realistic Budget (February 2015)
- What's Your Spending Personality? (March 2015)

The programs were well attended, and staff agree that the sessions are interesting, useful, and appropriate for increasing the staff person's financial acumen. Future plans include building financial literacy information into departmental meetings and forming partnerships with Atlanta University Center business schools.

HUMAN RESOURCES

The human resources department at the Robert W. Woodruff Library has also been quite involved in promoting financial literacy among library employees. The HR department sponsors the financial literacy of library employees in two ways:

- An employee assistance program for financial services: consultation, debt management, house purchasing, financial planning, online financial resource center
- A session on retirement accounts

Like many professional human resource departments, the HR department at the Robert W. Woodruff Library sponsors an employee assistance program (EAP). The EAP available at the RWWL is extensive and provides assistance on mental health, disabilities, conflict resolution, and more. A large portion of the EAP is devoted to financial literacy. Library employees are encouraged to make use of the EAP online financial resource center, including consultations on debt management, home buying and home ownership, and financial/estate planning. The EAP is easily accessible to library employees, as it is linked through the human resources management system and is explained in depth at each new employee orientation.

The RWWL human resources department also holds a session about financial literacy during the library's Spirit Week—a weeklong event each summer given over to internal projects and professional development. During Spirit Week the library closes to the Atlanta University Center community and employees are encouraged to dress casually and interact with each other informally in order to foster camaraderie and cooperation among departments and units. All employees attend, from administration to security officers, and participate in professional development sessions together.

Part of each Spirit Week is a session on financial well-being, in particular the library's retirement plan benefits, investments, and savings. The director of human resources reports on the annual meeting with the retirement plan fund managers. All library staff participate in the discussion, as the director of human resources shares information on demographics, assets, distribution of funds, and effects on payout benefits.

MONEY SMART WEEK

Many other initiatives were born of the Financial Literacy and Education Commission. Those concerning the library world are the American Library Association initiative Money Smart Week and the Reference and User Services Association initiative Smart investing@your library. The RWWL financial literacy taskforce chose Money Smart Week as its primary focus.

Money Smart Week is a financial literacy initiative created by the Federal Reserve Bank of Chicago in 2002. The American Library Association partnered with the Federal Reserve Bank of Chicago in 2010 to provide financial literacy programming to users of all ages to better manage their personal finances. Money Smart Week takes place annually in April, and hundreds of libraries—public and academic—participate each year (Money Smart Week 2015). At the Robert W. Woodruff Library, Money Smart Week is marked by presentations regarding financial literacy and specially created "research guides."

RWWL first participated in Money Smart Week in 2014. During this celebration, the library used several tactics to aid student and staff understanding of financial literacy:

- Messages sent out via the human resources management system
- Tips shared via social media
- A research guide created for the event

During the event, librarians sent out daily financial literacy tips from *Money magazine*. For example, these tips appeared on the library's Twitter feed:

> It's ALA's financial literacy week! Tip: Automate Your Financial Life: your monthly utility, cell & cable payments. Never pay late fees again

> Financial literacy tip: Have a Financial Plan: hire a financial planner to review your retirement & college savings plans. Get on track now!

> Today's financial literacy tip: "Don't Take It With You" Give money to your kids now rather than inheritance. Gifts of $11K/yr are tax-free

On the library's Facebook page, other tips were given:

> AUC Woodruff Library Presents Financial Literacy Tips in Honor of Smart Money Week. Tuesday's Tip: Know your credit score—The Fair Credit Reporting Act (FCRA) requires each of the nationwide credit reporting companies—Equifax, Experian, and TransUnion—to provide you with a free copy of your credit report, at your request, once every 12 months. Visit annualcreditreport.com to get your free credit report. True, you're entitled to free copies of your credit reports once a year, but one detail will be missing: the magic number that lenders and insurers use to judge your credit-worthiness. Currently, the credit bureaus make individuals pay for that.

> AUC Woodruff Library Presents Financial Literacy Tips in Honor of Smart Money Week. Wednesday's Tip: Don't take it with you—Pass on money to your children now rather than bequeathing it. Gifts of up to $11,000 a year are tax-free. Besides, your kids and grandkids will thank you—which they can't do if you have passed away.

During Money Smart Week, the librarians also sent out messages via the library's human resources management system:

> Stop assuming you're immortal—Hire a lawyer to craft a will, a durable power of attorney, a living will and a health-care proxy. It may cost $1,500 to $2,000 (more for large or complicated estates), but could save your heirs thousands in taxes and fees. Unless, of course, you live forever.
>
> Automate your financial life—Call your mutual fund or broker to have monthly investments routed from your bank. Do the same for your monthly utility, cell phone and cable payments. You'll find it easier to budget, and you'll never pay a late fee again.
>
> Don't toss the spare change—At six-month intervals, find a coin sorter and deposit your change in a savings account.

This initiative served two purposes: marketing and education. The target audience became aware of the event and were directed toward more information about programming. By using social media platforms as well as the library's human resources management system, librarians were able to expand their scope of communication, including through both the formal workspace (human resources management system) and the informal (Facebook and Twitter). The target audience also received edifying finance tips from a popular source (*Money* magazine).

The final initiative for the 2014 observance of Money Smart Week was a research guide dedicated to financial literacy. Though geared toward Atlanta University Center students, the guide was marketed to all library staff as well. This research guide contained information on banking and saving, credit and debt, security and ID protection, and library resources.

The RWWL next participated in Money Smart Week in 2015. The programming for this event was more complex than the previous year's, involving four different speakers and an updated research guide. The library forwent posting on Twitter and Facebook in order to concentrate resources and energy on the engaging list of speakers and their presentations. The events were advertised to library staff through flyers posted on stanchions, emails on the library's staff listserv, and the RWWL calendar located on the website.

Beginning in January 2015, librarians began soliciting Atlanta University Center faculty to speak on a financial literacy topic during the upcoming Money Smart Week. Integral to this process was the business librarian, who extended personal invitations to business and finance faculty from each AUC school. The business librarian also tapped contacts in the community and was fortunate enough to engage a local businesswoman to speak on the subject of entrepreneurship.

The resulting speakers were a mix of Atlanta University Center faculty and community businesspersons. Each spoke on entrepreneurship and wealth creation. The presentations were given throughout Money Smart Week and generally lasted an hour. The schedule was as follows:

- Monday: "Wealth Creation" by Arthur Toole, founder, Toole Group
- Tuesday: "The Pitfalls and Perils to Avoid When Starting a Business" by Delores Epps, CEO, Quality Associates
- Thursday: "Effective Credit and Debt Management: Understanding the Premise upon Which Wealth Is Built" by Dr. C. W. Copeland, American College of Financial Services
- Friday: "Investment and Wealth Building" by Dr. John Young, assistant professor of finance, Clark Atlanta University

Overall, the event was successful. The weeklong event garnered sixty-two participants, thirty-eight of whom were library staff (the rest were faculty, students, and members of the community). Librarians distributed a survey to each attendee. The combined results are listed in table 7.1. As indicated by these results, the majority of participants agree that the sessions they attended were valuable, that they learned something useful to their interests, and that they would recommend a Money Smart Week event in the future.

Money Smart Week is a simple, scalable event that can be adapted to the needs of any library—big, small, public, or academic. Libraries can create their own programs, as at the Robert W. Woodruff Library, or find local events to partner with using the Money Smart Week website. The website also includes many free resources such as recorded lectures and interactive activities to start with (Money Smart Week 2015).

Table 7.1. Evaluation Survey Results

Evaluation Questions	Not at All/Very Unlikely	Valuable/Likely	Very Valuable/ Very Likely
How valuable did you find the Money Smart Week session you attended?	0	10	23
How likely are you to apply or take action on something you learned in today's session?	3	8	23
How likely are you to recommend a Money Smart Week event in the future?	1	7	26

CONCLUSION

Financial literacy goes beyond discussions of debt consolidation, retirement plans, investments, and savings. Financial literacy is the ability to understand how money works and how to make informed and effective decisions regarding it. A financially literate library staff is capable of assisting patrons and students navigate their own financial issues and arrive at sound decisions. The activities described in this chapter can be easily adapted for other libraries in order to create an informed and efficient workforce.

REFERENCES

Dawes, Trevor A. 2013. "Libraries, ACRL, and Financial Literacy: Helping Students Make Sound Decisions." *College & Research Libraries News*, October. http://crln.acrl.org/content/74/9/466.full.

International Foundation of Employee Benefit Plans. 2014. "*Financial Education for Today's Workforce: 2014 Survey Results*." https://www.ifebp.org/bookstore/financialeducation/Pages/default.aspx.

Money Smart Week. 2015. "Resources." http://www.moneysmartweek.org/resources.

Redzic, Adi. 2013. "Financial Literacy: Why Students Need Librarians to Get Involved." *College & Research Libraries News*, December. http://crln.acrl.org/content/74/11/556.full.

U.S. Department of the Treasury. 2015. "Financial Literacy and Education Commission." http://www.treasury.gov/resource-center/financial-education/Pages/commission-index.aspx.

Chapter Eight

Myths and Realities of Consumer Credit

Jenny Brewer

The idea that supporting financial literacy in their communities might involve helping patrons in ways that could affect their credit score can be highly intimidating to library staff. This is an area where libraries may need to support internal literacies on the way to helping the community.

The consequences of a potential misstep combined with the personal nature of the issues and information involved can create a situation where staff dread questions of this nature. This feeling of intimidation can lead to ineffective or incomplete assistance. However, library staff can be trained to feel confident in assisting patrons with credit questions, and this training can lead to especially rewarding reference experiences, as knowledgeable support in this area can pay off for the patron in ways that have immediate and measurable results.

SAMPLE CASE STUDY: REFERENCE WITHOUT FEAR (PART 1)

Maple Glen Public Library has recently lost their reference librarian to a better opportunity in Maple Valley. Recruitment is underway for her replacement, but the process may take up to two months. In the meantime, there is an urgent need for help on the reference desk.

Library Director Jane Smith has reached out to other library departments requesting volunteers to fill in on the reference desk for several hours per week. There are no replies.

She walks down to the children's department and asks the librarian if she will work the reference desk on Monday morning. The children's librarian confides that she finds the adult desk intimidating.

"Some of those questions are really serious," she says. "If I get it wrong, bad things could happen to that patron."

Mrs. Smith hears similar concerns from the other librarians. Because the situation is urgent, she needs to build confidence in these librarians quickly. She collects a list of these "really serious" questions and assigns reference staff to create "crash courses" in a wide variety of topics, such as e-book downloading; real estate, wills, and divorce; software applications installed on public workstations; public document services; equipment troubleshooting; and the like.

She realizes that a significant part of the fear her staff feels has to do with being made responsible for sensitive information. She remembers a patron named Mr. Jones from her days on the reference desk. Mr. Jones came in on his way home from the bank, having just been declined for a home loan based on his low credit score. He asked Mrs. Smith for information on credit repair. Because Mrs. Smith had worked as a loan officer while she was attending graduate school, she had actually repaired credit scores for clients in the past.

Because she knew what had worked in the past, she was able to take Mr. Jones to the shelf and recommend a credit repair book that had instructions that matched her experience. Over the next several months, she met with Mr. Jones on multiple occasions and guided him through the book's recommendations, resulting in significant improvement of his score.

It had been a very delicate situation, however, because Mrs. Smith knew she could not give advice as herself or appear to influence any decisions that could have an impact on Mr. Jones's finances. She feels like retracing her steps in this process would provide a good example of the role a librarian can play in this aspect of a patron's life, and of best practices for the handling of sensitive information or situations.

She further realizes that her starting point in this situation had been more advanced than most other librarians, and that it would not have been possible for her to have found so many resources if she had not been able to limit her search to those which gave authoritative confirmation to her preexisting knowledge. She concludes that before they get to Mr. Jones, her lesson plan should begin with a credit primer that will quickly provide trainees with the same baseline understanding she had brought to Mr. Jones's original reference interview.

She recalls her early months as a mortgage processor. She had been surprised several times when her assumptions about how credit scoring and reporting were incorrect. She reflects that it is probably like this for everyone and decides that the best way to establish baseline credit awareness is to correct these misunderstandings. She starts a document:

HANDOUT: MYTHS AND REALITIES OF CONSUMER CREDIT

This list was compiled from consumer information published by the credit bureaus themselves (Transunion, FICO, and Experian) along with the consumer resources provided at Bankrate.com.

Myth: Living debt-free should be everyone's goal.

Reality: It's a good idea to avoid taking on unnecessary debt, but you should keep your options open in case taking on debt does become necessary to meet your family's basic needs (Experian 2015a).

Myth: Secured credit cards are undesirable.

Reality: Just because anyone can get one doesn't mean a secured credit card counts for less on a patron's credit report than an unsecured one (Experian 2007).

Myth: Checking a credit report will hurt your score.

Reality: Checking your own credit will not affect your score, and multiple inquiries are no longer as detrimental as they once were (Experian 2015a).

Myth: There's only one score that all lenders use to determine creditworthiness.

Reality: You have at least forty-nine different credit scores. "While you receive only one type of FICO score, lenders can choose from a variety of scores based on the kind of loan you're applying for. So if you want an auto loan, the lender can look up your FICO auto score. Apply for a credit card and there's a specific FICO bankcard score lenders can use" (Ellis 2012a).

Myth: Once a delinquent loan or credit card balance is paid off, the item is removed from a credit report.

Reality: "Negative information such as late payments, collection accounts and bankruptcies will remain on a person's credit reports for up to seven years. Certain types of bankruptcies stick around for up to 10 years. Paying off the delinquent account won't remove it from a credit report, but it will update the account to indicate it as 'paid'" (Experian 2015a).

Myth: If bills aren't paid on time because a consumer believes the bill is incorrect, the consumer can't be held accountable.

Reality: "If a bill is not paid in a timely manner, the delinquent payment may be reported as late to a credit bureau. If a bill was never received or was incorrect, it's best to contact the provider or company to resolve or discuss the matter prior to the bill becoming past due" (Experian 2015a).

Myth: Paying cash for everything can help a credit rating.

Reality: "Using cash for everything isn't better than using credit responsibly because consumers have to have some sort of history of responsible credit usage in order to establish solid credit histories and credit scores" (Experian 2015a).

Myth: The three credit reports and credit scores from the three credit bureaus will be the same.

Reality: Not all accounts are reported to all three bureaus, and accounts that are reported to all three bureaus may not be updated at the same interval. "Because the credit reporting companies' computer systems are different, the credit score formulas can be slightly different to work with a particular system. That difference in the formula can result in a difference in the scores" (Experian 2015a).

Myth: The best way to improve credit scores is to pay off all accounts and close them.

Reality: The score I see on an online credit reporting site is the same score the lender sees. "A lender looks at one kind of score, like a FICO score, and a consumer looks at a type of score called an 'educational score' that uses a different scoring formula and isn't used by lenders. You can often get these scores online for free from private companies like Quizzle.com, Credit-Sesame.com or CreditKarma.com" (Ellis 2012b).

Myth: Having bad credit won't hurt you if you make enough not to need credit.

Reality: "Federal law allows potential and current employers to view a modified version of your credit report for employment purposes such as hiring and promoting" (Experian 2015a).

Myth: FICO scores are locked in for six months.

Reality: Your most recent payments are reported every month and your score can change with each one: "your FICO score changes as soon as data on your credit report change" (Bankrate.com 2015).

Myth: I don't need to check my credit report if I pay my bills on time.

Reality: "When the Consumer Federation of America and the National Credit Reporting Association analyzed credit scores in the summer of 2002, they discovered that 78 percent of the files were missing a revolving account in good standing, while 33 percent of files lacked a mortgage account that had never been late. Twenty-nine percent contained conflicting information on how many times the consumer had been 60 days late on payments" (Bankrate.com 2015).

Myth: Bad news comes off in seven years.

Reality: "Some of it does. Chapter 13 (reorganization of debt) disappears seven years from the filing date. But if you filed Chapter 7 bankruptcy (exoneration of all debt), the window is 10 years from the filing date" (Bankrate.com 2015).

Myth: It helps to close old accounts.

Reality: "This credit myth advocates closing old and inactive accounts to hike up your score. However, this might inadvertently have the opposite affect and lower your credit score because now the credit history appears shorter. If you don't trust yourself to put a card away in a safe place and not use it, then consider canceling newer accounts" (Transunion.com 2015).

Myth: It's possible for a credit repair service to guarantee a certain number of points clients can gain.

Reality: "Contrary to this credit myth, credit reporting agencies determine your credit score via a complex algorithm that uses hundreds of factors and values to calculate it. It's almost impossible to calculate the difference in points changing one factor might make. It's wise to pay your bills on time, work to lower your debts and ask that any inaccuracies be corrected. A proven record of sound financial behavior and time will have the most significant impact on your score" (Transunion.com 2015).

Myth: Once an automobile company has pulled your credit, shopping around for a better rate will result in multiple inquiries and harm your score, possibly making you ineligible for the original offer.

Reality: "Looking for new credit can equate with higher risk, but most credit scores are not affected by multiple inquiries from auto or mortgage lenders within a short period of time. Typically, these are treated as a single inquiry and will have little impact on the credit score" (MyFICO.com 2015).

Myth: I can always pay someone to fix or repair my credit.

Reality: "Companies claiming to fix your credit deliver on their promises by generating a flood of dispute letters to the credit reporting agencies, which in turn ask the creditor to verify or document the entry. If they cannot, the listing must come off at that time. But if the creditor later does verify or document it, the agency slaps it right back into the file after 30 days" (Bankrate.com 2015).

Furthermore, the steps credit repair companies take to repair credit can be taken just as easily by the individual, and library staff can help them. See "Sample Case History: Librarian-Assisted Credit Repair" for details.

Mrs. Smith feels pretty good about her handout, although she is forced to set the font size at ten and the margins to three-quarters of an inch to keep the information on the front and back of a single sheet of paper. She realizes that this could be a barrier to access for vision-impaired patrons and makes a note to train staff to reprint the handout in whatever font such a patron might request.

She prepares to recount the experience of helping Mr. Jones. She recalled that she had used *Credit Repair Kit For Dummies* by Steve Bucci to begin the initial process. This title came with a "Cheat Sheet" that confirmed the continued relevance of strategies she had employed as a loan officer. Mrs. Smith then sets about crafting a narrative illustrating the ways she applied Mr. Bucci's "Cheat Sheet" to Mr. Jones's situation and achieved net gains to Mr. Jones's score without incurring legal risks for the city:

SAMPLE CASE HISTORY: LIBRARIAN-ASSISTED CREDIT REPAIR

On the day Mr. Jones was declined for a home loan, he drove directly from the bank to the library. He presented himself at the Reference Desk seeking assistance with credit repair, and Mrs. Smith pulled *Credit Repair Kit For Dummies*, 4th edition, by Steve Bucci. Mrs. Smith opened the book to the "Cheat Sheet." She pointed to the first item on a list titled "8 Tips for a Top Credit Score": "Clean up your credit reports every year. Use the Annual Credit Report Request Service to access your report and dispute errors and out-of-date data to boost your score. Up to 25 percent of credit reports have errors; yours may, too" (Bucci 2014). Mrs. Smith explained that she had some familiarity with the process and offered to help him apply the book's advice, providing he was satisfied with the quality of the material and wanted to proceed. She told him she would look at his report with him provided he brought it to her with identifying information blacked out. To be safe, she also provided him with a copy of the library's patron confidentiality policy.

Mr. Jones went to a public workstation and printed out his reports. He borrowed a Sharpie and blacked out the account numbers on each entry along with his Social Security number at the top. When he came back to the desk, Mrs. Smith sat down with him and showed him which entries were derogatory. She asked him to assert what he believed to be the correct date of last activity and balance owed for each entry. Mrs. Smith then assisted Mr. Jones in disputing a late payment on a department store card, which Mr. Jones believed had occurred in the same month as a late payment on his auto loan.

Mrs. Smith then explained that this was the extent of what could be done to address negative entries. She went back to the checklist and showed Mr. Jones how five of the remaining eight tips refer to preventing future negative activity:

- Keep balances below 50 percent of your credit limits. High credit balances mean lower scores.
- Pay your bills on time. It's that simple.
- Keep accounts open longer. Older accounts score higher because they establish the length and stability of your credit history.
- Limit new credit because it lowers your score. New credit and more inquiries on your account increase your risk profile and lower your score, especially if you don't have a long credit history. Add new credit only when it makes sense, not just to have another card or to get an incentive gift.
- Avoid cosigning; it's dangerous to your credit score. If the person for whom you cosign defaults, you may not know about it for months. As a cosigner, you're 100 percent responsible for the debt, including any penalties, and your credit score suffers as well.

She then explained how the remaining two tips have the potential to involve taking on new debt:

- Use more than one type of credit. Doing so shows that you can manage different types of credit and different types of payments (fixed or variable). Have a variety of credit cards, retail accounts, installment loans, and other types of credit.
- Use secured cards to help establish or reestablish credit. Secured cards are accepted by merchants and scored like regular credit cards, and the balance is guaranteed by a bank deposit. This makes credit easier to get and builds or rebuilds your score faster.

She explained that it was possible to strategically open certain types of accounts for the sole purpose of building credit history. She said that, as a loan officer, she had seen it done to good effect, but that she had also seen people who already had a lot of negative entries end up with a lot more, as they had not changed the habits that originally led to their low scores. She emphasized that she is providing this information on the assumption that he has a responsibility to gauge for himself what is appropriate to his individual circumstances.

Mrs. Smith showed Mr. Jones how, providing the dispute to his department store account was resolved in his favor, both of his late payments would age past the two-year mark in ninety days. She suggested that he ask the bank to update his scores at that time and then consider whether to open more accounts.

When Mr. Jones returned, he stated that the bank had praised his efforts but ruled his score still twenty points short. He said that the loan officer had suggested he open one or two more accounts, and then asked for her advice. Mrs. Smith reminded Mr. Jones that she could not make recommendations but conceded that their credit repair "Cheat Sheet" had covered this (Bucci 2014). She encouraged him to cross-reference additional credit repair manuals to confirm this recommendation. Furthermore, she referred him to a recognized "Credit Card Buying Guide" to help him decide which cards to apply for if he chose to proceed (Consumer Reports 2014).

Finally, she suggested that he ask the bank to update his credit again in 120 days, and to let her know the results. She did not actually see him until the following summer, when he informed her that he had finally become a homeowner!

SAMPLE CASE STUDY: REFERENCE WITHOUT FEAR (PART 2)

Mrs. Jones presented her two-part "crash course" to reference staff and participated in demonstrations of the "crash courses" that she had assigned to them as well. Together, they assembled a two-day "working retreat." Mrs. Smith worked out a retreat schedule that allowed children's department and reference desk duty to rotate among herself and the remaining three reference staff over the following Monday and Tuesday, with one person always in the boardroom with the designated trainees. On their evaluation forms, all of the participants rated themselves as "much more prepared to provide reference services." Outside staff were able to rotate into the Reference Desk schedule immediately, providing much-needed support to the department throughout the seven weeks it took to hire a new reference librarian.

CONCLUSION

Consumer credit is an area of financial literacy that may be as confusing to staff as it is to patrons. In situations such as this, supporting financial literacy in the community may require a train-the-trainer approach. Once staff competency has been addressed, librarians might also consider mounting a public awareness campaign using Bucci's "Credit Repair Cheat Sheet," possibly accompanied by an abbreviated version of the case study presented above and the "Myths and Realities of Consumer Credit" handout. Pathfinders and programming could also be adapted from this material.

Fostering a high level of community awareness about credit issues might even have an effect on a library's local economy, as people begin to find themselves with more discretionary cash due to the lower monthly payments that result from higher scores!

REFERENCES

Bankrate.com. 2015. "11 Credit Report Myths." http://link.bankrate.com.akadns.net/finance/debt/11-credit-report-myths-1.aspx.

Bucci, Steve. 2014. *Credit Repair Kit for Dummies*. Hoboken, NJ: John Wiley & Sons.

Consumer Reports. 2014. "Credit Card Buying Guide." http://www.consumerreports.org/cro/credit-cards/buying-guide.htm.

Ellis, Blake. 2012a. "You Have 49 FICO Credit Scores." *CNNMoney*, August 12. http://money.cnn.com/2012/08/28/pf/fico-credit-scores/.

———. 2012b. "Your Credit Score: Not the Same Score Lenders See." *CNNMoney*, September 25. http://money.cnn.com/2012/09/25/pf/credit-scores-cfpb/.

Experian.com. 2007. "Using Secured Credit Cards to Improve Credit History." *Ask Experian*, August 22. https://www.experian.com/ask-experian/20070822-using-secured-credit-cards-to-improve-credit-history.html.

———. 2015a. "20 Common Credit Myths." http://www.experian.com/credit-education/credit-myths.html.

———. 2015b. "Employment and Credit." http://www.experian.com/blogs/ask-experian/2015/04/08/employment-and-credit/.

MyFICO.com. 2015. "Credit Score Facts & Fallacies." http://www.myfico.com/crediteducation/factsfallacies.aspx.

Transunion.com. 2015. "Credit Myths and Misconceptions." http://www.transunion.com/article/credit-score-myths.

Chapter Nine

The Public Library as Financial Literacy Promoter and Provider

Maryann Mori

Public libraries have long been providing information to promote financial literacy. Copies of Morningstar and Value Line reports (publications that provide investment information and updates about stocks, funds, etc.) were always standard inclusions in public library collections, along with various books on personal finance such as *The Richest Man in Babylon* (Clason, 1926), *The Intelligent Investor* (Graham, 1949), and *Common Stocks and Uncommon Profits* (Fisher, 1958)—all still considered classic writings about finances. It is, however, doubtful that the phrase *financial literacy* was used much in past years when libraries were providing books about retirement planning, investing, paying for college, and purchasing a home. But those kinds of resources—heartily recommended by librarians eager to help the public understand these kinds of consumer topics—have been staples in public libraries for decades. (For a list of current recommended titles for library collections, see the appendix of this chapter.)

In recent years, public libraries have been turning their attention to more formal education on financial literacy for people of all ages. While it is debatable when the phrase *financial literacy* came into vogue, its description certainly encompasses public libraries' past offerings that would have fallen into this category, for according to Investopedia, financial literacy is "the possession of knowledge and understanding of financial matters. Financial literacy is mainly used in connection with personal finance matters. Financial literacy often entails the knowledge of properly making decisions pertaining to certain personal finance areas like real estate, insurance, investing, saving (especially for college), tax planning and retirement" (Investopedia 2015). Libraries still provide resources such as Morningstar and Value Line, albeit those sources are now available as online subscription offerings, and public library shelves still abound as they always have with financial books on all of the aforementioned categories of real estate, insurance, investing, saving, tax planning, and retirement, including titles by the latest investment/money gurus and the tried-and-proven publishers such as the *Wall Street Journal* and Wiley.

This chapter will discuss how public libraries have traditionally been equated with literacy and how that concept positively affects financial literacy promotion and warrants numerous partnerships with major finance-related institutions. It will also discuss why public libraries are good providers of financial literacy information. Finally, the chapter will discuss ways public libraries are providing lifelong learning opportunities in the realm of financial literacy.

PROMOTERS OF LITERACY

Because libraries are most often associated with books and reading, they are natural places to promote literacy. While the public library's traditional role in this respect was to promote literacy in the sense of reading, libraries are now promoting transliteracy skills, with financial literacy being among these. Within the past few years, the American Library Association (ALA) has developed two large partnerships that help public libraries further promote financial and investment literacy.

Although Money Smart Week, "a public awareness campaign designed to help consumers better manage their personal finances," has been around since 2002, it developed into a partnership with ALA in 2010 (Federal Reserve Bank of Chicago 2015). This partnership with ALA means libraries are getting even more attention as viable promoters of financial information. Money Smart Week coincides with National Financial Literacy Month in April. During Money Smart Week, public libraries make an extra effort to remind the public of their usual offerings of financial information, such as books, online publications, and databases. Libraries also host special programming during Money Smart Week, not only to highlight their resources but also to bring in guest speakers (financial experts) and conduct various learning opportunities on consumer education topics to help members of their community become more financially literate.

The second partnership, known as Smart investing@your library, is between ALA and the Financial Industry Regulatory Authority (FINRA). FINRA has recognized the public library's value in promoting financial literacy. Gerri Walsh, president of FINRA's Investor Education Foundation, has said, "Libraries are uniquely well positioned in their communities to help residents with their personal finance information needs. Library patrons can be confident that their own best interests are at the heart of programming" (FINRA 2015). Walsh made the comments in a news release dated February 2, 2015, that announced the organization's continued partnership with ALA in awarding grants to public libraries specifically for the purpose of supporting financial literacy. Libraries do not need to win the grant, however, in order to benefit from Smart investing@your library; the Smart Investing website offers plenty of unbiased resources that librarians can share with patrons or use to develop in-house programs for all ages—from children to teens to retirees. The site even offers tutorials and tests for library staff in order to help train the trainer, as it were.

Many other financial institutions have recognized the value of public libraries in promoting financial literacy. The Consumer Financial Protection Bureau (CFPB) partnered with the Institute of Museum and Library Services (IMLS) in 2014 "to develop financial education tools and share best practices with the public library field" (IMLS 2015). According to the IMLS website, "The goal of our partnership is to provide tools and materials to help libraries provide free, unbiased financial information and referrals in their communities, and to build local partnerships and promote libraries as community resources." The CFPB includes on its website a page devoted to helping libraries develop sound financial literacy information. The organization provides librarian training in "monthly webinars for library staff on how to discuss financial education topics with patrons," program ideas, a partnership guidebook, as well as online, print, and marketing resources (CFPB 2015). In June 2014, the CFPB collaborated with the Rhode Island Office of Library and Information Services to unveil a statewide initiative "to improve financial literacy" (Reed 2014). Jennifer Bone, president of the Rhode Island Library Association, said, "Libraries are in the business of providing access to free, objective, reliable information resources so all citizens have opportunities to gain knowledge and skills throughout their lives. By unveiling vetted financial information tools and resources, the CFPB will help libraries deliver more fully and effectively for our patrons when it comes to personal finance matters" (Reed 2014).

As mentioned, public libraries often expand their finance-themed programming efforts during Money Smart Week (MSW). Examples of these special programs include activities such as a "piggy bank parade" for young children—a program where youngsters hear stories about saving money and about pigs, and then make and decorate a piggy bank (possibly from recycled materials such as bleach bottles, or from cardboard cutouts or by painting purchased ceramic banks). The banks can be put on display at the library during MSW, or photos of the banks can be "paraded" on the library's website or social media sites (Facebook, Pinterest, etc.). Iowa hosts a statewide Great Piggy Bank Savers Pageant as part of MSW activities through the United Way and the MSW Iowa committee (United Way of Central Iowa

2012). The Great Piggy Bank Savers Pageant is popular not only with young children but also with teens and college students; libraries have been known to tie the event to MSW as well as Earth Day (both of which occur in April), and this connection seems to appeal to young adults. Teens have attended MSW programs at public libraries where they have had opportunity to learn about buying a first car, withholding taxes from a first job's paycheck, saving for wants/needs, or living on a budget as college time draws near. Public libraries have conducted programs for adults by developing partnerships with extension education and various local financial institutions to host sessions about consumer credit, retirement investing, identity theft, online banking/shopping, purchasing a first home, and paying for college.

Because so many established financial organizations have recognized public libraries as valuable places for financial literacy information, the public library's role as provider of this information continues to grow. Not only are large financial organizations taking note of public libraries, but the public is realizing the local library's role in providing reliable and unbiased financial information.

A 2013 report from Pew Internet and American Life Project showed that 95 percent of Americans over the age of sixteen believe public libraries are important places for their communities because the public library "provides free access to materials and resources" (Zickuhr et al. 2013). Those same Americans agree that "the public library plays an important role in giving everyone a chance to succeed" (Zickuhr et al. 2013). This public perception, tied with the new opportunities created by programs such as Money Smart Week and Smart investing@your library, has turned the public library into a viable and recognized resource for financial information.

Perhaps one of the reasons public libraries are perceived as ideal locations for promoting and providing financial literacy is that, traditionally, public libraries have been known as neutral territory for idea sharing. Public libraries have long been recognized as places for lifelong learning. Libraries do not have an agenda, or a sales margin to meet, and librarians are viewed as helpful, knowledgeable, and nonjudgmental persons who freely disseminate information. Even when partnering with financial institutions to provide programming, the library is careful to ensure that such programs remain "sales pitch free." In fact, a requirement of Money Smart Week is that no services can be sold or promoted through any programs. These facts are especially important in regard to financial information. Citizens have come to realize and expect that the public library is a place where their questions can be answered free of charge, free of judgment, and free of bias.

While many libraries highlight their financial resources and provide special financial information during Money Smart Week, other libraries actively promote these resources and information all year long. One such library is the New York Public Library (NYPL). NYPL has a "Money Matters @

Financial Literacy Central" page on its website, which allows patrons to see ongoing programs (including topics as diverse as living on a fixed income or learning about stock investments), obtain reliable information online, access help for taxes, and learn about the library's online investment resources (such as Value Line and Morningstar). The library's Money Matters resource is made possible through a partnership with McGraw-Hill Financial.

One of the most creative ways a public library has chosen to develop financial literacy among its patrons comes from Chesapeake Public Library in Virginia, which developed an online game in 2011 called $ave $teve (*Library Journal* 2012). The library received a FINRA grant and partnered with Norfolk State University and local artists to develop the game. The game "links to unbiased financial information" that gives players "the knowledge to help $teve overcome his money challenges" (*Library Journal* 2012). Three different playing levels mean the game can be played by children, teens, and adults. In fact, "the library is partnering with local schools to use the game to supplement learning" (*Library Journal* 2012).

Brooklyn Public Library developed an online resource titled MyOwnBiz that allows young people (ages twelve to twenty-one) to investigate aspects of entrepreneurship (MyOwnBiz 2015). Funded by a grant from the JPMorgan Chase Foundation, the site includes five considerations of business ownership: knowing where to start (educational and legal requirements), funding the business (grants, costs, money goals), identifying customers, marketing the business, and developing a business plan (MyOwnBiz 2015). The resource was launched in 2003 as "Someday Soon . . . I'll Start My Own Business" after the library surveyed area youth and learned that "90% of youth surveyed reported that they were interested in learning more about starting a business" ("Brooklyn! Build My Business" n.d.). These examples may seem extreme; after all, not every public library has the resources or audience to launch such big projects. But even the smallest of public libraries often offers financial literacy information via links from the library's website, printed in-house materials, and regular displays that highlight the library's collection of personal finance information.

A successful example of small libraries impacting their communities' financial literacy awareness is the Smart investing@your library story from Iowa. The state library of Iowa, known as Iowa Library Services, received a Smart Investing grant from FINRA in 2010, and an additional grant in 2012 that was used to continue the effort begun in 2010 (Iowa Library Services 2015). Public libraries were offered the opportunity to apply to the state-sponsored program for nearly six hundred dollars' worth of investment books and materials, and selected libraries partnered with Iowa State University Extension staff to host face-to-face and online classes for library patrons to learn more about investing, preparing for retirement, and retiring. Iowa Library Services selected as its participants public libraries that were "located in rural communities of under 25,000 population" (Iowa Library Services 2015). In the first round of grants, twenty-five libraries were selected (Iowa State Extension and Outreach 2011). Over four hundred rural Iowans participated in the classes offered at those libraries, with noticeable improvements in the participants' financial literacy knowledge. "Pre- and post-surveys indicate that participants not only increased their knowledge about investing, but also took action"; participants began looking at their retirement plans more seriously, developed an "investment philosophy," and "assessed risk tolerance" (Iowa State Extension and Outreach 2011). Participants said "they appreciated learning about investing without any pressure to buy particular investment products. They also said they had shared information from the course with family members, friends and neighbors, and planned to use local and state library resources in the future to learn more about investing and other personal finance topics" (Iowa State Extension and Outreach 2011). Another eighteen rural libraries participated in the second round of grants through Iowa Library Services (Iowa Library Services 2015). This program proved that even smaller libraries can actively provide quality financial literacy resources and opportunities to patrons.

PROVIDERS OF LIFELONG LEARNING

As noted elsewhere in this chapter, public libraries are known as places of learning for all ages. Andrew Carnegie is the person most often associated with deeming public libraries as "the people's university." Although the phrase's attribution is debatable, the sentiment is true; public libraries are places where anyone of any age or socioeconomic background can learn about anything—all without fee to the user. The public knows this fact, and librarians know it. Librarians are eager to keep up the image, so they are eager to participate in and offer new ideas for helping the public gain better understanding of a topic. It is often because of librarians' endorsement of lifelong learning activities that public libraries offer financial literacy information in the first place. As an example of librarians' eagerness to develop new ideas to promote lifelong learning activities, the Money Smart Week Iowa committee annually offers new ways to get financial literacy learning opportunities into the hands of the public and has received excellent responses from public librarians who are eager to introduce those ideas at their libraries. In 2014, the committee unveiled a program known as Dash for the Stash that asked public libraries to put up a series of four posters that shared various financial and investment information. The posters included a QR code that participants could scan to access an investment question to answer (with answers gleaned from the posters). Public libraries across Iowa were quick to accept the program and oversee its operation at library facilities.

Another program initiated by Money Smart Week Iowa was a "read" where public librarians were asked to sponsor intergenerational programming that allowed parents or grandparents to interact with a child to learn about saving money. The pilot program proved so successful that it was repeated in 2015 with the theme of entrepreneurship as its focus.

Investment clubs are another finance-themed lifelong learning activity that public libraries often provide, whether by directly hosting the club at the library, sponsoring a virtual club (such as Brooklyn Public Library does), or allowing existing clubs to utilize library space. Santa Clara County Library District in California offers investment club kits—packets of information that library patrons can borrow to start their own investment club (Santa Clara County Library District 2013).

Kansas City Public Library features an H&R Block Business and Career Center that is "a dedicated service center for patrons doing research in . . . entrepreneurship, job seeking and career development, grant research and writing, business and financial news, [and] youth financial literacy" (Kansas City Public Library 2015). The Business and Career Center offers personal consultation appointments with the library's business librarians. According to the library's website, "Business librarians are available to help you to understand and use Library resources, find information, make referrals to local agencies for additional assistance or training, and answer questions related to new business, job hunting, education, personal finance, and more" (Kansas City Public Library 2015).

Developing extensive "path finders" (lists of reference resources) to other existing financial literacy websites and information is yet another way that public libraries make personal finance education a lifelong focus among library patrons. Denver Public Library has such a page on its website. A simple online search for "public libraries personal finance" will result in numerous public libraries that have pages similar to the one at Denver Public Library. The Public Library Association, a division of the ALA, has an annotated list of online financial information resources that public libraries can use to develop their own path finders on their local library websites (ALA 2015a).

In addition to Money Smart Week observations in April, many public libraries also observe Financial Wellness Month in January. The Programming Librarian website, an initiative of the ALA, encourages libraries to observe this month and offers suggested examples of programs that have been successful in other public libraries (ALA 2015b). The observation is appropriately timed at after-holiday spending seasons, so the public is often more interested at this time in learning about ways to pay off debt, spend less, and save for future purchases. Librarians understand the value of providing information at the appropriate time and are accustomed to highlighting national observances; participation in financial literacy events during this month makes good sense for public libraries.

Whether providing physical books or virtual databases, printed newspapers or online investment news, do-it-yourself tutorials or in-person programs, public libraries continue to provide personal finance, investment, and assorted financial literacy information. Public libraries have always provided this kind of information, and with new and continually expanding partnerships with major financial institutions, it is obvious that public libraries will continue to be major players in helping the public become more financially literate.

APPENDIX: RESOURCES FOR DEVELOPING FINANCIAL LITERACY COLLECTIONS IN PUBLIC LIBRARIES

- Lydia Dallett, "11 Personal Finance Books Everyone Should Read before Turning 30," *Business Insider*, February 5, 2014, http://www.businessinsider.com/personal-finance-books-to-read-before-30-2014-2#. A brief description of each title is given, as well as an explanation of "why it's great for young people."
- Matthew Boesler, "The 22 Most Important Finance Books Ever Written," *Business Insider*, December 3, 2013, http://www.businessinsider.com/the-most-important-finance-books-2013-12#. List includes titles from the twentieth and twenty-first centuries.
- Lisa Aberle, "The Ultimate Round-Up Collection of Personal Finance Books," Get Rich Slowly: Personal Finance That Makes Sense, January 21, 2016, http://www.getrichslowly.org/blog/2007/03/07/building-a-personal-finance-library-25-of-the-best-books-about-money/. Includes a brief description of each title; titles are listed in categories such as "frugality," "kids and money," and "investing."
- Peter McKay, "Business Books: Core Collections," George A. Smathers Libraries, UF Business Library, http://businesslibrary.uflib.ufl.edu/businessbooks. Includes links to bibliographies of "best books" in various money-related categories such as business, consumer behavior, economics, and investment.
- Geoffrey James, "Top 10 Personal Finance Books of All Time" James, . "Top 10 Personal Finance Books of All Time," *Inc.*, May 8, 2013, http://www.inc.com/geoffrey-james/top-10-personal-finance-books-of-all-time.html. Lists older publications along with newer ones that that are considered classics or core titles.

REFERENCES

ALA. 2015a. "Financial Literacy: Resources for You and Your Patrons." Public Library Association. http://www.ala.org/pla/tools/financiallit.

———. 2015b. "Financial Wellness Month." Programming Librarian. http://ozzie.ala.org/library/events-and-celebrations/financial-wellness-month.html#.VPOLseEYOFI.

———. 2015c. "Money Smart Week." http://www.ala.org/offices/money-smart-week.

"Brooklyn! Build My Business: Teen Entrepreneurial Competition Case Overview." n.d. *Shaping Outcomes*, 2. http://www.shapingoutcomes.org/course/cases/Brooklyn%20Case%20final.pdf.

CFPB. 2015. "Library Training." http://www.consumerfinance.gov/library-resources/librarian-training/.

Denver Public Library. 2015. "Investing and Personal Finance." http://denverlibrary.org/content/investing.

Federal Reserve Bank of Chicago. 2015. "About Money Smart Week." Money Smart Week. http://www.moneysmartweek.org/.

FINRA. 2015. "FINRA Investor Education Foundation and the American Library Association Announce $1.8 Million in Grants to Public Libraries to Support Financial Literacy." February 2. http://www.finra.org/Newsroom/NewsReleases/2015/P602379.

IMLS. 2015. "Financial Literacy." https://www.imls.gov/issues/national-initiatives/financial-literacy.

Investopedia. 2015. "Financial Literacy." http://www.investopedia.com/terms/f/financial-literacy.asp.

Iowa Library Services. 2015. "Smart investing@your library: Iowa's Story." http://www.statelibraryofiowa.org/ld/q-s/smart-invest-lib/smart-invest-iowa.

Iowa State University Extension and Outreach. 2011. "'Smart Investing' Course Reaches Rural Communities." http://www.extension.iastate.edu/content/smart-investing-course-reaches-rural-communities.

Kansas City Public Library. 2015. "H&R Block Business & Career Center." http://www.kclibrary.org/business-career.

Library Journal. 2012. "Jim Blanton: Movers & Shakers 2012—Recession Busters." March 13. http://lj.libraryjournal.com/2012/03/people/movers-shakers-2012/jim-blanton-movers-shakers-2012-recession-busters/#_.

MyOwnBiz. 2015. http://somedaysoon.brooklynpubliclibrary.org/.

Reed, Jack. 2014. "CFPB, Sen. Reed, RI Libraries Launch Financial Literacy Partnership in Johnston" Jack Reed: United States Senator for Rhode Island, June 16. http://www.reed.senate.gov/news/releases/cfpb-sen-reed-ri-libraries-launch-financial-literacy-partnership-in-johnston.

Santa Clara County Library District. 2013. "Santa Clara County Library District Announces Investment Club Starter Kits to Go." January 13. https://www.sccl.org/About/Library-News/Press-Releases/Santa-Clara-County-Library-District-Announces-Inve.

United Way of Central Iowa. 2012. "Great Piggy Bank Downloads." Everyone Can Save. http://www.everyonecansave.org/page54/downloads-2/bank.html.

Zickuhr, Kathryn, Lee Rainie, Kristen Purcell, and Maeve Duggan. 2013. "How Americans Value Public Libraries in Their Communities." Pew Internet, December 11. http://libraries.pewinternet.org/2013/12/11/section-3-perceptions-of-public-libraries/.

Chapter Ten

What Is Financial Literacy and Why Should We Care?

Shin Freedman and Marcia Dursi

> "Financial literacy is a basic but essential skill for living in the 21st century. It is what reading and writing was for previous generations; somebody who could not read and write could not fully participate in society, just as today, somebody who is not financially literate cannot fully participate in the modern economy." (Lusardi 2013)

Financial illiteracy among the U.S. population, including college students, is a fast-growing concern for all. The problems—poor borrowing behavior, failure to understand the consequences of college tuition borrowing, student loans, failure to save money, and lack of participation in retirement programs—are not limited to those with low education, women, African Americans, or Hispanics. For most students, college will be the first time they have been responsible for financial decisions that can have a long-term impact on their future. For some, these decisions may be made without significant support from home. Financial decision making can lead to success or failure in our current and future lives.

But what exactly is *financial literacy* and all the other terms used so interchangeably with this phrase, such as *financial education*, *financial capability*, *financial awareness*, and *financial knowledge*? Unfortunately, even after so many years of studying the problem, no one clear definition of the phrase *financial literacy* has emerged. Financial literacy has been defined in multiple ways:

- Possessing the skills and knowledge on financial matters to confidently take effective action that best fulfills an individual's personal, family, and global community goals (Council for Economic Education 2013).

- The ability to use knowledge and skills to manage financial resources effectively for a lifetime of financial well-being. Financial literacy encompasses financial education—the process by which individuals improve their knowledge and understanding of financial products, services, and concepts (Cackley 2014)
- Possessing the skills and knowledge on financial matters to confidently take effective action that best fulfills an individual's personal, family, and global community goals (National Financial Educators Council 2014)
- People's ability to process economic information and make informed decisions about financial planning, wealth accumulation, debt, and pensions (Lusardi and Mitchell 2014).
- The ability to recognize the financial implication of nonfinancial information (Wilson, Abraham, and Mason 2014).

Despite the U.S. government's early policy and now classic document to encourage financial literacy among all Americans, without a definitive financial literacy definition it is challenging to create programs to teach, train, or strengthen college students' skills and abilities in this area. The policy was not put in use until the National Standards for Financial Literacy were developed in 2013 by the Council for Economic Education, yet these standards were developed only to grades four, eight, and twelve. The need to improve college students' financial literacy skills is so apparent! As revealed by the FINRA Investor Education Foundation's National Financial Capability Study conducted in 2012, Millennials (those born between 1978 and 1994) make ill-informed financial decisions and engage in behaviors that result in poor individual financial health. A startling statistic from this study shows that 23 percent of Millennials spend more than their income (FINRA 2014).

With 71 percent of college graduates carrying an average of $29,400 in student loan debt upon graduating, with the disappearance of pensions, mounting credit card debt, and high default rates, and with saving plans becoming more diversified, personal finance has become "like rocket science: hard and complicated," noted Singletary (2014). Furthermore, student credit card loan debt averages more than $4,100, according to Sally Mae's National Study of Usage Rate. College students with a credit card reach over 28 percent, of whom about a quarter have more than one credit card. It should come as no surprise then when a Yahoo search conducted in February 2015 using the search terms "college students financial literacy" brings up a credit card ad as its first result.

In the 2014 Money Matters on Campus (MMOC) survey, researchers expressed concern that financial literacy among young adults does not appear to be improving, especially among those who may need these critical money management skills the most—minorities, those from low socioeconomic backgrounds, and those with little financial knowledge (EverFi 2014). The report also suggested that while financial knowledge alone plays a strong predictive role in increasing healthy fiscal outcomes, financial literacy education programs should also be augmented with attitudinal and behavioral components to increase their impact on real-world decision making.

WHAT ROLES DO ACADEMIC LIBRARIES PLAY IN FINANCIAL LITERACY?

What roles do academic libraries play in promoting, teaching, and informing college students, staff, and faculty of the importance of financial literacy? As with information literacy, the library and librarian role is to help users determine when they need financial information and what type of financial information; how to locate the financial information needed to fulfill their need; how to evaluate the source, quality, and reliability of that information; and how to develop the skills needed to use the financial information to accomplish a specific purpose. Whether text, image, or data, whether information, visual, or financial literacy, academic libraries and librarians are in the unique position of providing direction and guidance through our expertise in information management and behavior modification. Through numerous library instruction sessions, we enable students to grow from poor or low-quality information literacy skills to higher-quality skills. Financial literacy provides an opportunity for students to develop higher-quality financial behaviors that will be a strong building block for a more financially sound future.

Because of concerns about the high cost of college education and because most people do not know how to manage money, Trevor Dawes, the Association of College & Research Libraries president in 2013–2014, urged academic librarians to develop financial literacy programs and resources that can have an impact on the lives of our faculty and staff members, our students, and other members of our communities (Dawes 2013). Despite Dawes's urging of financial education as a natural extension of information literacy and the presence of financial literacy forums at American Library Association conferences, academic libraries and librarians have been slow to respond in developing financial literacy for college students.

An article by Redzic (2013) in *College & Research Libraries* lamented that the epicenters of academic life and depositories of knowledge do not actively offer financial literacy education resources. In that article, he urged librarians to connect with other campus stakeholders, including faculty, students, and the larger community, to deliver much-needed financial literacy services to students. The reason cited was that libraries and librarians are generally trusted to bring unbiased, well-researched knowledge to users.

The American Library Association recognized the need to help librarians deliver financial literacy services. The Business Reference Services Section (BRASS) of the Reference and User Services Association, under the direction of an expert panel of financial literacy advisors, wrote the document "Financial Literacy Education in Libraries: Guidelines and Best Practices for Service" (Reference & User Services Association 2014).

There are many tools academic librarians can use to guide students to resources that will equip them to develop lifelong financial literacy skills. The key, though, is to help students understand that the skills and knowledge they are learning are as important now as they will be several years out. Much research has been conducted showing that financial education done in advance of time of need is not conducive to long-term memory or use (Fernandes, Lynch, and Netemeyer 2014). This is similar to the issues faced by librarians when conducting a library instruction session; too soon and students cannot place the instruction in context to an assignment nor remember what to do when they need to locate information. Conduct a library instruction session too late and it serves no purpose as students have already located the information they will use.

Other similarities between information literacy and financial literacy exist. For example, an analysis conducted by the TIAA-CREF Institute and the Global Financial Literacy Excellence Center using the 2012 National Financial Capability Study data found that many college-educated young adults suffer from a lack of awareness that they lack financial knowledge (Scheresberg, Lusardi, and Yakoboski 2014). This problem is also found in information literacy, in which students do not know they do not know.

LIBRARIAN LIAISON WORK

The results of a recent study showed that it is not the financial education students receive that impacts their financial literacy skills. Rather, it is the students' strong mathematics skills that transfer into lifelong financial skills (Cole, Paulson, and Shastry 2014). Financial knowledge, like all knowledge that is not used or tapped into on a regular basis, can deteriorate over time, yet each year there are more and more complex financial tools and options from which consumers (former students) can choose. Without a strong mathematics background, it is difficult to differentiate between these many options. As a result of our liaison work, there are many opportunities to facilitate discussions, speaker events, student workshops, and sharing of resources between and with the finance and mathematics faculty. As with information literacy skills, students need to come to the realization that financial literacy skills are indeed lifelong skills.

As behavioral finance gains importance as an academic field, insights gained from the field of behavioral cognitive psychology are helping to explain consumers' money management, financial, and investment behaviors. While there is much discussion of the definition of financial literacy, there is little disagreement among researchers on the set of behaviors needed to ensure financial success. These behaviors include saving, cash flow management, absence of debt or debt payment budgeting and scheduling, and investment decisions and character traits such as self-control, frugality, and wisdom and responsibility (Fernandes, Lynch, and Netemeyer 2014). Terms such as *self-control*, *positive feelings*, *societal and cultural differences*, and *behavior management techniques* are finding their way into the literature of the finance, economics, and psychology disciplines (Austin and Arnott-Hill 2014). The liaison work conducted with finance and mathematics faculty can be replicated with finance, economics, and psychology faculties.

LIBRARY WEB PRESENCE ON FINANCIAL LITERACY

Through the use of content management systems such as LibGuides, academic librarians can present high-quality information resources for financial literacy to the academic community at large.

LIBRARIAN ACADEMIC SUPPORT

The following partial list describes best practices on financial literacy activities initiated by libraries.

- At Penn State University, the university libraries sponsored financial literacy presentations and workshops on budgeting, identity theft, credit cards, student loans, and other personal finance topics relevant to college students. The Student Financial Education Center, a peer-to-peer financial education program, is housed in the library.
- The University of Tennessee, Knoxville, planned a three-part "Financial Literacy Boot Camp" program for the 2014–2015 academic year to introduce students to financial knowledge and skills. The program was a supported by a grant from the UT Alliance of Women Philanthropists to the Hodges Library.
- Tennessee Technological University's Volpe Library offered instruction on personal finance topics, including savings, budgeting, debt, college student essentials, and philanthropy, in fall 2014. The library licensed presentation materials from Dave Ramsey's Foundations of Personal Finance for College Campuses (http://www.daveramsey.com/school/college). The library is collaborating with the Learning Villages and athletics

to develop sessions designed for these students in addition to the open-attendance sessions.

- At Marymount University, an information literacy curriculum mapping concept, adapted from Wartburg College, was added to the introductory finance course of the School of Business Administration, in which the fundamentals of business finance and financial well-being of college students are taught. Collaboratively, the librarian and the School of Business Administration department chairs determined which courses should be included in the initial mapping process. The curriculum map has been updated on a yearly basis. See the "Curriculum Map Worksheet" in the appendix to this chapter. All freshmen students and transfer students take the English composition component of the University's Liberal Arts Core (EN101 and EN102), so the School of Business Administration curriculum map started with these two courses. The business courses listed on the curriculum map begin with MGT291, Business Communication, a writing-intensive course offered every semester in which two library instruction sessions are provided to the students. Next is FIN301, the introductory finance course, in which the fundamentals of business finance are taught. MKT301, the introductory marketing course, is the last course on the map. In this course, a marketing plan is created to deliver goods and services to customers and includes understanding demographics, pricing models, and advertising rates. These courses are taken by every student enrolled in the bachelor of business administration (BBA) program and are selected for the curriculum map since each course requires knowledge of completely different resources to solve the information needs of the discipline. Not all the information literacy competency standards were selected for inclusion on the curriculum map for the BBA program. Through this close connection with the students and faculty, ideas for writing assignments related to financial literacy topics are provided by the librarian.

CONCLUSION

To be financially literate, students and individuals must demonstrate knowledge and skills needed to make choices within a financial marketplace that all consumers face regardless of their particular characteristics. A successful measure of financial literacy will allow librarians/educators to identify education to achieve desired outcomes.

Thorough awareness of the importance of financial literacy skills and the similarity between these skills and information literacy skills, librarians are in a unique position to help college students develop lifelong financial literacy. Collaboration with other areas and departments throughout a higher education institution is the key to successful implementation of a financial literacy curriculum plan. Academic libraries and librarians cannot work in isolation to promote financial literacy. Nor can aspects of financial literacy be taught in one-shot library instruction sessions, as librarians have seen how less than successful such sessions have been for information literacy instruction. As the need for higher levels of financial literacy are recognized not only on college campuses but throughout countries and their economic bodies, it is important that academic libraries and librarians are involved in that conversation.

APPENDIX: CURRICULUM MAP WORKSHEET

1. LI: Librarians introduce a concept
2. LR: Librarians reinforce a concept
3. LM: Librarians teach a concept so students master it (LI move to LR and then move to LM)
4. F: Teaching faculty responsibilities

Standard One

1. The information-literate student defines and articulates the need for information.

Outcome	EN101	EN102	MGT 291	FIN301	MKT 301
Explores general information sources to increase familiarity with the topic.	LI	LR	LI	LI	LI
Defines or modifies the information need to achieve a manageable focus.	LI	LR	LI	LI	LI
Identifies key concepts and terms that describe the information need.	LI	LR	LI	LI	LI

2. The information-literate student identifies a variety of types and formats of potential sources for information.

Outcome	EN101	EN102	MGT 291	FIN301	MKT 301

Knows how information is formally and informally produced, organized, and disseminated.	N/A	N/A	LI	LI	LI
Recognizes that knowledge can be organized into disciplines that influence the way information is accessed.	N/A	N/A	LI	LR	LR
Identifies the value and differences of potential resources in a variety of formats (e.g., multimedia, database, website, data set, audio/visual, book).	LI	LI	LI	LR	LR
Identifies the purpose and audience of potential resources (e.g., popular vs. scholarly; current vs. historical).	N/A	N/A	LI	LR	LR
Differentiates between primary and secondary sources, recognizing how their use and importance vary with each discipline.	N/A	N/A	N/A	LI	LI
Realizes that information may need to be constructed with raw data from primary sources.	N/A	N/A	F	LI	LI

3. The information-literate student considers the costs and benefits of acquiring the needed information.

Outcome	EN101	EN102	MGT 291	FIN301	MKT 301
Determines the availability of needed information and makes decisions on broadening the information-seeking process beyond local resources.	N/A	LI	LI	N/A	LR

4. The information-literate student reevaluates the nature and extent of the information need.

Outcome	EN101	EN102	MGT 291	FIN301	MKT 301
Reviews the initial information need to clarify, revise, or refine the question.	LI	LR	LR	LR	LR
Describes criteria used to make information decisions and choices.	LI	LR	LR	LR	LR

Standard Two

1. The information-literate student selects the most appropriate investigative methods or information retrieval systems for accessing the needed information.

Outcome	EN101	EN102	MGT 291	FIN301	MKT 301
Investigates the scope, content, and organization of information retrieval systems.	N/A	N/A	LI	LI	LR
Selects efficient and effective approaches for accessing the information needed from the investigative method or information retrieval system.	LI	LI	LI	LI	LR

2. The information-literate student constructs and implements effectively designed search strategies.

Outcome	EN101	EN102	MGT 291	FIN301	MKT 301
Identifies keywords, synonyms, and related terms for the information needed.	LI	LR	LR	LI	LI

Selects controlled vocabulary specific to the discipline or information retrieval source.	N/A	N/A	LI	LI	LI
Constructs a search strategy using appropriate commands for the information retrieval system selected.	LI	LI	LI	LR	LR
Implements the search strategy in various information retrieval systems using different user interfaces, search engines, and search parameters.	LI	LI	LR	LR	LR
Implements the search using investigative protocols appropriate to the discipline.	N/A	N/A	LI	LI	LI

3. The information-literate student retrieves information online or in person using a variety of methods.

Outcome	EN101	EN102	MGT 291	FIN301	MKT 301
Uses various search systems to retrieve information in a variety of formats.	LI	LI	LR	LR	LR
Uses various classification schemes and other systems to locate information resources within the library or to identify specific sites for physical exploration.	LI	LR	LR	N/A	LR
Uses specialized online or in-person services available at the institution to retrieve information needed (e.g., interlibrary loan, professional associations, institutional research offices, experts and practitioners).	N/A	LI	LR	N/A	LR

Uses surveys, letters, interviews, and other forms of inquiry to retrieve primary information.	N/A	N/A	N/A	LI	LR

4. The information-literate student refines the search strategy if necessary.

Outcome	EN101	EN102	MGT 291	FIN301	MKT 301
Assesses the quantity, quality, and relevance of the search results to determine whether alternative information retrieval systems or investigative methods should be utilized.	LI	LI	LI	LR	LR
Identifies gaps in the information retrieved and determines if the search strategy should be revised.	LI	LI	LI	LR	LR
Repeats the search using the revised strategy as necessary.	LI	LI	LI	LR	LR

5. The information-literate student extracts, records, and manages the information and its sources.

Outcome	EN101	EN102	MGT 291	FIN301	MKT 301
Creates a system for organizing the information.	LI	LR	LI	LR	LR
Differentiates between the types of sources cited and understands the elements and correct syntax of a citation.	LI	LR	LI	LR	LR
Records all pertinent citation information for future reference.	LI	LI	LR	LM	LM
Uses various technologies to manage the information selected and organized.	N/A	N/A	LI	LR	LR

Standard Three

1. The information-literate student summarizes the main ideas to be extracted from the information gathered.
2. The information-literate student articulates and applies initial criteria for evaluating both the information and its sources.

Outcome	EN101	EN102	MGT 291	FIN301	MKT 301
Examines and compares information from various sources in order to evaluate reliability, validity, accuracy, authority, timeliness, and point of view or bias.	LI	LI	LR	LR	LR

3. The information-literate student synthesizes main ideas to construct new concepts.
4. The information-literate student compares new knowledge with prior knowledge to determine the value added, contradictions, or other unique characteristics of the information.

Outcome	EN101	EN102	MGT 291	FIN301	MKT 301
Determines whether information satisfies the research or other information need.	LI	LI	LI	LR	LR
Uses consciously selected criteria to determine whether the information contradicts or verifies information used from other sources.	LI	LI	LI	LR	LR
Determines probable accuracy by questioning the source of the data, the limitations of the information gathering tools or strategies, and the reasonableness of the conclusions.	LI	LI	LI	LR	LM

Selects information that provides evidence for the topic.	LI	LI	LI	LR	LR

5. The information-literate student determines whether the new knowledge has an impact on the individual's value system and takes steps to reconcile differences.
6. The information-literate student validates understanding and interpretation of the information through discourse with other individuals, subject-area experts, and/or practitioners.
7. The information-literate student determines whether the initial query should be revised.

Outcome	EN101	EN102	MGT 291	FIN301	MKT 301
Determines if original information need has been satisfied or if additional information is needed.	LI	LI	LI	LR	LR
Reviews search strategy and incorporates additional concepts.	LI	LI	LI	LR	LR
Reviews information retrieval sources used and expands to include others as needed.	LI	LI	LI	LR	LR

Standard Four

1. The information-literate student applies new and prior information to the planning and creation of a particular product or performance.
2. The information-literate student revises the development process for the product or performance.
3. The information-literate student communicates the product or performance effectively to others.

Standard Five

1. The information-literate student understands many of the ethical, legal, and socioeconomic issues surrounding information and information technology.

Outcome	EN101	EN102	MGT 291	FIN301	MKT 301
Identifies and discusses issues related to privacy and security in both the print and electronic environments.	N/A	N/A	F	LI	LI

2. The information-literate student follows laws, regulations, institutional policies, and etiquette related to the access and use of information resources.

Outcome	EN101	EN102	MGT 291	FIN301	MKT 301
Uses approved passwords and other forms of ID for access to information resources.	LI	LR	LR	LR	LR
Complies with institutional policies on access to information resources.	LI	LI	LR	LR	LR
Legally obtains, stores, and disseminates text, data, images, or sounds.	N/A	N/A	LI	LI	LI
Demonstrates an understanding of what constitutes plagiarism and does not represent work attributable to others as his/her own.	F	F	LI	LI	LI

3. The information-literate student acknowledges the use of information sources in communicating the product or performance.

Outcome	EN101	EN102	MGT 291	FIN301	MKT 301
Selects an appropriate documentation style and uses it consistently to cite sources.	LI	LR	LI	LR	LR

This curriculum map is based on the following: http://library.wartburg.edu/infolit/Curriculum%20MapComplete%20Document2005.pdf.

REFERENCES

Austin, Percy, and Elizabeth Arnott-Hill. 2014. "Financial Literacy Interventions: Evaluating the Impact and Scope of Financial Literacy Programs on Savings, Retirement, and Investment." *Journal of Social, Political, and Economic Studies* 39 (3): 290–314.

Cackley, Alicia Puente. 2014. "Financial Literacy: Overview of Federal Activities, Programs, and Challenges." Testimony, Subcommittee on Financial Institutions and Consumer Credit, House Committee on Financial Services, U.S. General Accountability Office. Washington, DC: U.S. General Accountability Office.

Cole, Shawn A., Anna Paulson, and Gauri Kartini Shastry. 2014. "Smart Money? The Effect of Education on Financial Outcomes." *Review of Financial Studies* 27 (7): 2022–51.

Council for Economic Education. 2013. *National Standards for Financial Literacy.* New York: Council for Economic Education.

EverFi. 2014. *Money Matters On Campus: How Early Financial Attitudes, Knowledge, and High School Preparation Influence Financial Decisions.* http://moneymattersoncampus.org/wp-content/uploads/2014/04/MMOC_Report_FINAL-4-4-14.pdf.

Dawes, Trevor A. 2013. "Libraries, ACRL, and Financial Literacy." *College & Research Libraries News* 74 (9): 466–67.

Fernandes, Daniel, John G. Lynch Jr., and Richard G. Netemeyer. 2014. "Financial Literacy, Financial Education and Downstream Financial Behaviors." *Management Science* 60 (8): 1861–83.

FINRA. 2014. *National Financial Capability Study.* Washington, DC: FINRA Investor Education Foundation. http://www.usfinancialcapability.org/.

Huston, Sandra J. 2010. "Measuring Financial Literacy." *Journal of Consumer Affairs* 44 (2): 296–316.

Jagman, Heather, Krystal Lewis, Brent Nunn, and Scott Walter. 2014. "Financial Literacy across the Curriculum (and Beyond): Opportunities for Academic Libraries." *College & Research Libraries* 75 (5): 254–57.

Kell, Peter. 2014. "Early Financial Literacy Education Key to Informed Financial Decisions." *Keeping Good Companies* 66 (11–12): 685–88.

Lusardi, Annamaria. 2013. "Keynote Address." CITI-FT Financial Education Summit, December 9.

Lusardi, Annamaria, and Olivia S. Mitchell. 2014. "The Economic Importance of Financial Literacy: Theory and Evidence." *Journal of Economic Literature* 52 (1): 5–44.

National Financial Educators Council. 2013. "Financial Literacy Definition." http://www.financialeducatorscouncil.org/financial-literacy-definition/.

Redzic, Adi. 2013. "Financial Literacy." *College & Research Libraries News* 74 (11): 556–57.

Reference and User Services Association. 2014. "Financial Literacy Education in Libraries: Guidelines and Best Practices for Service." http://www.ala.org/rusa/sites/ala.org.rusa/files/content/FLEGuidelines_Final_September_2014.pdf.

Scheresberg, Carlo de Bassa, Annamaria Lusardi, and Paul J. Yakoboski. 2014. *College-Educated Millenials: An Overview of Their Personal Finances.* Washington, DC: Global Financial Literacy Excellence Center.

Singletary, Michelle. 2014. "ACRL President's Program: Financial Literacy @ Your Library." American Library Association Annual Conference, Las Vegas, NV.

Wilson, Richard M. S., Ann Abraham, and Carolynne L. J. Mason. 2014. "The Nature of Financial Literacy." In *The Routledge Companion to Accounting Education*, edited by Richard M. S. Wilson, 50–80. New York: Routledge.

Chapter Eleven

Why Financial Literacy Matters

Ashley E. Faulkner

While financial literacy has been an advantageous skill set since the advent of financial systems, many of the arguments used to justify financial literacy education today are posited in the realm of "twenty-first century literacies" and the general perception that as the world grows increasingly complex, the number of nuanced literacies required to navigate that world grow likewise (Jagman et al. 2014). Few would argue life doesn't seem increasingly complex, and as regards interaction with financial instruments in the modern world, few can avoid it. From widespread bartering, to nearly ubiquitous monetary systems, to our current reality of leveraging and consumer credit, most people now face financial decisions daily: use of credit cards, home financing options, ongoing retirement considerations, portfolio management, employment security, insurance, personal savings accounts . . . the list could go on. Considering this increasingly complex financial world, it is not much of an exaggeration to say, as Operation HOPE founder John Hope Bryant phased it recently, "In today's world, a solid understanding of financial matters is as fundamental as learning to read and write" (Operation HOPE 2015).

But are you satisfied with such a simple explanation? Financial literacy matters because the world is increasingly complex. That's it? If so, you can stop reading here. If not, this chapter will explore three main trends that make financial literacy particularly imperative:

- Economic turbulence
- Digitization
- A disproportionately high impact on at-risk groups

There are, of course, myriad additional reasons why financial literacy is imperative on a personal, national, and global scale, but time is limited. We will conclude with a discussion of why libraries, in particular, should address financial literacy.

ECONOMIC TURBULENCE

This first trend is a cyclic and intertwined phenomena for which, as yet, no one has been able to parcel out precise causality. One argument for financial literacy education in light of modern economic turbulence is that it will help people weather difficult economic times, like the recent 2008 recession, and all the inevitable downturns to come. An interesting argument chorused right alongside the first is that financial literacy will help *prevent* economic downturns in the future. In one argument, economic turbulence is caused by macro forces and financial literacy is the means of treating resulting economic wounds. In the other, poor financial literacy, in part, actually *causes* economic turbulence as poor consumer decisions, en masse, affect macroeconomic forces.

Regardless, the solution is the same: improve financial literacy. Better financial literacy will either help us treat the personal aches we feel when the economy heads south. Or, improved financial literacy will actually prevent consumers from making poor financial decisions on a massive scale and thus prevent economic crises. Or, perhaps a bit of both.

The Macroeconomic Impact of Financial Literacy

The U.S. federal government has made it quite clear how important they consider financial literacy. The 2003 formation of the Financial Literacy and Education Commission was followed by the 2006 publication of "Taking Ownership of the Future: A National Strategy for Financial Literacy" and a 2011 update, "Promoting Financial Success in the United States: National Strategy for Financial Literacy" (Financial Literacy and Education Commission 2006, 2011). Statements relating this strategic emphasis to an underlying belief in the macroeconomic impact of personal financial literacy come from such heavy hitters as former chairman of the Federal Reserve Ben Bernanke and former chairperson of the U.S. Securities and Exchange Commission Mary Schapiro. Ben Bernanke has said, "Financial education supports not only individual well-being, but also the economic health of our nation," while Schapiro equated investor ignorance and unethical investment advisers as potentially equal threats to the overall health of our financial markets (Olen 2014; Dixon 2015).

Though there has yet to be a definitive empirical study on the issue (as known to the author), a link between individuals' financial literacy and the overall health of the economy within which they operate makes intuitive sense. The most obvious argument is probably the case of small businesses.

Individuals are not only consumers in the economy, of course, but also producers. Small businesses, as only one way individuals are active producers, account for a significant portion of the U.S. economy. According to the U.S. Small Business Administration, small businesses account for roughly 46 percent of the nonfarm private gross domestic product (GDP) of our nation and employ roughly 56 percent of the nation's private workforce (Dahmen and Rodríguez 2014; U.S. Small Business Administration Office of Advocacy 2015). In addition, as one recent *Inc.* article pointed out, all big business was once a small business, so when politicians opine that small businesses are the "backbone of the economy" it may actually be more accurate to say they *are* the economy, or at least where it begins (Hecht 2014).

How does financial literacy affect small businesses? The most direct affect may be found in cases where the financial *illiteracy* of small business owners and managers might well account for the failure of their enterprises. One recent case study at the Small Business Development Center of the University of South Florida, for instance, found that the three main causes for financial distress in the small businesses they studied were loss of revenues, insufficient cash flow, and excessive debt. All three causes could be partially addressed through better management of finances via increased financial literacy. The study found that 50 percent of small business owners in their sample did not regularly review financial statements, that 86 percent of these businesses were experiencing financial difficulties, and that 100 percent of the companies that both didn't review their statements and were experiencing difficulties could link their avoidance of financial statements to the owner's lacking literacy (Dahmen and Rodríguez 2014). Intuit, a well-known vendor for financial planning software, has stated that poor financial literacy is *the* most common cause of business failure. When one considers that the questions on Intuit's financial literacy quiz (which a majority of Canadian small business owners failed in another recent study) are things such as, "What is the role of the balance sheet?," it is easy to understand how illiteracy could sink the small business ship (Jackson 2015).

There are also more nuanced ways one can follow the thread of financial illiteracy to negative macroeconomic consequences. Consider, for instance, that student loan debt now represents the second largest type of debt owed by Americans, trailing only home mortgages. The average student graduating from a four-year college has more than twenty-five thousand dollars in personal debt, and most of these students will be paying off their loans well into their thirties. This debt has the potential to affect the economy as a whole, because these indebted students are less likely to start businesses (see above) and are also potentially less likely to purchase their own home (Eisler and Garrison 2014). There are also less immediate potential impacts, such as the fact that if the government thinks American consumers don't understand financial products, this might eventually lead to greater regulation of the financial industry, bogging down competition beneath increased costs of compliance, and the colloquially argued tendency of uninformed investors to be not only the most gruesome victims of speculative bubbles of all varieties (when prices on stocks, houses, and so on increase without a reasonable basis in concrete value) but also the most egregious perpetrators (Dixon 2015).

To Help People Weather Economic Turbulence, Regardless of Its Source

It will likely take little argument to convince you that improved financial literacy can help individuals weather poor economic conditions. Just ask yourself, if someone had three months', six months', or a year's worth of living expenses in an emergency savings account (recommendations vary), would he or she be better able to handle an unexpected period of unemployment or a sharp downturn in the market and the value of their investment portfolio? Would someone with more financial literacy be better able to fend off the potential financial disaster of an unwise mortgage or a scam investment with a "guaranteed" return of such-and-such percent? Would someone with an adequate understanding of their personal finances be better able to adjust their investments, savings, and spending habits in accordance with *any* economic reality? The answer is, instinctively, yes.

DIGITIZATION

An increasingly online environment has impacted every facet of life, and our financial life is no exception. An online environment has increased access to financial markets, reduced or at times outright eliminated the role of traditional intermediaries between the everyman and the market, increased our access to *information* about financial markets (and thus fed our general tendency toward overconfidence), and moved everything to a faster pace. Day trading has become potentially hour trading: a worrying shift when one considers most individuals should be trading with a long-term investment horizon in mind.

More Financial Products, Offered to More People

When we talk about "increased access" to financial markets we mean many things, but in our case we will discuss mainly:

- Due to reduced barriers to entry, access by novice investors to financial products that might in the past have been de facto reserved for more sophisticated investors; and

- An increasing number of investment opportunities available to all as financial firms have grown their product offerings.

The online environment has provided low transaction costs and easy access to trading. Add in a combination of aggressive marketing by online brokerage companies and the pure necessity for individual investors to take more responsibility for their financial well-being due to a shift from defined benefit to defined contribution pensions, and the world has seen an exponential increase in the number of active investors (O'Connor 2013; Scheresberg 2013). The combination of access and the increased individual responsibility for one's own financial perpetuity has led many individual investors into areas of the market once reserved for institutional investors. Unfortunately, these individual investors rarely have the financial acumen of their institutional counterparts. And they often have poor returns to prove it.

Disintermediation and Overconfidence

A reduction in the number of middlemen required to participate in various financial markets and an increase in access to *information* about these markets would seem, at first glance, like positive changes. Unfortunately, investment results paint a different picture. If individual investors were, on a whole, highly financially literate, then these likely would be positive changes. But individual investors are, on a whole, financially *illiterate* and, in a strange quirk of human nature, not just blissfully ignorant of their own ignorance but actually vehemently convinced they're more knowledgeable than they are.

Psychology offers us two main explanations: (1) the tendency of individuals to exhibit confirmation bias in their search for information, and (2) a form of cognitive bias called the Dunning-Kruger effect. The first relates to the way people search for information in an online environment, which offers near perfect disintermediation of information: users can access almost any and every type of information directly and with minimal filters. This, of course, has an empowering impact on individual research, but it also allows researchers to fall prey to a tendency to seek out only the information that confirms what they already believe. In the case of online investors, this tendency is potentially devastating to one's investment strategies as not only are alternate viewpoints not considered but the investors with the strongest confirmation bias also exhibit the greatest overconfidence, as shown in one recent study. Overconfidence negatively impacts investing in a number of ways, most notably in the tendency of those with higher expectations about their performance to trade more speculatively and frequently (day trading becomes hour trading) and almost always to realize lower returns (O'Connor 2013).

The second psychological explanation, the Dunning-Kruger effect, is almost entirely a matter of overconfidence, and an interesting explanation for why the *least* financially literate individuals will likely be the *most* overconfident investors and thus face the very *worst* returns in the modern free-for-all markets. The Dunning-Kruger effect, as explained in a recent *Pacific Standard* article, is the inability of incompetent people to recognize their own incompetence and, in fact, often to exhibit a sense of superiority. Interestingly, the article explored financial literacy in particular as one area where many individuals suffer from this cognitive bias. In the 2012 National Financial Capability Study conducted by the Financial Industry Regulatory Authority (FINRA), twenty-five thousand Americans were asked to rate their own financial knowledge, after which their *actual* financial literacy was measured. Those that displayed the *worst* financial literacy were more likely to give themselves the highest possible self-rating (Dunning 2014).

Unfortunately, overconfidence in one's financial literacy can have a particularly devastating monetary impact. While it is tempting to blame some of this overconfidence and its impact on Wall Street and a tsunami of brokerage advertising, ultimately, this is only more reason why financial literacy is imperative for every individual. The only way to spot, understand, and resist financial propaganda is to be financially literate enough to know it when you see it, and know better.

THE DISPROPORTIONATELY HIGH IMPACT ON AT-RISK GROUPS

One of the most insidious aspects of financial illiteracy, and one of the most poignant arguments for why financial literacy education is imperative, is the disproportionately high impact financial literacy has on already at-risk groups. What we mean when we talk about "at-risk groups" varies, of course, depending on what risk we're discussing. When we talk about financial literacy, at-risk groups are those groups of individuals most likely to suffer from financial hardship, particularly low-education achievers, low-income individuals, youth, and women.

Low education and low income attainment appear to precipitate a vicious monetary cycle wherein limited means and financial illiteracy combine to perpetuate financial hardship indefinitely. One study found that nearly three-quarters of those without a college degree were unable to answer even simple financial literacy questions (Scheresberg 2013). A 2014 study found socioeconomic status accounted for nearly 17 percent of the variation in performance on a financial literacy test (Shin 2014). Intuitively, it's hardly surprising then that these low-income, financially illiterate individuals are the most likely to use high-cost borrowing methods. They're in more need of such tools as payday loans, pawn shops, auto title loans, and rent-to-own options, and they're less likely to know these borrowing methods come with the highest interest rates and that this means they are actually the worst deal for someone who needs to be using what money they have wisely (Scheresberg 2013).

Sadly, both low education and low income are further correlated with certain demographic groups for which financial illiteracy is also particularly high: youth and women. The financial illiteracy among youth is particularly concerning in light of our national push for higher education. While a college education might well correlate with higher financial literacy, one might almost wonder if this is less to do with the level of education students have achieved and more to do with an unfortunate acquaintance with backbreaking debt. The sad fact is that young adults in the United States are taking on tens of thousands of dollars in student-loan debt (not to mention the average of over four thousand dollars in credit card debt they'll amass over four years) when they have yet to be exposed to financial matters sufficient to improve their literacy and when taking on debt could have a profound effect quite literally on the rest of their lives (Scheresberg 2013; Z.G. 2014; Farrington 2014).

Students need to understand that student loans are a loan against their expected future income and that, yes, they must be repaid (Farrington 2014). The number of borrowers past due on their student loan payments has been growing, and one recent study from the Brookings Institute found that 14 percent of students with loan debt didn't even know they *had* student loan debt (Scheresberg 2013; Farrington 2015). This debt, and its potentially delinquent repayment, is an issue that will affect these students' financial security for many years to come.

Women are a particularly at-risk group for a number of reasons: the persisting gender pay gap at play in many countries (including ours), the fact that women are more likely to take breaks in their careers, and the fact that women generally live longer than men while subsisting on an annual median retirement income eleven thousand dollars below men in the same demographic group (Picchi 2014). They are also less likely to seek out financial education, have traditionally been socially conditioned to be financial enablers and to avoid discussing finances as a matter of "femininity," and tend to feel less confident regarding their financial abilities, regardless of their actual level of literacy (Jarecke, Taylor, and Hira 2014; Landers 2014). In one recent study, while 38 percent of men could correctly answer the three posed financial questions, only 22 percent of women were able to do so, and women were far more likely to say they didn't know the answers (Picchi 2014). Without a serious improvement in their financial literacy, these women are either subservient to a relationship with someone with greater financial acumen or must face a frightening financial world unarmed and unconfident.

WHY FINANCIAL LITERACY MATTERS TO LIBRARIES

If you are satisfied that financial literacy does, in fact, matter, perhaps your next question is, well, why does it matter to us? Why should libraries, in particular, care about the financial literacy of our patrons? Again, there are succinct answers:

- Because we are an institution that upholds the ideal of democratized education across all subject matter.
- Because the other institutions addressing financial literacy concerns have thus far done so haphazardly.
- Because we are positioned in such a way that we might act as "anchors," bringing together a number of disparate groups for this sole aim (Monsour 2012, 37).

In this case, perhaps the succinct answers suffice. Libraries have long been a hub of democratized education and have a history particularly of providing business reference and other financial-literacy-related services that spans more than a century (Smith and Eschenfelder 2013). Financial literacy concerns have thus far been primarily addressed through commercial ventures and in K–12 education, but both providers have serious flaws. Financial literacy skills being taught by financial service providers seems to pose a severe risk of bias. As Lauren Willis, a professor at Loyola Law School in Los Angeles, slyly phrased it, "The idea that the fox is going to teach the hen is a bit much" (Braham 2013). While K–12 educators pose much less risk of bias, many educators with disparate backgrounds feel unprepared to teach personal finance and economics material. Even if they did feel prepared to teach financial literacy, while most states have K–12 financial education standards in place, relatively few require a full course on personal finance be taken to graduate, and very few require students be tested on this knowledge (Council for Economic Education 2014).

Librarians have much in common with their K–12 educator counterparts. They report similar levels of apprehension regarding providing financial literacy instruction and services, perhaps because many lack formal financial literacy training (Smith and Eschenfelder 2013). There are a number of arguments in favor of libraries providing financial literacy services though—namely, that a number of programs like Smart investing@your library have begun to put considerable emphasis on library staff development to help address the ability of frontline staff to provide financial literacy services, and the record of successful joint financial education ventures libraries and community partners have begun to establish (Monsour 2012). Library partners report the perception that they benefit from the trust our patrons already place in libraries, allowing us to act as facilitators of financial literacy education, even if we are not the educators ourselves (Smith and Eschenfelder 2013). The simple answer might be that while libraries are not more prepared than others to offer financial literacy education, we are ideally positioned and, as public institutions of education for the everyman, are obligated to address this literacy that truly *every man* requires to navigate our increasingly complex financial world.

REFERENCES

Braham, Lewis. 2013. "With Great Power Comes Great Responsibility." *BloombergBusiness*, October 23. http://www.bloomberg.com/news/2013-10-23/with-great-power-comes-great-responsibility.html.

Council for Economic Education. 2014. "Survey of the States: Economic and Personal Finance Education in Our Nation's Schools." http://www.councilforeconed.org/wp/wp-content/uploads/2014/02/2014-Survey-of-the-States.pdf.

Dahmen, Pearl, and Eileen Rodríguez. 2014. "Financial Literacy and the Success of Small Businesses: An Observation from a Small Business Development Center." *Numeracy* 7 (1). doi:http://dx.doi.org/10.5038/1936-4660.7.1.3.

Dixon, Drew. 2015. "Former Securities and Exchange Commission Chairwoman Says Financial Illiteracy Pervades U.S." *Florida Times-Union*, January 20. http://jacksonville.com/news/metro/2015-01-20/story/former-securities-and-exchange-commission-chairwoman-says-financial.

Dunning, David. 2014. "We Are All Confident Idiots." *Pacific Standard*, October 27. http://www.psmag.com/health-and-behavior/confident-idiots-92793.

Eisler, David L., and Scott Garrison. 2014. "Addressing College Student Loan Debt: Strategies for Success." *College & Research Library News* 75 (7): 374–91.

Farrington, Robert. 2014. "The Financial Literacy Gap Costs College Graduates Thousands." *Forbes*, July 16. http://www.forbes.com/sites/robertfarrington/2014/07/16/the-financial-literacy-gap-costs-college-graduates-thousands/.

———. 2015. "Failure to Follow Up: The Sad Truth about Millennial Financial Literacy." *Forbes*, January 8. http://www.forbes.com/sites/robertfarrington/2015/01/08/failure-to-follow-up-the-sad-truth-about-millennial-financial-literacy/.

Financial Literacy and Education Commission. 2006. "Taking Ownership of the Future: The National Strategy for Financial Literacy." http://www.treasury.gov/about/organizational-structure/offices/Domestic-Finance/Documents/Strategyeng.pdf.

———. 2011. "Promoting Financial Success in the United States: National Strategy for Financial Literacy." http://www.treasury.gov/resource-center/financial-education/Documents/NationalStrategyBook_12310%20%282%29.pdf.

Hecht, Jared. 2014. "Are Small Businesses Really the Backbone of the Economy?" *Inc.*, December 17. http://www.inc.com/jared-hecht/are-small-businesses-really-the-backbone-of-the-economy.html.

Jackson, Brian. 2015. "4 in 10 Canadian Small Business Owners Get 'F' for Financial Literacy." *IT Business*, January 20. http://www.itbusiness.ca/news/4-in-10-canadian-small-business-owners-get-f-for-financial-literacy/53311.

Jagman, Heather, Krystal Lewis, Brent Nunn, and Scott Walter. 2014. "Financial Literacy across the Curriculum (and Beyond): Opportunities for Academic Libraries." *College & Research Library News* 75 (5): 254–57.

Jarecke, Jodi, Edward W. Taylor, and Tahira K. Hira. 2014. "Financial Literacy Education for Women." *New Directions for Adult and Continuing Education* 141 (Spring): 37–46. doi:10.1002/ace.20083.

Landers, Jeff. 2014. "Financial Literacy: The Key to Every Woman's Financial Stability." *Forbes*, March 6. http://www.forbes.com/sites/jefflanders/2014/03/06/financial-literacy-the-key-to-every-womans-financial-stability/.

Monsour, Margaret. 2012. "Libraries Innovate with New Financial Education Programs." *Public Libraries* 51 (2): 36–43.

O'Connor, Lisa G. 2013. "Investors' Information Sharing and Use in Virtual Communities." *Journal of the American Society for Information Science and Technology* 64 (1): 36–47. doi:10.1002/asi.22791.

Olen, Helaine. 2014. "The Quest to Improve America's Financial Literacy Is Both a Failure and a Sham." *Pacific Standard*, January 7. http://www.psmag.com/business-economics/quest-improve-americas-financial-literacy-failure-sham-72309.

Operation HOPE. 2015. "Operation HOPE and Kaplan University Launch Free Non-Credit Financial Literacy Certification." Press Release, January 13. http://www.operationhope.org/news/nid/1698.

Picchi, Aimee. 2014. "Women Trail Men in Financial Literacy." *Moneywatch*, December 31. http://www.cbsnews.com/news/the-troubling-financial-literacy-gap-for-women/.

Scheresberg, Carlo de Bassa. 2013. "Financial Literacy and Financial Behavior among Young Adults: Evidence and Implications." *Numeracy* 6 (2): 1–21. doi:http://dx.doi.org/10.5038/1936-4660.6.2.5.

Shin, Laura. 2014. "American Students Score below Average in Financial Literacy." *Forbes Personal Finance*, July 10. http://www.forbes.com/sites/laurashin/2014/07/10/american-students-score-below-average-in-financial-literacy/.

Smith, Catherine Arnott, and Kristin Eschenfelder. 2013. "Public Libraries in an Age of Financial Complexity: Toward Enhancing Community Financial Literacy." *Library Quarterly* 83 (4): 299–320.

U.S. Small Business Administration Office of Advocacy. 2015. "Small Business Profiles for the States and Territories." February. https://www.sba.gov/sites/default/files/advocacy/SB_Profiles_2014-15.pdf.

Z.G. 2014. "Financial Literacy: Crediting the Classroom." *Economist*, August 08. http://www.economist.com/blogs/freeexchange/2014/08/financial-literacy.

Part Two

Library Resources

Chapter Twelve

Asking for Help

Finding Partners for Your Financial Classes

Kate Moody

Many libraries recognize the need for financial education in their communities; however, with limited staff, who have no formal financial training, no extra time, and no extra resources, they often find it difficult to address this need. The President's Advisory Council on Financial Capability (2013, 10) recommends libraries "align with, consolidate and boost, rather than supplant, existing efforts of the private, for-profit, non-profit, and governmental sectors." These "efforts" have outreach educators eager to engage new ways to communicate with the public; as one of the most trusted community institutions, your library is a natural collaborator. A good collaboration should be a win-win-win for the partner, library, and patron. Organizations such as your local cooperative extension system, credit counselors, and job centers want to get their message out to a wide array of people. Libraries want more fiscally informed patrons. Patrons want to learn personal finance while avoiding scams and bad advice. With so much to gain, finding partners and building a successful community program is simpler than it seems.

This chapter will outline how to find compatible community partners to aid in financial instruction. It will describe the process of identifying appropriate groups who can contribute to your objectives and how to choose among these groups to increase likelihood of success. It will then discuss how to ensure a smooth working relationship and identify some of the common pitfalls of working with outside partners. This chapter assumes that your library has already envisioned a program and chosen in-house staff to supervise its development, and thus focuses on forging the external relationships needed to make the program a success.

GETTING STARTED

Identifying Outcomes

- What are your goals and who is your audience?

Financial literacy is an umbrella term used to describe anything having to do with personal finance and how money works. Many different kinds of organizations exist that could be of use to teach financial literacy; your educational needs will be the largest factor in identifying whom to approach. Most likely you are trying to address a particular issues in your community: underwater mortgages, credit card debt, paying for college, taxes, or navigating social security, to name a few. The U.S. Census provides abundant resources that can illuminate possible educational foci. State and local governments typically also provide reports and data. Once you have determined this need, those establishing the program (hereafter referred to as the financial literacy committee) must create goals or outcomes to guide program development and provide assessment mechanisms.

During goal development, discuss what segment of the population you are trying to serve. Knowing this population will narrow the list of organizations that you consider partnering with. For example, if you are planning a program about paying for college, you would probably want to connect with local high school students, and thus you should be in contact with high school counselors and administration. If you will be trying to bring in a particular group of immigrants, you may need educators that speak their language, and so you should contact bilingual educators.

Needs and Values Assessment

- List what you need to achieve your goal
- Prioritize your needs
- Know your value

A partnership based on an equal exchange of needs and values is a strong signifier that the partnership will be successful because the organizations are mutually dependent and will succeed or fail together. Once you know your goals and audience, the next step is to determine everything the program will need, from basics like pencils for attendees to multimedia advertising. Write out a list of all items needed to get your program up and running, separated into items that you have and, more importantly, what you need. Do you need a space for the programming? Someone with expertise? Increased service to a particular community? These needs are what you will use to determine which partnership is more likely to succeed, so be as clear and as precise as possible.

Once you have your list of needs written out, weigh the importance of each. Some items on the list will be integral in your programming, and other things will be optional. Prioritize your list, putting the most important items at the top and least important at the bottom. The American Library Association (n.d.) has a chart template in their Partnership Tool for the more quantitatively inclined to help select the right partner. The first step in this method is to assign a percentage to each item correlated to how important it is to the success of the program, with a total of 100 percent. Further steps are discussed below.

Next, consider what your library may have to offer to potential partner organizations—this is your "value." Just as you will only be contacting those that can meet your needs, your value must be in line with their needs. When you approach organizations, you should be able to eloquently and clearly define your value to them, so spend a few minutes considering what you can offer. Every library, no matter the size, staffing, or funding level, has much to offer. One of our most valuable assets is our reputation as a nonpartisan, unbiased institution that welcomes everyone. We are a community hub. Our staff is service oriented, knowledgeable, and often technologically savvy, among other things. The library itself may provide meeting spaces, technology, and resources. Possible partners may not fully grasp all the benefits of working with the library, so you will want to be sure you are able to tell them exactly why they will be glad they chose to work with you.

IDENTIFYING POSSIBLE PARTNERSHIPS

As you research possible partner organizations, do not overlook partnerships your library has established in the past, as it is simpler to continue an ongoing relationship than to develop a new one. Create a list of preexisting partnerships your library has. If one or more of these partners can help you secure your needs, you may be more than halfway through the partnering process already. Next, consider the types of partnership requests you have received and the types of partnerships you may want to pursue (Consumer Financial Protection Bureau 2014). In Smith and Eschenfelder's (2013) study, almost all partnering organizations interviewed stated that they made the initial approach in partnering with the library. They also noted that it took three to four months for the library to respond. This data suggests that a possible partner has already contacted the library—check formal records and talk to staff who may have been contacted. This stage of the process can benefit from a lot of informal chatting with anyone willing to listen to your plan. Potential partners don't necessarily advertise their wish to engage in community development. Discussing your plan to develop a financial literacy program with friends, patrons, and associates can often unearth possible partners you may not have thought of or known about.

Smith and Eschenfelder's (2013) research also indicates that the most successful financial literacy partnerships libraries have are with state and local government agencies or offices, job centers, K–12 schools, and other nonprofits. Other organizations of this sort you may want to pursue include the following:

- A local college—community, state, or nonprofit
- Your state's cooperative extension system
- Counseling agencies (housing, employment, credit)
- Community centers (ethnic, religious, etc.)
- Credit unions
- Established nonprofits, such as the United Way and Goodwill Industries International
- Your regional Federal Reserve office
- State Department of Education or Department of Treasury

If your library has limited community resources or your patrons have very specific issues best addressed by a person who works in the field, consider collaborating with a financial professional. Accountants, bankers, and financial advisors have a depth of expertise that may benefit your patrons. Many businesses would like to offer their help because they value community service and encourage their employees to serve in the community. As long as this partner is able to provide unbiased, thorough information without attempting to sell anything to your patrons, the collaboration should go well. Having an explicit agreement such as a memorandum of understanding, a legally nonbinding document outlining the terms of the collaboration, or contract are effective tools to ensure all parties have a clear understanding of their responsibilities and expectations.

PICKING THE RIGHT PARTNER

There is more to choosing the right partner than comparing needs, goals, and values. The Consumer Financial Protection Bureau (2014, 21) recommends that you partner with organizations who have "good standing within the community, that will be courteous and respectful to all, and that are knowledgeable and reliable. You may want to evaluate the organization's mission, operations, and the reputation and conduct of the organization, its administrators and staff." For private companies, check with the Better Business Bureau or your state attorney general. For individuals in the financial industry, the Commodity Futures Trading Commission's SmartCheck website (http://www.smartcheck.gov) is an invaluable resource to ensure that the professional is properly registered and to identify any disciplinary actions on their records.

Once you are comfortable with the credibility of your potential partners, you should have your list of possible community partners as well as the following:

- A financial literacy need you want to address
- Basic goals
- Target audience
- Your needs
- Your values

Using this information, compare your list of possible partners to these qualifiers. Identify organizations that jump out as hitting more of the qualifiers than others as well as those that may only hit one but would be excellent in that category. Remove any that do neither, have bad standing in the community, or whose mission, operations, or conduct are at odds with your library's. The more overlap between your partners' missions and the goals of your program, the greater the chance of success.

While building a relationship with another organization can certainly be a nuanced process, and may feel like something one does on the basis of instinct, the success of your program is important enough to spend some time doing by the numbers (it is a financial literacy program after all). The ALA (n.d.) recommends using a spreadsheet, listing the qualifiers in the left column and the partners along the top row. Each qualifier should be given a weighted percentage so that they equal 100 percent. Then give a numerical value to how well the qualifier is met by each organization, from one to ten. Multiply the percentage by the numerical value and sum the totals for each organization. See their publication for more details. The organization or organizations with the highest scores are the ones you should be working with.

INTRODUCTIONS AND ESTABLISHING THE PARTNERSHIP

- Determine if your needs and values match up
- Create a shared vision
- Lay out all expectations and responsibilities in writing

Before you decide to jump into a partnership, discuss your goals, plans to achieve them, common ground, and what you can do for each other. The more mutually beneficial the partnership, the greater the likelihood of success. Discuss what resources you have and what you are looking for from the partners. Especially if you are working with a for-profit group, discuss the importance of unbiased, thorough information, and highlight the fact that this is not a chance to solicit new business. If after these initial meetings you feel your organizations meet each other's needs and values well, develop a contract or memorandum of understanding so that all parties understand their responsibilities and expectations.

ENSURE A SMOOTH WORKING RELATIONSHIP

Once you have your partner or partners, there are many ways you can encourage success. A little planning and effort on the part of leadership can pay sizeable dividends down the road.

Communication

Good communication reduces frustration, focuses efforts, and increases motivation. Many problems can be traced back to either miscommunication or a lack of communication. Depending on factors such as the size of your library, scope of the project, and nature of your collaboration, you will need to tailor your communication methods to best suit your situation. Shared timetables will help keep everyone on the same page throughout the process. Open lines of communication will keep small problems from becoming big problems down the road. You may find it useful to have a standard list of questions to ask of all partners before your programming to cover small details that are easily missed (Consumer Financial Protection Bureau 2014).

Especially if you are creating a large-scale collaboration, schedule regular meetings to provide updates and further refine the project. Send a meeting agenda beforehand and stick to it to make the meeting as efficient as possible. Remember, no one wants to be in a meeting any longer than it takes to go over the necessary information. Everyone should leave the meeting knowing what is expected of them. The chair of the library financial literacy committee should then follow up the meeting by distributing meeting notes to everyone involved, including administrators or officials, in a timely manner. Within this communication, there should also be a written list of party expectations to eliminate confusion and ensure that everyone understands what should happen before the next meeting.

Each organization should have a liaison to the other partners. Having a single person in charge of this streamlines the flow of information, reduces staff time spent on tasks, and reduces internal friction. Without a liaison, multiple people may respond to a partner's inquiry, possibly with conflicting answers, or no one will respond thinking that someone else will take care of it. Each organization will need to determine one person to act as a liaison to outside partners. This is an important job that requires attentiveness and responsibility; do your best to give it to someone who is up to the task. Everyone involved should have the contact information for each group's liaison.

Different libraries with different resources and different needs will find that they have different communication styles. However your library decides to communicate, be sure the lines of communication are open, all parties know what their role is, and all parties are consistently updated with news of their collaborators' actions.

Encouraging Ownership

Those who feel that they "own" this program will work harder and with higher-quality output because they will feel its success, or failure, also belongs to them. A simple way to do this is to give those working on this project increased responsibility for the program and the authority to develop it without being micromanaged. This will increase personal investment and ownership.

Initial meetings should be a dialogue to discuss what the objective is, how it can be addressed, and what value each organization can contribute to help achieve it. When all parties are included from the very beginning, participants feel responsible for the end result. Through these open dialogue meetings, you may find that you are more able to meet each other's needs and values than you had originally thought. For larger initiatives, this is when you can develop a unique goal, achieved only through collaboration. Programs are more likely to be successful when all parties are working toward the same goal, which they have created together, and everyone is getting something they need out of the partnership.

Compromise

Part of creating your unique goal will probably include compromise, as it ensures everyone benefits from the partnership. Having the event take place at the community college instead of the library is a compromise you could live with. Having the event be an advertisement for a local bank is a compromise you would never make. Know that the programming probably will not end up being what you had initially envisioned; some things are essential for success, but most aspects are probably more malleable than you think. Sharing control over the project can make people uncomfortable (librarians doubly so). To avoid this, keep an open mind, know the return on your investments, remind yourself that everyone wants to achieve the same goal, and be aware of the fact that no matter how brilliantly earth shaking your thoughts on the matter are, someone else just may have an idea better than yours.

Position the Right People to Shine

As with so many other endeavors, the quality and success of the program will come down to the individuals. Many people have a strong interest in financial literacy and helping the community; find out who on staff is this person and make sure they are on, or maybe even the chair of, this committee. Chances are, your library is starting a financial literacy program because you have someone on staff like this. Encourage, guide, and support them. Their enthusiasm and drive will strengthen the program.

Set Yourself Up for Success

Try to include short-, mid-, and long-term goals. Small achievements along the way bolster morale and tend to improve everyone's performance. Short-term goals can also help you identify ways your program may need modification as it develops. Most importantly, if you can succeed early on, administration will be more likely to provide resources for future events.

BEWARE COMMON PITFALLS

A good partner can provide things like expertise, marketing, funding, a wider audience, increased library visibility, and reduced costs. Unfortunately, there are libraries that have hosted unscrupulous financial literacy speakers who were only working for their own future profit. There are also less nefarious but more commonplace pitfalls, all leading to overly stressed staff and mediocre programming. Most of these pitfalls can be avoided through planning and strong communication.

Self-Interest

A major risk when dealing with outside speakers for financial literacy programming is bringing in someone whose goals differ from those of your program. Libraries must guard against "implicit or implied endorsement of financial products or services, by libraries or their partners" (Reference and User Services Association 2014, 15). Before this person interacts with your patrons, you should have done the following:

- Searched the Better Business Bureau and SmartCheck.gov to ensure all certifications are up to date and there are no complaints against the group or person
- Had a frank discussion about your expectations and their responsibilities
- Signed a contract or memorandum of understanding

The formal agreement should state outright that they may not solicit business from your patrons, this person must present unbiased information designed for the public's best interest, and they may not collect patron data, mention financial products specific to their company, or cherry-pick data. Your specific library may have more restrictions. Administration should review the contract or memorandum before signing. Avoiding all this extra hassle is a good reason to work with government and nonprofit speakers.

Lack of Time and Resources

Some of your needs are likely not the result of an inability to get something done but simply not having enough time to get it done. Be realistic about how long each step will take and give yourself the time you need. Create generous timetables in case, or more likely when, you have to make changes due to unforeseen circumstances. Understand what your resources are and list the needed resources as part of your "needs" when determining partners. The partners you work with are there to fill any gaps in your resources.

Dependency on a Single Staff Member

Although many business partnerships are started through personal friendships, be sure that this new relationship evolves so that it is between the library and the partner. If it remains dependent on one staff member, you will find yourself back at square one should that staff member leave or have a falling out with the partner (Reference and User Services Association 2014).

Loss of Enthusiasm

As time passes, people tend to lose enthusiasm, especially when confronted with obstacles. Keeping everyone's focus on the ultimate goal of the project through consistent and full updates on all aspects of the project can help maintain enthusiasm and commitment. Phone or chat with those involved in the program when there is good news to spread, such as the achievement of medium-term goals. The liaison may hear that a particular speaker has agreed to be a part of your program and then share this information with the committee chair. The chair should not wait until the next meeting to tell others on the committee; stop by their offices to give them the good news. This may spark another person to make an extra couple of phone calls and get a professional graphic designer to make the advertisements rather than using the same tired template you use for all your other programming.

Mistrust

Trust is an essential component of collaborative work. Putting unreliable people in a position where others depend on them will rarely end well. Do your best not to partner with those who you cannot trust. Keep an eye out for red flags, such as not coming through with what is expected of them or your having a hard time getting a hold of an otherwise responsive partner at an inopportune time. If you find yourself not trusting your partner, nip it in the bud. Talk to them to get to the heart of the issue. If it is not resolved, you may need to dissolve the partnership as chances are the same problem will come up again.

Breaking Up

Despite all the work you have done to make sure you and your partners will be a good match, it is possible that at some time in this process you find that you must break the partnership. Your contract or memorandum should set up a termination procedure that allows the partnership to be dissolved (TechSoup for Libraries n.d.). This should increase the likelihood of a smooth break and reduce the chance of negative repercussions. Hopefully, your partnership will be a resounding success and lead to many collaborations throughout the years.

REFERENCES

American Library Association. n.d. "Smart investing@your library: Selecting Strategic Partners." http://smartinvesting.ala.org/wp-content/uploads/2010/07/Partnership-Tool.pdf.

Consumer Financial Protection Bureau. 2014. "Community Partnership Guidebook for Libraries." June. http://files.consumerfinance.gov/f/201406_cfpb_partner-guidebook.pdf.

President's Advisory Council on Financial Capability. 2013. *Final Report.* January 29. http://www.treasury.gov/resource-center/financial-education/Documents/PACFC%20final%20report%20revised%2022513%20%288%29_R.pdf.

Reference and User Services Association. 2014. "Financial Literacy Education in Libraries: Guidelines and Best Practices for Service." American Library Association. http://www.ala.org/rusa/resources/guidelines.

Smith, Catherine Arnott, and Kristin Eschenfelder. 2013. "Public Libraries in an Age of Financial Complexity: Toward Enhancing Community Financial Literacy." *Library Quarterly* 83 (4): 299–320.

TechSoup for Libraries. n.d. "Planning for Success." http://www.techsoupforlibraries.org/Cookbooks/planning-for-success.

Chapter Thirteen

Best Practices to Implement Financial Literacy in a Large Public Library

Melissa Jeter

Popular reference questions from patrons warrant in-depth information that only programming and specific services can provide. Before implementing programs and services on financial literacy at the large public library system where I work, a popular reference question resembled the following scenario:

A patron asks me if I could help him or her at the computer. I walk over to the computer with the patron only to have a patron point to the screen and ask, "What does this mean? I'm trying to get my credit report, but I don't even know what this means. Plus, there's stuff on here I don't even recognize!" As I look at the information on the computer screen, I get a little nervous. First of all, there is sensitive, private information like social security numbers, credit card numbers, and even bank information on the screen. Second, I'm not sure how the patron wants me to assist. I'm a librarian not a credit counselor, so I am not equipped to address such issues. Repeated experiences like these and reflections on the matter of financial literacy led me to initiate more in-depth programming as well as specific reference assistance, programming, and services for adults.

In this case, by large public library system I mean one that serves a county population of over four hundred thousand people. Of that four hundred thousand, more than three hundred thousand county residents are cardholders and use their library on a regular basis. Moreover, this large public library system is characterized by having a legacy foundation organized and operated exclusively for the purpose of advancing the mission, long-range goals, objectives, and priorities of the library as well as balancing the quality and range of the library's services beyond the level supported by taxpayers.

Lastly, this large public library system also includes a main library and nineteen agencies throughout the county.

Over the last four years, as an adult services librarian, I partnered with the grant specialist librarian in the business technology department to initiate more in-depth financial literacy programming as well as specific reference assistance, programming, and services for adults. As we gained momentum for the subject matter, more librarians throughout the system actively participated in facilitating financial literacy programming, collection development, and, of course, reference services. This large public library system can serve as a case study from which best practices can be derived. From this case, public libraries of similar characterization have an opportunity to learn what best practices to use as they embark on financial literacy in their community.

To determine how our library could better serve the financial literacy needs of our patrons, we took the following actions that I suggest as best practices for librarians in large public libraries:

1. Research financial literacy, including its definition, and librarian and patron information needs.
2. Design programming and dissemination of financial literacy information that works in harmony with research and provides measurable outcomes.
3. Compile information and make it accessible to librarians and patrons.
4. Seek collaboration and partnerships within the library as well as in the community.
5. Provide in-depth information through training for librarians and programming for patrons.

1. RESEARCH FINANCIAL LITERACY

Definition of Financial Literacy

Financial literacy is education on issues such as budgeting, credit reporting, investing, mortgages, school loans, savings, building resources or wealth, and consumer protection and fraud. In the public library, patrons often seek information on getting a credit report. However, the question that arises is which resources are reputable. There are many websites that offer a free credit report, but through research we have found that there is really only one place that will provide a free credit report from all three credit reporting agencies: AnnualCreditReport.com. Defining financial literacy will be helpful in identifying the information needs of librarians and patrons.

Librarian Needs for Financial Literacy

After researching the definition of financial literacy, study the need that librarians have for financial literacy. I found out what librarians at my library were thinking by asking them in an online survey. An online survey is a nice way to get information quickly and compile data and statistics to later use to state your case for financial literacy programming and reference services.

Based on the survey of eighty-four librarians, those who responded indicated that they mostly saw their role was to refer patrons to books when asked about financial information. Though the library has access to many financial databases, librarians were more likely to refer patrons to books or AnnualCreditReport.com. Moreover, librarians had concerns about providing accurate information, locating that information, and maintaining the privacy of patrons when using a public computer.

Patron Needs for Financial Literacy

Surveying the librarians also provided information on the needs of patrons. In this case, the survey of librarians asked what questions they received from patrons about financial matters. The responses from eighteen of eighty-four librarians indicated that getting an annual credit report and investing were the topics most asked about. In terms of popularity, however, credit reports were the most significant. At least once a week, librarians said they received questions about how to obtain a credit report.

Thus, the needs patrons have can be deduced from the regularity of reference questions. In addition, patron needs can be assessed by exploring the existence of high school, state, or college requirements in educational institutions or relevant articles in newspapers as well as the presence and number of community organizations focused on budgeting, credit repair, investing, mortgages, and saving for particular large purchases. For example, the Ohio Education Department has addressed the need for financial literacy and has even codified it in the Ohio Revised Code (http://codes.ohio.gov/orc/3313.603). By doing minimal research, the degree to which there is a need in your city, county, or state for financial literacy can be found. According to a Pew Charitable Research study in March 2014, there were at least seventeen states requiring financial literacy programming and reference services (Prah 2014).

2. DESIGN PROGRAMMING AND DISSEMINATION OF FINANCIAL LITERACY

Through researching financial literacy, I uncovered that there are seasons for financial literacy. These seasons informed decision making on the time of year to implement programming. One such season is February. In February, there is a weeklong national campaign called America Saves Week. America Saves Week is a campaign created by the Consumer Federation of America and the American Savings Council. Also, in April there is Money Smart Week, usually held the third week of April. Money Smart Week was started by the Chicago Federal Reserve and partners with the American Library Association (American Library Association 2015). Holding programs around these times maximizes the importance of financial literacy in a particular community and also lends initiative to even more resources that can help in creating a successful program.

Seasons for financial literacy can also be determined based on observation of the times in which patrons most often ask financial literacy questions. For example, experience has taught us that tax season, usually January through April, is a time when patrons have questions about tax preparation. The New Year is also a time when people think about creating new habits—spending and budgeting being two of them. By aiming for the times when a topic is popular, you can reach patrons when their minds are most receptive to such information. It is also helpful to keep track of the questions patrons have at these times to get a qualitative and quantitative measure of the need.

Observation and the online librarian survey indicated certain objectives of programming. Designing objectives for programming allows measurement of outcomes. The outcomes must be conceptualized as tasks that patrons will know, feel, or create. For example, one measurable outcome can be that patrons leave programming knowing that AnnualCreditReport.com is the only reputable online website from which to obtain their credit report. Measurable outcomes can be obtained by simple pre- and post-tests administered during the program. Polling is another way to obtain measurable outcomes. In the very initial programs, in the case of this large library system, pre- and post-tests were administered as a part of the presentation. These showed patrons that they were able to learn something of value in the program. Also important to note is that using instruments to obtain measurable outcomes is different than a general evaluation. In this case, presenters were asked for their three main objectives in their presentation. Those objectives were used as the measurable outcomes for the program. General evaluations assist program presenters in determining how to set up the rooms in a better fashion or help the speaker to learn to speak louder or have handouts. Programming outcomes determine if the patrons have reached the objective of the program subject matter. Compiling the data from programming outcomes can let you know if the financial literacy program is making an impact in the lives of people in your community.

The measurable outcomes can be used to demonstrate the effectiveness of the programming. Such information can be invaluable in large public library systems when proving the effectiveness of financial literacy programming in the community. This information could be used later in various ways, but I especially think of using measurable program outcomes to demonstrate to the voting public that libraries are not only serving the public good but benefiting the overall health of the community. The ability to demonstrate how financial literacy programming meets the needs of the community is important if your large library system is dependent on tax levies.

3. COMPILE INFORMATION

As research is done, compile the information and make it accessible to librarians and patrons. In this case, the research that we found was initially compiled and organized in an online wiki. A wiki is a collaborative sharing information technology tool. The wiki allowed collaboration between me and the grant specialist librarian asynchronously, yet in one digital place. The benefit is that two librarians working in physically different spaces with different times of work can still work in one digital workspace. The wiki allowed us to have a mutual location to place information we researched while maintaining open communication. The wiki worked as a living document that could be updated at any time, and that constant communication and feedback facilitated sharing and collaboration without always having to meet to work. In this case an online wiki was used to organize information, maintain the results of the survey of librarians, and plan and design programs for financial literacy.

Using the wiki allowed us to collaborate and share information as needed. Once we were ready to start implementing what we researched about financial literacy, we worked with the information technology department to put this information on our intranet for librarians. Also, we were trained in the content management system and later WordPress in order to continue to compile financial literacy information on the library website for patrons. So if your library has an intranet or website, specific information can be posted or published for librarian and patron use.

Researching and compiling information are two practices that foster collaboration and partnership. Implementing financial literacy in a large public library takes collaboration and partnership with every department and agency within the library as well as organizations outside the library that are dedicated to financial literacy. Another important way to make information accessible is staff training. Training works especially well when led by a librarian and a representative of a community-based organization who addresses the personal finance needs of folks in the community.

4. SEEK COLLABORATION AND PARTNERSHIPS

Researching and compiling information are two practices that lead to seeking collaboration and partnership. Implementing financial literacy in a large public library takes collaboration and partnership inside as well as outside the library, with organizations that are dedicated to financial literacy.

The compilation of the information sources or subject guides can provide librarians with more resources that can assist the patron. In our case, a list of local community organizations and financial coaches has helped patrons interested in interpreting their credit report.

Partnering within the Library

Your coworkers are essential partners, and one way to partner with them is to ask them about their experiences. The "ask" can be done in different ways, but in this case, as I have said earlier, I conducted an online survey. Surveys not only obtain useful information but also inspire colleagues to think about financial literacy as a part of their regular reference, programming, and service duties. It helps to pave the way for financial literacy programming and services. As librarians learned that there were two librarians leading the project, they were more inclined to suggest ideas and even participate in a committee through which programming, training, collection development, and more services were being planned and facilitated.

With our survey results in hand, the grant specialist librarian and I asked to meet with the manager of human resources. We met with human resources to tell her about our plans to conduct financial literacy programming and services, but also about the need for librarians to be trained in financial literacy. In this meeting, we discussed the possibility of having librarians trained and the organizations and businesses who could provide that training. Moreover, we made sure to request training incentives that were relevant to staff interests. In this case, the training incentives requested were dress-down financial Fridays once a month. So those librarians who had taken the training could wear jeans or comfortable shoes on a specific Friday agreed upon with human resources. Later, as financial literacy programming and services became funded by a Smart Investing ALA/FINRA grant, the incentives included a T-shirt with the logo of the financial literacy program. On several occasions, we met with human resources as well as the branch services department to discuss the need for financial literacy training. We were able to determine the dates and times when training could be administered. In the process, we also discussed which librarians, either children's, adult, or generalist, might be included in that training.

In addition to meeting with human resources and branch services, we also met with the manager of the main library, where the business and technology department resides. In meeting with the managers of the different departments, we were able to gain ideas and information that allowed us to plan better for the upcoming programming.

The process of implementing financial literacy was not a linear one, but one where we constantly asked questions, conducted research, and acted on that research. Practical theories and plans of action were proposed, implemented, and adapted as necessary. This evolving process allowed us to gain more information and grow our initial programs. In the beginning, my branch and the business technology department led the later systemwide programming on financial literacy. From these initial programs, we gathered measurable outcomes as well as evaluations. In addition, we worked through the marketing department in order to gain publicity that led to the program being covered in the local newspaper. We compiled the program feedback and later provided it to the managers of the participating branches. So one aspect of partnering within the library is to think about the library as an open system. Thinking about the library as an open system means transcending the bureaucracy of the organization and working with everyone at every level as a partner. That being said, make sure to meet individually and provide information about the research and possible solutions to address financial literacy needs of librarians and patrons. Listen to how colleagues in various departments can best serve financial literacy programming, reference, collection development, and staff training needs. In our case, administrators and managers of the marketing department, technical services, branch services, information technology, and legacy foundation all wanted to know more about the research and possible solutions on financial literacy. This openness allowed everyone at all levels to contribute their best work. Moreover, as colleagues in different parts of the system saw enthusiastic librarianship, they wanted to participate in the novel initiative. As the small initiatives to conduct financial literacy programming and services grew, we became interested in having speakers and sponsors from outside of the library. Thus, we partnered with local, state, and federal agencies outside the library.

Partner with Local, State, and Federal Agencies

Similar to partnering with colleagues within the library, creating partnerships with organizations outside the library involves providing information about the need for financial literacy. In this case, the grant specialist met the income manager for the local United Way. This interaction developed into a partnership that led to introductions to another community partner who worked at the Local Initiatives Support Corporation (LISC). In our ever-evolving conversations with our library colleagues, our community partners were also invited alongside managers and administrators in human resources and branches services. In our case, the United Way and LISC have been essential in providing staff training, specifically on navigating credit reports for reference librarians; programming, including measurable program outcomes; and collection development book suggestions.

Local agencies, such as the United Way and LISC, who regularly help people understand their personal finances can be very helpful as informational resources to whom librarians can refer patrons. In this case, LISC has a community network of Financial Opportunity Centers with financial coaches. These financial coaches are free to the public and thus a great resource to whom patrons can be referred during reference transactions. Thus, at the point in the reference interview when the librarian has provided as much information as possible without interpreting a document such as a credit report, the librarian can suggest free financial coaching from the community-based Financial Opportunity Center.

Because the United Way and LISC have programs that assist people with their personal finances, we enlisted them to conduct their five-week series on financial fitness in library programming. The financial coaches regularly conduct these series, so the measurable outcomes were already embedded in the financial fitness programs. This was a great benefit to the larger financial literacy library programs to determine the difference that the programs were making in the financial lives of patrons, but also as our financial literacy programming became grant funded.

Lastly, the financial coaches served as an additional resource from which we could gather information about books they would recommend for patrons. Those book recommendations were used in collection development in addition to using resources such as Edelweiss and Ingram. In some instances, books purchased were also used as door prizes for patron attendance.

In addition, local agencies, financial institutions, state agencies, and federal agencies are great resources to draw on for programming. State agencies, including the Attorney General's Office and Department of Commerce, as well as a federal agency such as the Federal Trade Commission often have a speakers bureau that will send speakers to programs for low to no cost. In the initial programming, programs on consumer fraud from the Better Business Bureau as well as the Attorney General's Office were held. Partnering with public and private agencies as well as individual speakers on topics of home economics, such as couponing or shopping to stretch the bills, built our financial literacy program and piqued individuals' interest in the more intensive programs later to be conducted through United Way and LISC. Partnerships with your local community, state, and federal agencies are not only beneficial but critical. Consequently, in order to appreciate the relationships built with partners, we made sure that any and all publications included their logos and public information.

5. PROVIDE IN-DEPTH INFORMATION

Training for Librarians

Preparing librarians for financial literacy reference transactions actually begins by surveying librarians about their concerns in answering patrons' questions. With the survey results, training can be organized to address those needs. In this case, our United Way partner presented information about navigating credit reports for librarians because our survey indicated that questions about credit reports were most popular with patrons. A financial coach presented the information, including pre- and post-testing to measure the outcomes of the training.

Programming for Patrons

When our financial literacy programming started around 2008, I created some of the content and contacted a few speakers. Partnering was mostly done internally among me, another branch, and the business technology department. However, as we started partnering, programming included a series of workshops, "Rebuilding Your Credit," sponsored by Huntington Bank, Advocates for Basic Equality, Consumer Credit Counseling Service, the Lucas County Treasurer, and the Ohio State Treasurer's Office. During consumer protection week in 2010, we had a sort of "consumer protection fair," which involved the Better Business Bureau, the Northwest Ohio Development Agency, and the Ohio Attorney General's Office. In these programs, the library provided a venue where partners could put on presentations. In instances where for-profit partners, like banks, were involved, no one partner ran the show. They either alternated as speakers or had different display tables at the same event. They might give away small gewgaws, but they did not sell their products.

The best practice is to join together with your partners in community organizations to conduct programs. Most community-based organizations have some idea of financial literacy needs based on their administration of programming. Partnering with community organizations allowed us to abdicate reinventing the wheel. Once we partnered with LISC, we could let financial coaches from their Financial Opportunity Centers administer patron programming. Patron programming consisted of budgeting, increasing credit scores, and recovering from financial disaster. Their programming included built-in measurement of outcomes as a regular practice. This regular practice of measurable outcomes created statistics that could be later used to demonstrate program success.

CONCLUSION

The success of our financial literacy reference, programming, and services can be attributed to the best practices we used in this large public library system. Once a need for financial literacy was discovered, it made sense to research and compile information. Sharing that information with colleagues and patrons was just a natural next step. Programming and reaching out to community organizations also boosted success by getting the word out about financial literacy at this large public library. To meet the needs of patrons, librarians also needed to be prepared through training. Finally, meeting the financial literacy needs of patrons must be accessible and relevant.

BIBLIOGRAPHY

American Library Association. 2015. "Money Smart Week." http://www.ala.org/offices/money-smart-week.

America Saves Week. 2015. "About America Saves Week." http://www.americasavesweek.org/about/about-america-saves-week.

Fairest, Jon. 2014. "Leading Employees through Major Organizational Change." *Ivey Business Journal*, July/August, 4.

Federal Trade Commission. 2015a. "Consumer Information." http://www.consumer.ftc.gov/.

———. 2015b. "Contact the Federal Trade Commission." http://www.ftc.gov/contact.

Ohio Department of Education. 2015. "Financial Literacy." http://education.ohio.gov/Topics/Ohio-s-New-Learning-Standards/Financial-Literacy.

Ouellette, Russ. 2014. "Speeding Up the Pace of Organizational Change." *New Hampshire Business Review*, July 25.

Prah, Pamela. 2014. "Financial Literacy Requirements Lag in States." Pew Charitable Trusts, March 4. http://www.pewtrusts.org/en/research-and-analysis/blogs/stateline/2014/03/04/states-lag-in-educating-students-about-personal-finance.

United States Census Bureau. 2015. "Lucas County, Ohio, QuickFacts." http://quickfacts.census.gov/qfd/states/39/39095.html.

Chapter Fourteen

Career Information Literacy at the Academic Reference Desk

Frans Albarillo

Improving financial literacy involves enabling students to make good choices based on their ability to identify, find, and evaluate the information they use to make financial decisions. University students are at a point where they make all kinds of decisions that have a financial impact on their lives; many of these decisions are in some way career related. These choices include what they should study, whether they need to pursue specific certifications, and whether it is worth considering additional graduate work that can increase the cost and time it takes them to finish their education. The more financially literate they are, the better information they can use to inform their educational decisions. Academic libraries can play an important role in providing students with the information and financial literacy they need to make career-related decisions. The new Association of College & Research Libraries "Framework for Information Literacy for Higher Education" threshold concepts make it clear that librarians have an opportunity to teach students that professional literature is a conversation, and that business information, because it is highly structured, demands strategic searching; otherwise the student will be overwhelmed.

At the author's library, the reference desk is a place of teaching and student–librarian dialogue. It is a place where the library attempts to provide an answer to any academic-related question. Many of those questions are career related, even if they don't appear so at first glance. Biology students looking for MCAT review books might ask, "What happens if I don't get into medical school?" A fine arts student interested in sculpture once asked, "How do I become a gunsmith?" Students come with a wide range of questions: "What can I do with a music degree?" "How can I become a producer?"

The premise of this chapter is that knowing how career information is structured improves the individual's financial literacy. In this case, the outcome is better career choices by students who are learning to navigate professional and business literature in electronic and print formats. The information in this chapter is drawn from the experience of the author, a business librarian at a four-year public liberal arts college in Brooklyn, New York, who has several years of experience at the reference desk, where inevitably a student (whether at the beginning or end of their undergraduate degree) comes up and asks: "How do I learn about careers?" This chapter provides insight into how to make the academic library a useful resource for students with career-related information needs, including reference interview tips, information about core career resources, and additional resources, as well as guidelines for improving services and offerings.

The audience is novice business librarians and academic librarians who are new to business and career information. Prior to becoming a librarian, the author worked for four years providing career information support to undergraduate, MBA, and doctoral business students and in six years of librarianship has taught career-focused instruction and workshops in addition to providing regular reference desk support.

THE REFERENCE INTERVIEW

When engaging with a career-related question, context is very important. Ask students about their educational history. It's important to know where they are in their studies. People near the end of their university studies will require resources to help them transition to life after undergraduate study, while incoming freshmen or sophomores are seeking resources that might help them decide on a major. Age is another important consideration: Is the student a traditional or nontraditional student? Is this a second career? Of course you can't just ask a person their age, but asking questions about their professional interests or course of study will help determine if you're working with a nontraditional student enrolled in an executive MBA program or a student who has just finished high school. You may learn that the student has an undergraduate degree from another country that is not recognized in the United States and as a result is repeating some coursework. Building a professional understanding of the student's educational history will inform the kinds of sources you present.

CORE RESOURCES

The core career-related resources a librarian can offer students include the library catalog as well as information from the Bureau of Labor Statistics, associations and trade journals, databases, and industry reports and profiles. Most public and university libraries have access to these items in one format or another. This section on core resources focuses on what's typically available in an academic library, which can be supplemented with other resources described later in the chapter.

Catalog

One of the distinguishing features of academic libraries is that they're organized using Library of Congress subject headings. One popular question that is surprisingly difficult to answer quickly in an academic library is, "Where is the career section?" To provide a quick answer, it is useful to prepare a guide with keywords and call number ranges for subject terms such as vocational guidance, job hunting, résumé writing, and employment interviewing. As subject headings subdivide, it will be useful to add subject terms for subject-specific career-related books such as "music—vocational guidance," "biology—vocational guidance," and "business—vocational guidance."

Labor Statistics

The United States Department of Labor's Bureau of Labor Statistics is a good one-stop shop for career exploration. It's a free, authoritative, and up-to-date website that contains career, salary, association, and industry data collected by the government. If students are interested in looking up career information by occupations, they can start with the *Occupational Outlook Handbook*. A related site is the Occupational Information Network (O*NET) Resource Center, which provides a highly structured database of knowledge, skills, and abilities needed to perform occupational tasks. Users can search by specific skills, or they can take an online self-assessment that will suggest professions and careers. *Occupational Outlook Quarterly*, a journal published by the Bureau of Labor Statistics, has recently changed its name to *Career Outlook* and publishes articles and career profiles, which are helpful for students who are exploring a career. You can browse the archives by subject to get a full idea of the content.

State labor offices also provide their own labor and workforce statistics. Doing a quick search on Google will usually lead you to a state labor office. These sites provide their own analysis and reports on employment projections, local industries, and special studies. As an example, the New York State Department of Labor provides regional employment and unemployment reports, including special reports on large private company employers and the emerging green industry. Students can learn from these regional reports before they move to a particular region. The New York Department of Labor also provides information for job seekers with links to statewide career events and career offices. These websites have career development links to job search tools that help users prepare résumés and cover letters and gives interview tips. The website also lists information on immigration, youths, and veterans services.

Associations and Trade Journals

Professional associations and societies are nonprofits that are established to further a particular profession or interest. They vary widely in size and resources—some are very large and influential, while others might consist of members from a particular geographic area. The obvious example for librarians is the American Library Association and the variety of activities and publications it provides to the library profession. The information that associations may provide, either freely or at a price, includes salary surveys, job banks, Listservs, networking opportunities, membership listings, and local chapters. You can find a list of associations on the Occupational Outlook Handbook website. These tend to be the larger associations. Most of the publications are promotional advocates and offer a very positive view of the profession or special interest (think National Rifle Association), so it's always useful to show students other resources to complement an association's advocacy agenda. I include special interest associations and scholarly associations in this category of resources because they are often commentary to a particular profession. A fine arts metalsmithing student who is interested in the American Custom Gunmakers Guild could also review the National Rifle Association's website.

Databases

Business databases such as LexisNexisAcademic and EBSCOs Business Source, as well as multisubject databases like Gale's OneFile, often include trade and association journals. Most subscription databases can search by the North American Industry Classification System (NAICS) or its predecessor, Standard Industry Codes (SIC). The Bureau of Labor Statistics has a list of these codes on their website. Showing students how to use these codes in library databases allows them to strategically search and access trade and professional journals that may not be available freely on association or interest group websites. Teaching students how to search by industry code and occupational keywords gives them a highly effective way of using business databases to sort and filter through hundreds of local, national, and international periodicals. The search filters are very important when first introducing these databases since students are likely very used to natural language searching. At the reference interview, showing students database search filters gives the librarian an opportunity to reinforce how business content is more structured than other kinds of information. In addition to occupational keywords, showing students how to narrow their search for reports is another feature of business information where it is more common to find reports of different kinds. This could give them access to information like salary surveys, guides to best places to work, or lists of top companies and reports on industry leaders. Once students are aware that there are other ways to access information about companies and professions, they will be better able to help themselves find good information during the course of their studies, as their interests evolve. In turn this will help them get the best information on which career and educational path to take, so it is critical to teach these skills early in their studies.

Industry Reports and Profiles

Industry reports are third-party documents that cover trends in a particular industry or sector. Reports are in a particular format for business information, which I often emphasize is not freely available outside of a library context. There are many different business databases that produce reports on public and private companies and industries. Some examples of these kinds of databases include ReferenceUSA, Hoovers, IBISWorld, Mergent, and S&P NetAdvantage. Information that is useful to nonbusiness students includes company histories, business descriptions, listings of the top companies, and industry reports. Some of these databases are more difficult to search, but the advantage is that they are third-party reports that give people a deeper, less biased overview. The author always encourages students (usually graduating seniors and graduate students) to find business reports and use them to compare businesses for a more nuanced view of industries and career outlooks. Databases like IBISWorld are very well suited to giving students a deeper understanding of small industries, while Mergent and S&P databases are geared toward finance majors. Even if the business database is complex and seems like overkill, it's worthwhile to show the student one report or publication that might make a difference on the course of study they decide to pursue. As an accidental business librarian, the author learned how to use specific components of complex databases depending on what users needed. The author encourages nonbusiness librarians to explore business databases because financial and business information is very practical and once a user knows how it's structured, with practice, it's not that difficult to search these databases for commonly asked career information.

OTHER RESOURCES

Career Center

Outside of the library's physical and online collections are more sources of information that can help students with career-related questions. Most universities have a career center with counselors providing résumé, interview, and career exploration programming. Some departments and larger programs (MBA, education, law, health, nutrition, or medicine) also have their own career center, so it may be good to ask around about these kinds of services for current students and alumni. Career centers often have information on different graduate school exams (GRE, LSAT, MCAT) and other professional examinations, as well as lists of job and internship resources. They may subscribe to specialized career resource databases such as Vault or CareerBeam. The library is very much complementary to campus career centers, and it is useful to meet with career center staff in order to understand their intake process for students and possibly to collaborate with them on purchasing resources like books.

Social Media

Social media offers another way to find and explore career information, and reference librarians can share information about this approach with students. Career centers sometimes offer workshops on professional networking websites such as LinkedIn. Following companies or career centers helps students to find out about jobs and local recruiting events. Companies, as part of their branding strategy, often maintain Facebook and LinkedIn pages that give students and job seekers more insight into their organizational culture. LinkedIn recently launched a new tool called the Field Study Explorer, allowing users to compare their academic field of study and where they currently work, what they do, and the university they attended.

Social media skills are important to students beginning to explore career options. This includes preparing your social media for your job search, a privacy-related topic that is important to today's students. Sometimes a career center will have workshops or resources for this, but other times a librarian can be the only resource who can help a student find out about taking down online pictures or best ways to delete and restart a Facebook account.

Public Library

The public library is a great resource for students, especially if the library system includes a business library. It's important to make students aware that they may not have access to the university library or the career center after graduating, but they can always go to the public library for job hunting and career exploration resources. If they have the funding and staffing, public libraries also provide career-related programming. The author often searches public library catalogs and web pages for former students and alumni who no longer have access to the university's career services. As an example, Brooklyn Public Library has a job hunting topic page with a variety of resources including links to the public library's databases such as ReferenceUSA (a company directory), in addition to job sites like Wetfeet and Idealist.org. Alerting students to the fact that there are also librarians that can help them find information at a local public library is a good practice and sometimes gives students a better idea of the role the library plays in helping people meet their information needs. Many library systems have a dedicated business library, and it's good to show students where they can find career and job search programming in those more specialized branches. Compared to academic libraries, public libraries with a business emphasis will have more resources for entrepreneurs, personal finance, and small businesses. Pointing out this distinction is another good teaching moment, especially if the student is new to academic libraries and the kinds of collections maintained by academic libraries.

MAKING THE LIBRARY A BETTER RESOURCE

In September 2014 the Business Reference in Academic Libraries Committee (part of ALA's Reference and User Services Association) developed an important document called "Financial Literacy Education in Libraries: Guidelines and Best Practices for Service." The learning guidelines in this document clearly state that "career choices, education choices, and skills have a direct impact on income" (Reference and User Services Association 2014, 1). The document provides a comprehensive framework for financial literacy that covers a wide variety of personal finance questions and resources, as well as excellent advice on best practices for financial literacy services and partnerships. The appendix has a list of useful resources and definitions that could be used in workshops or on web pages, and all of the information in the report is useful for a librarian looking to improve career-related offerings.

Another way to enhance the library's usefulness is to take advantage of opportunities to create collaborations with career services, first-year and pre-college programs, and separate academic departments. At Brooklyn College, one librarian is assigned as a formal liaison to career services, and this includes a small collection development budget for career books. Communicating with career services is especially important so that the library can complement their work and avoid duplicate subscriptions to material, books, or workshop content.

Many academic libraries have a career and jobs LibGuide or web page that informs students, faculty, and other external audiences about how career information is organized. Emailing this guide, or physically meeting with departments to gain feedback on the content, can often be a good starting place for conversations with departments external to the library. Recently, there is a trend to link skills taught in humanities and the social science disciplines to valuable career skills. For example, English departments are stressing the ability of their graduates to communicate effectively in writing and critical thinking, while sociology departments are highlighting how their students learn how to gather and analyze social data in the form of surveys, interviews, and focus groups.

Ultimately, the library can be made into a place to demystify personal finance, business, and career information by purchasing career resources, showing nonbusiness students how to access authoritative business sources, and actively collecting and making accessible this information. It is important that the librarian not give financial advice but rather show students the sources they need, both primary and secondary. Business databases are quite expensive, and there is no reason why the practical aspects of business information seeking should only be taught or shown to business majors by business librarians. Financial literacy and business information are everybody's concern.

CONCLUSION

Librarians can help increase students' financial literacy by giving them the best possible range of information on careers and job searching on which to base their decisions. With guidance through some of these resources at the reference desk and advice about how career information, such as business information, is structured, the students can become smarter and strategic searchers so that they take advantage of the resources available to them. While the library is not a career center, the library as a career information center can make the student aware that this type of information is organized in a specific way. The reference desk is one great place to provide this service, and in chapter 19 I show how to teach these resources together as part of a career information library instruction session.

REFERENCES

Association of College & Research Libraries. 2016. "Framework for Information Literacy for Higher Education." http://www.ala.org/acrl/standards/ilframework.

Jagman, Heather, Krystal Lewis, Brent Nunn, and Scott Walter. 2014. "Financial Literacy across the Curriculum (and Beyond): Opportunities for Academic Libraries." *College & Research Libraries News* 75 (5): 254–57.

Reference and User Services Association. 2014. "Financial Literacy Education in Libraries: Guidelines and Best Practices for Service." http://www.ala.org/rusa/financial-literacy-education-libraries.

Roggenkamp, John. 2014. "Financial Literacy and Community Colleges: How Libraries Can Get Involved." *College & Research Libraries News* 75 (3): 142–43.

Sheley, Christina. 2014. "Get Hired! Academic Library Outreach for Student Job Seekers." *Indiana Libraries* 33 (2): 71–72.

Chapter Fifteen

Developing a Personal Finance Collection for a Public Library

Lisa G. Liu and Roslyn Donald

Balancing a checkbook and understanding how to calculate the interest on a car loan used to be the epitome of financial literacy. Today even ordinary financial lives are much more complicated. Life insurance, credit cards, long-term care insurance, health-care spending accounts, 401(k) retirement plans, home equity lines of credit, 529 college savings plans, and car leases are all common financial challenges that demand a sophisticated approach. Financial literacy is an essential skill for all adults, yet students receive little guidance in domestic economics. Some high schools teach a consumer math course that covers a few basics, but no institution prepares students to juggle the products and tools that the average family needs to manage its financial life.

Poor financial management is endemic in the United States population. According to the FINRA Investor Education Foundation's 2012 National Financial Capability Study (FINRA 2013), 30 percent of U.S. citizens used nonbank borrowing such as payday loans, pawn shop loans, or advances on a tax return in 2012; furthermore, 34 percent only paid the minimum payment on their monthly credit card statement. These facts demonstrate how poorly many U.S. citizens manage their finances. As the preeminent resource for lifelong learning, the personal finance collection of a public library is the obvious resource for adults who need help dealing with new financial challenges. Sadly, many personal finance collections are outdated, worn out, and irrelevant to the local population; consequently, they cannot meet this urgent need.

The question is how do librarians reinvigorate personal finance collections and create a systematic maintenance plan. Unfortunately, there are few tools available to librarians to help manage a personal finance collection. Personal finance materials are rarely covered in review journals; as a result, items are added to collections in a haphazard fashion. Our goal as authors of this chapter is to outline a process that will help you overhaul the personal finance collection of your library and ensure coverage of the most useful topics. We developed this process for Santa Clara County Library District (SCCLD) as part of a Smart investing@your library grant project. We conclude with strategies for maintaining the collection going forward so that it becomes a resource for lifelong learning.

CHALLENGES

When you set out to revamp the personal finance collection at your library, you will find that there are few helpful guides. General review resources such as *Publishers Weekly* or *Library Journal* cover budgeting or investment titles, but only on an irregular basis. Business periodicals such as *Inc.* or the *Wall Street Journal* do cover personal finance topics, but their book reviews tend to be focused on business or career management. *Public Library Core Collection: Non-Fiction* (15th ed.) has a few titles, but it is a minimal starting point at best. For a librarian without a business or finance background, it is a daunting task to select authoritative, credible titles for a personal finance collection. Finding those same materials in languages other than English is an even greater challenge.

STRATEGY AND PROCESS

We recommend developing a personal finance collection in phases. This approach works well for library systems with diverse demographics across branches as well as for libraries with limited funding. At SCCLD, we implemented a three-phase strategy. The objectives of Phase One were to assess current holdings, decide what to weed, and assess the needs of the community. The goal of Phase Two was developing a list of personal finance titles that all libraries in a system should have as a core collection. Finally, the goal of Phase Three was to compile a list of recommended optional titles that each library's selectors could use to customize collections to fit the unique needs of their broader community.

Phase One: Analyze Your Collection and Community

Step 1: Assess Your Current Holdings

Assess the state of your personal finance and investing collections by focusing on holdings in the Dewey ranges of 332.024–332.8 and 640–640.73. Include the e-book collection in this analysis. Depending on the collection development tools available, generate a report on the personal finance and investing holdings with the following information:

- Titles by format with number of items per title
- Age of items
- Circulation: number of checkouts and holds per item across libraries
- Condition

This inventory report forms the basis for decisions about your current holdings of personal finance materials.

Step 2a: Weed Holdings

In this step we recommend weeding criteria. The goal is to sort the list of titles generated in Step 1 into three categories:

- Titles to discard
- Titles to replace with new copies or newer editions, if available
- Titles to keep

To decide what to discard, consider criteria based on the circulation, age, and condition of the materials, such as the following:

- Titles published more than five years ago
- Worn or damaged copies
- Titles that have not circulated within the past one or two years
- Titles that circulate sporadically, not more than a couple of times per year

Step 2b: Refresh Classics

Classic titles and those recommended by the *Public Library Core Collection: Non-Fiction* are exceptions to the above criteria. There are several authors writing on personal finance topics who have been popular for many years. These evergreen authors are worth keeping in the collection, in every format you can afford. Consider keeping or replacing old copies of books by these evergreens with new copies or updated editions:

- David Bach

- Ric Edelman
- Benjamin Graham, especially *The Intelligent Investor: The Classic Text on Value Investing*
- Napoleon Hill (extremely popular with Hispanic readers)
- Robert Kiyosaki
- Suze Orman
- Dave Ramsey
- Thomas J. Stanley

Lists of evergreen authors should be vetted periodically, despite popularity of their titles. It is important to stay current on their recent activities. For example, Kiyosaki's Rich Dad, Poor Dad series still has high circulation despite his company's recent financial troubles. This is a perennial problem that librarians face: balancing what is in demand versus what is good quality material. Different librarians will make different decisions based on individual libraries' selection policies.

To better understand the topic gaps in your collection, the next step is to generate an environmental scan of your library's community. If staff resources allow, the collection analysis can be conducted simultaneously with the community analysis.

Step 3: Conduct a Community Analysis

To understand the personal finance information needs of your patrons more specifically, collect the following data about the communities served by your library system:

- Population of service area and growth or decline from previous year; projections for the next five years
- Demographics: ethnic backgrounds, socioeconomic levels, education levels, age groups, income levels, primary languages spoken at home
- Employment: unemployment rate, common professions and occupations, military bases
- Housing: home ownership rates, mortgage rates, median monthly rental rates, and year-over-year increases of these statistics
- Financial literacy levels
- Local financial institutions

The QuickFacts tool developed by the U.S. Census Bureau is a helpful resource to gather demographic data quickly about a state, county, or city of five thousand people or more. The websites for local governments and organizations such as chambers of commerce can also be useful sources for demographic data.

For direct measures of financial literacy, the 2012 National Financial Capability Study of the FINRA Investor Education Foundation is very helpful. It provides several measures of the financial behavior and knowledge of American adults state by state. The study measures multiple aspects of this behavior. These include how individuals manage their resources and how they make financial decisions such as how much to save, how much to pay on their credit card balances, and where to borrow money. The study also evaluates how these indicators vary with underlying demographic, behavioral, attitudinal, and financial literacy characteristics. The findings are accessible through a user-friendly online tool for generating state-specific reports.

The purpose of a community analysis is to determine the personal finance information needs of your community. It is also a systematic guide to select topics that would be of most interest or use to your patrons.

Phase Two: Develop a Core Collection

The next phase of your collection development is to develop a core collection by identifying specific personal finance topics of interest to your patrons and selecting new titles to meet those interests.

Step 1: Identify the Personal Finance Topics of Interest to Your Community

Using the community analysis developed in the prior step, work with your reference staff to brainstorm financial topics that would have the widest appeal. Subjects that appeal to younger people in the community include buying versus renting a home, finding a financial advisor, financing college, paying off college debt, researching stocks, or managing credit card debt. Other topics such as retirement and estate planning, wealth distribution, and Social Security are of interest to older patrons. Group similar topics into four or five broader subject areas such as the four key components of financial capability used in the FINRA study:

- Making Ends Meet
- Planning Ahead
- Managing Financial Products
- Financial Knowledge and Decision Making

Other useful classifications include My Money Five, published by the Federal Financial Literacy and Education Commission, or the Consumer Information categories designated by the Federal Trade Commission. At SCCLD, we used the following:

- Budgeting and Money Management

- Life Stages and Financial Planning (e.g., starting a family, saving for college, retirement)
- Investing
- Insurance
- Real Estate

The materials selected to address each topic will make up the core collection of financial planning resources for each library in your system.

Step 2: Determine Selection Criteria for New Materials

To select new materials to address the identified topics, develop criteria for a core collection. Possible criteria to apply include:

- Publishers
- Publication date
- Format
- Language
- Price points and vendors

Detailed recommendations for each bullet point are discussed below.

Publishers: A quick search of personal finance titles in two vendors' online catalogs reveals thousands of titles and dozens of publishers. As you gain experience vetting personal finance materials, note which publishers produce reliable content that fits the needs of your community. In our experience, the following publishers consistently produce high-quality, accessible materials:

- Sphinx
- Aspatore
- Wiley
- FT Press
- Praeger
- Nolo
- AMACOM

Publication date: Economic conditions and laws change frequently. These factors can affect patrons' financial planning; therefore, make sure your holdings are current. Topics such as income tax laws, estate planning, and real estate investment are especially volatile and need regular updating. In general, we recommend that holdings for topics subject to constant change be no more than three years old.

Format: The format of materials is another important selection criterion, necessary to accommodate the learning preferences of as many patrons as possible. In addition to printed materials, seek titles available in other formats such as large print, audio, video, online, and downloadable. Be especially careful when selecting e-book titles. The publication date listed by some e-book vendors reflects the text's conversion to digital format, not the publication date of the title in its original format.

Language: Many libraries serve sizable bilingual and even multilingual communities. Ideally, personal finance collections should include titles in all the community's languages. Unfortunately, there is limited availability of such materials even in the most common languages, such as Spanish and Chinese. The few that are available are often written for financial professionals, not the general public. Materials in less common languages such as Hindi, Vietnamese, Persian, Polish, Russian, and Cambodian are even more difficult to find. Often the only alternative to serve these populations is to use online materials provided by the federal government. A good starting point to find these materials is USA.gov, the U.S. government's official web portal.

Price points and vendors: Many widely marketed consumer and financial planning guides are expensive. Of course, price is not necessarily an indicator of quality. The market offers a range of topics and materials from reliable publishers in the twenty- to thirty-five-dollar price range from most library vendors. In comparison, a few specialized topics such as technical analysis or candlestick charting are routinely very expensive, often starting at fifty dollars per title. If your community analysis shows that your patrons are interested in sophisticated investing techniques, it is worth purchasing a few of these titles. Otherwise, stick with the cheaper prices. Set your maximum price points to stay on budget.

Step 3: Acquire Your Core Collection

After completing the above steps, you are ready to finalize the second phase of your collection's improvement plan: acquiring a core collection for each library in your system. Determine a schedule to have the new items in place given typical constraints of budget, staffing, and other projects in progress. The schedule will provide a time frame to start promoting the new items. Set clear benchmarks to assess how well you are meeting your goals before the deadline of this phase so that you can make timely adjustments.

Phase Three: Compile a List of Supplemental Recommended Titles

Step 1: Add Topics Unique to Different Communities

The goal of the core collection is to meet the information needs of a wide range of patrons in each of your system's libraries. However, each community may have distinct financial planning needs. To meet the specific needs of individual communities, assign staff to develop a list of other topics not covered in Phase Two. For instance, topics such as bankruptcy, foreclosures, or setting up charitable foundations may not be covered in the core collection, but they could be of interest to some communities; in this case, develop a list of supplemental titles to meet these specific needs. Other topics with appeal to specific communities include sophisticated investing techniques, special needs trusts, veterans, and eldercare.

Step 2: Fine-Tune Individual Library Collections to Meet Disparate Needs

Individual branches can fine-tune their collections to meet local needs during this phase. For example, SCCLD has community libraries not only in urban, very affluent areas but also in rural, low socioeconomic areas. Libraries in affluent areas are more likely to need specialized investment titles on technical analysis and options trading; those in less affluent areas may need more titles on managing a tight budget and avoiding nonbank borrowing. Libraries can choose titles from this supplemental list to customize their collections to meet the unique needs of their communities and broaden the range of topics covered.

ASSESSMENT

To ensure the needs of your community are being met, follow up the acquisition of new material with an assessment to understand what areas of your personal finance collection are circulating and what is just sitting on the shelf. Metrics include the following:

- Number of checkouts per item and title
- Number of holds per item and title
- Number of renewals per item and title
- Patron feedback and requests for purchases

For SCCLD's Smart Investing project, we conducted an analysis of the checkout rates for the new personal finance core titles after they had been in circulation for about seven months. We generated a report using our ILS on the number of checkouts per title. During this period of time, the 63 print titles of the core collection were checked out a total of 1,365 times, or an average of 22 times per title across the seven libraries (the standard checkout period is three weeks). The supplemental titles were checked out a total of 485 times or an average of 17 times per title.

The checkout report on the personal finance materials will enable you to explore a number of questions about the collection. Rank the list of titles by number of checkouts and the number of holds, and consider questions such as the following:

- Is there a pattern in what is in demand?
- Are particular formats preferred?
- Are there differences among the different branches in your system? What are they?
- What were the most requested purchases, if any?
- Were items in languages other than English checked out?
- What were the circulation differences before promoting the collection compared to after?

PROMOTION AND MAINTENANCE

After all phases of the collection development process have been completed, the personal finance collection at your library will be more current and therefore more useful to patrons. The next step is to market the collection. At SCCLD we tried not only traditional programming but also some online promotion. We partnered with the local chapter of the Financial Planning Association to offer free seminars on topics such as asset accumulation and estate planning. We promoted the new holdings with online and paper book lists, all with the tagline "Smart investing@the library." We also started a blog focused on money and finance topics, and still maintain the blog three years later.

Before promoting your personal finance collection, take some baseline circulation measurements as described under "Assessment" above. After the promotional period, take the same measurements so you can gauge the effectiveness of your publicity plan. You can also take advantage of the analytics provided by social media platforms to measure your community's interests.

Your findings will provide a systematic basis to decide how to improve the collection and marketing plan. Consider the following:

- Adding a wider range of financial topics
- Targeting the needs of more specific user populations, such as those of different economic levels or language backgrounds
- Adding more copies of the most popular titles
- Adding titles of the most popular authors
- Shifting the collection if some titles are more popular at some libraries than at others

It is also important to update the community needs analysis to account for any changes since the last analysis as you plan for the continued maintenance and updating of the personal finance collection. As the collection changes, collect data on circulation after a period of time to see if there is an increase or decrease in the usage of personal finance resources. Based on findings, you can determine a schedule for periodic updating of that collection. Try to weed your personal finance collection at least once a year for condition and every other year to remove outdated material.

Buy new titles from the evergreen authors as they come out, and replace worn copies. But also review the list of evergreen authors periodically, removing or adding to it according to new information about financial experts. To keep current with resources that meet your community's needs, regularly check sources that cover financial planning and investing, such as the following:

- USA.gov
- National Public Radio's *Planet Money*
- Bloomberg BusinessWeek
- Wall Street Journal
- The business or money section in local newspapers
- FINRA's investor education site (http://www.finrafoundation.org/resources/index.htm)

CONCLUSION

Modern financial lives demand a sophisticated approach to managing the many economic tools available to U.S. residents. Developing a current, clean, and useful personal finance collection is not easy, but it is certainly possible using some basic collection management techniques. It requires an understanding of local information needs, taking stock of the collection, weeding systematically, keeping current with popular authors, researching financial trends, and analyzing circulation statistics. Though professional tools for personal finance subjects are sorely lacking, most librarians will be able to make informed choices of materials using their knowledge of major publishers and popular authors. As libraries position themselves to be lifelong learning centers, financial literacy is a major focus for adult services. The purpose of this chapter has been to give library professionals concrete tips and guidelines to assist in maintaining a current and relevant collection in good condition that will enable lifelong financial literacy for patrons at their libraries.

REFERENCES

Federal Trade Commission. 2015. "Consumer Information." http://www.consumer.ftc.gov/.

FINRA. 2013. "2012 National Financial Capability Study." http://www.usfinancialcapability.org/.

MyMoney.gov. 2015. http://www.mymoney.gov/Pages/default.aspx.

USA.gov. 2015. http://www.usa.gov/index.shtml.

ACKNOWLEDGMENTS

We acknowledge the support of the Santa Clara County Library District, the FINRA Investor Education Foundation, and the American Library Association for making it possible for us to work on the Smart investing@your library grant project. We also appreciate the help of our colleagues Annapurna Dandu and Patricia Lorenzo, who assisted with the collection development efforts. Finally, thanks to Dr. Roslyn Knutson for her thorough review of our chapter and excellent, much-needed editorial advice.

Chapter Sixteen

Financial Literacy Collection Development

Karen Evans

Libraries are often faced with a multitude of decisions when choosing materials to purchase for their patrons. Several factors can influence a librarian's decision about what to purchase and when to purchase it. Cost, currency, patron reading level, library user need, library or shelf space, and accessibility of materials are a few of the considerations involved when developing a collection. The type of library also influences selection; academic and public institutions often have vastly different collection and patron needs.

This chapter examines collection development for financial literacy materials in libraries. Financial literacy affects every stage of life, and the lessons we learn about money and finances can determine how we handle money for the rest of our lives. From teaching children the value of saving to exploring how advertising affects our spending with teenagers to creating budgets and education saving plans for new families and planning for a financially secure retirement, money is with us every day and affects our plans and goals. Before we can discuss collection development and financial literacy for library patrons, we need to define the terms; understanding what collection development and financial literacy are is an important step in understanding how librarians or staff select these items for their libraries. Without a core understanding of collection development, it would be difficult to understand how collection development functions and how it influences the choices libraries make when purchasing items.

What is collection development? Although collection development can cover a wide variety of definitions and duties in public and academic libraries, this chapter will use a core definition of developing and maintaining a set of resources on a specific topic for patron use. The definition is rudimentary, but it covers the gist of collection development. How does a library assess what patron needs are on a particular topic? After deciding those needs and the parameters of the topic, how do librarians select specific resources from the vast amount of print and electronic options available?

Financial literacy is the second component of this chapter and is defined as "the ability to use knowledge and skills to manage one's financial resources effectively for a lifetime of financial security" (Jump$tart! 2015). There are several key terms within this definition that assists the collection development librarian in deciding what items to order for a collection of resources on financial literacy. For someone to have knowledge about a subject, they must have access to items which explain a variety of terms, situations, and ideas for the reader to understand. *Skills* implies that the user can transfer the knowledge into everyday situations or activities. Developing skills (depending upon the patrons) may involve reading books or articles or completing worksheets or role-playing to fully understand how knowledge of the subject can translate into skills for use in everyday situations. Another significant aspect of the definition is the term *lifetime*. Financial literacy is not just for adolescents with a first job or single college graduates or new retirees worried about their financial outlook; financial literacy is a lifelong pursuit for every person.

BUILDING A FINANCIAL LITERACY COLLECTION: KNOWING YOUR PATRONS

Academic and public libraries have diverse patrons, and libraries strive to achieve a varied collection that will reflect their community and library users. To build a collection relevant to users, librarians and staff must be aware of several factors concerning their patrons; in other words, librarians and staff must know their patrons and know what they want and need.

There are several areas where patron information can assist librarians with choosing correct materials. Some questions to consider when looking for information on your patrons include the following:

- What age groups does your library serve?
- Do you have a children's area or a young adult area?
- Does your library serve primarily older, retired adults?
- Is your library a focal point for nonnative English-speaking residents or those for whom English is a second language?
- Does your library serve every age group?

If your library serves every age group, you need to collect materials for every age group. The age of your patrons can be an expensive factor in developing your collection of financial literacy sources. With a wide patron group, focus must be given to different age groups and their distinct financial literacy needs.

The reading level of your patrons is a significant factor in the types of material you purchase for your library. Financial literacy materials are available in a wide variety of reading levels, from children to adult. Purchasing materials at the correct reading level will ensure your patrons have the materials they need to become financially literate. In addition to reading levels, language can be another prominent area of concern, particularly for public libraries. Immigrant communities are scattered throughout small towns, rural communities, and big cities. The immigrants may have no language skills or only an elementary understanding of the common language spoken in the community where they live. Acquiring materials in a variety of non-English sources will provide access to your patrons and additionally make them feel welcome in your library.

Obtaining information concerning patron age, reading levels, and language abilities will provide tools to assist in creating a collection of materials the patrons will be able to use. An additional item to consider is the financial level of the patrons in your library. Perhaps your community has a mixture of financially solvent seniors, but young families are struggling with financial issues. Or your library may cater to single-parent families and immigrants who are working in low-wage positions. Understanding the general financial situation of the patrons in your community can help you build a collection of relevant and helpful resources.

Another area of concern for libraries is the barriers their patrons may have to using the materials the library provides. If patrons are visually impaired, print materials should be purchased in large print or braille to provide easier access to the materials. Patrons can be shown how to enlarge screens to provide better access to electronic resources. Libraries may want to consider purchasing magnifying glasses or other technologies that can assist visually impaired patrons in using the materials. Library users who have difficulty with arthritis may find it easier to use lighter paperback books rather than heavier, hardbound books or to use page-turning devices rather than try to turn pages with their fingers.

CHARACTERISTICS OF COLLECTION DEVELOPMENT

There are several areas to consider when developing a collection on financial literacy for your patrons. Questions to consider when developing a collection can include these:

- How will the materials be selected for your library?

- How will you evaluate the materials before you purchase them?
- How will you acquire the items, perhaps from a vendor or via an online company?
- What factor does your budget play in the purchase of an item for your library?
- What format do you order—electronic, print, video, games, or CDs?
- Can you ensure that all resources are available to all your patrons?
- How will you maintain the resources you purchase, and how will you determine when an item should be replaced?

When selecting materials for the library, the selector (person who orders the items) should be aware of the general characteristics of the library users as discussed earlier in this chapter. Armed with that knowledge, selectors can make informed decisions about the types of material to order. Selecting resources in different languages and reading skills may suit patrons much better than simply ordering all items at a high reading level and in English. Looking for a variety of resources about financial literacy, from adult books aimed to English-as-a-second-language patrons to resources for new families and items on enjoying retirement for older patrons, will ensure that your library has the right tools for all your patrons.

Another factor to consider when selecting materials is topic coverage. Financial literacy can cover a wide variety of subjects—including saving, budgeting, investing, retirement, credit, and bankruptcy. Each of these subjects can contain dozens of subareas of information to consider when purchasing for a library. Retirement interests could include IRAs (Roth and traditional), bonds, stocks, and money market accounts. It is important for the selector to knowledgeably select the correct item for the library.

One way to successfully select the correct items for your library is to evaluate before you purchase. Evaluating materials may include several factors:

- The reputation of the author or publishing company
- The timeliness and content of the material
- Popular and scholarly reviews of materials (books, CDs, videos, etc.)
- Price of the items (including publisher discounts)
- Relevance to the patrons

Libraries often rely on the reputation of the publisher in selecting materials; if the publisher is well known and established in the field, it is more likely the selector will consider purchasing materials from the publisher. The same applies to the author of the publication. If the author is well known, an authority in the field, or just had a successful television appearance, it is more likely the publication will be purchased. Often patrons contact their libraries after seeing someone on television discussing their publication and request the library purchase it for their collection. When patrons take the time to contact their library and request an item, it is a wise move for the library to listen and order at least one copy.

Another way to evaluate a source is to look at the publisher website or catalog. How does the publisher review the source? If the resource is academic, are there reviews by experts or academics? If the item is a popular source, are reviews listed by readers or other authors in the same genre? Reviewing bookseller websites is an additional way to evaluate an item; these sites include pertinent information on publisher and date of publication. Additionally, bookseller sites often have reviews listed by a variety of readers, giving many different points of view about a publication. It is often worth the time to review these sites and gain a better understanding of the book and how it is perceived by readers.

Libraries often purchase their materials from an established vendor or from a bookseller site. Often, contracts with specific demands are negotiated with vendors—books come into libraries ready for display and checkout. Or vendors are contracted to send a specific genre of books or authors. Using an online bookseller allows the selector to read a synopsis of the book and any reviews available, which can help the selector make an informed decision about purchasing the item. Often, online booksellers list additional items purchased with a particular title; this allows the selector to view items they may not have been aware of.

Budgets are an ever-increasing important factor in collection development for academic and public libraries. With often dwindling funds, selectors must ensure the items they purchase are the best choice for their library; often, additional funds to correct any purchasing mistakes do not exist. Should the item be purchased in hardback or softback? Should a large-print version be purchased? Would it be more beneficial to the library to purchase the item as an electronic book? E-books are easier to update if necessary, and the ubiquitous wear and tear on a print book would not be an issue with this format.

Making these budget decisions depends in part on the type of patron the library serves and the needs of those patrons. With an aging or older population, purchasing items in large print may be the best choice for the library; or if the population is more technology oriented, purchasing in electronic format may be best for the patrons. Again, this is an area where knowing the patrons served by your library can help you make the correct decisions in purchasing materials.

Has your library thought about a program allowing patrons to purchase books for the library? This is a way for libraries with stagnant budgets to increase their collection and library holdings. Library personnel select items for the library and display the book title and purchase price; patrons can select a title and give the purchase price to library staff. Book plaques could be placed inside the book thanking the donor or used as a way to memorialize a family member or friend. Or perhaps hosting a book sale would benefit your library. Selling outdated books, magazines, and other materials along with library themed items (bags, bookmarks, mugs, etc.) might be a way for your library to increase funds to purchase new items.

Maintenance is an issue affecting budgets. It costs money to repair or replace books. Books can become outdated and need to be removed or weeded from the shelf; for diseases and health issues or legal and criminal subjects, information may change and books may need to be discarded and replaced with items more current. Print items can also be damaged through heavy use or carelessness, necessitating the repair of an item. If the resource has worksheets, surveys, or recipes, the pages may have been removed by patrons, making the book useless for others.

Although the format of items has been discussed throughout the collection development process, it is an important aspect to consider when purchasing materials. Although claims have been made for several years that the print book is on the way to extinction, they still exist and are used by many. Purchasing an item in print can involve space, storage, and maintenance issues for libraries. These can be costly concerns, with off-site storage and maintenance fees claiming parts of ever-smaller library budgets. Electronic formats may not have the space and storage issues of print, but many patrons may not like browsing or reading an electronic book. For many reasons, patrons may not have access to electronic books outside of the library. They may not be technological savvy enough to use an electronic book, or they may not be able to afford a personal computer or Internet access at home. They may not remember passwords for accessing the system to retrieve the book. Electronic books do have many pluses for users: One can access the book using small electronic devices capable of fitting into pockets—most lighter than carrying a print book. Electronic resources can be updated to reflect new information or resources on the topic. One can enlarge the print as needed and may be able to change the language on an electronic resources. But if electronic books are not used or if the idea is not of interest to your patrons, why purchase these? If patrons will not use the item, why waste limited funds on it? Instead, purchase a resource with the format your patrons want on a topic they are interested in.

Print resources provide the "comfort" of holding the book in your hand and looking at the cover and browsing through the pages before you decide to purchase it. But print sources can be very heavy to carry, become outdated quickly, or become useless if a patron has removed pertinent pages from the volume. Printed material cannot be translated with the same ease as an electronic source; a different volume must be printed. As mentioned before, space and storage can affect print collection in libraries. The apparent issues with print and electronic sources mean the selector must take the time to evaluate both types of resources and determine the one most suited to the patrons in their library.

Finally, one of the most important ways to determine if an item should be purchased is to decide if it is relevant to your patrons. If you cannot determine what your patrons want, ask them. Have a survey they can fill out at the checkout desk or available online. If you send paper or electronic newsletters, include a survey. If your library staff does not spend time interacting with your patrons and do not know what they want or need, a survey may be your best choice to help you make the correct decisions in purchasing items for your library.

USING THE COLLECTION

The financial literacy items have been purchased and you are waiting for your patrons to rush in and check the items out and become financially literate. But nothing happens; the books sit on the shelves gathering dust. Perhaps you spent all of your time ensuring you selected the best materials for your patrons and did not give any thought to displaying or advertising the new materials. Displaying and publicizing new acquisitions is an important way to promote items and show patrons the importance of the collection. Setting up a display of books and providing a definition of financial literacy may be enough to interest your patrons in the benefits of understanding money.

There are several other ways to publicize a financial literacy collection and explain the importance of financial literacy and fitness to your users. Libraries could create a series of financially fit workshops, including sessions on the following:

- Creating a budget
- Managing your bills
- Using credit cards and debt
- Opening checking or savings accounts
- Understanding and applying for mortgages
- Federal and state taxes
- Retirement

The sessions could be geared toward general topics (understanding credit or mortgages) or focused on specific groups, such as college students and financial aid or resources for those retiring soon. Workshops or classes would be an opportune time for nonnative English-speaking residents to learn about American banking, credit, and tax systems. Patrons could practice filling out forms to open accounts or talking with bank personnel about financial issues. Worksheets on topics could be available for patrons to practice budgets or filling out mortgage forms. Perhaps local banks would be willing to give presentations on financial topics. If your library conducts classes for those learning to speak English, presenting information on financial literacy could be appropriate. Providing opportunities for all patrons to learn about financial literacy with resources appropriate for their skill level is an essential duty for today's libraries.

CONCLUSION

Financial literacy is an important aspect of life today for any person. Being financial literate is a lifelong goal and is pertinent at every stage of life. In today's multicultural societies, academic and public libraries have the ability to provide their patrons with the resources and information they need to become financially literate and secure in life.

REFERENCE

Jump$tart! 2015. "National Standards in K-12 Personal Finance Education." 4th ed. http://www.jumpstart.org/assets/files/2015_NationalStandardsBook.pdf.

Chapter Seventeen

"How to Present Your Best Self" Workshops

Jennifer Wright Joe

Librarians of many different stripes can help their patron population by offering workshops on how to get a job. In a series of workshops titled "How to Present Your Best Self," the author has identified key areas that are helpful for assisting patrons in finding the right job. Among these are how to research the job they want, how to write a résumé (and rewrite it, if necessary), how to present one's self at a job interview, how to prepare a presentation, and more. These workshops have been organized in such a fashion that they should work for either public libraries or academic libraries. While it is not necessary for an individual to attend all of these workshops, they do fit together in a nice series, should the institution want to make it a standing engagement.

The Great Recession has made seeking employment a daunting task in the minds of many. Part of that may be a shift in who is looking for work. While the average worker does not seem to be spending more time searching for a job, one study found that, "for nearly all age categories, unemployed males with at least a bachelor's degree spent much more time searching for a job after the recession than before it" (Aliprantis, Chen, and Vecchio 2014, 13). These jobs might require more expertise in job searching to be time efficient, with competition requiring more precise applications. It may also be that it takes more time to find these jobs among the rest. Both of these problems and many more might be helped by this set of workshops.

Librarians have a reputation on campus and in their communities for being information sources, being involved in their communities, and being persons of trust. This puts librarians in a unique position to help displaced workers and new graduates find their paths in life, as they have a ready patron base, already familiar with their other services, as well as partnerships within the community that might be able to help them build their workshops and give advice where needed. Librarians can partner with several different entities in the community or departments on an academic campus to make these presentations happen and to get whatever support they might need. In a midsized town, for example, they could reach out to major employers, such as a hospital or an educational institution, as well as career development centers and government offices. Academic librarians have all of those resources, in addition to the resources on their own campuses: career services, student affairs, professional development services, and alumni centers. Together, these different groups can help organize workshops to cover the following tasks.

STEP ONE: HOW TO RESEARCH THE JOB YOU WANT

Researching the job that the individual wants is often an overlooked step in the job-hunting process. While a patron may know what he or she wants to do and what he or she is capable of, they may not connect this to how a job is presented in a job listing. This is especially true of college students, who may never have worked more than a part-time job in their lives. By earning an advanced degree, they have, by default, put themselves in a new category of worker. Patrons who come into the public library looking for job-search help could very well be in the same category and not realize it, either because of education pursued or experience gained in previous employment. In the current economy, they may believe that they do not have the luxury of being picky in the jobs for which they apply and might think they should apply for anything they come across (Bourne 2014). However, researching the jobs that are available is not necessarily being picky, and patrons should be persuaded out of this notion as soon as possible. Instead, it should be seen merely as a fact-finding mission to make the patron aware of the company for whom they would be working and what their primary job duties would be. While some job listings can be incredibly detailed, others may have limited space, and any could have the phrase "other duties as assigned" attached to them. A cursory examination of the company might be able to shed better light on what those other duties might be. This would also be an excellent place to review some professional networking websites that might give patrons more insight into companies. One of the most recommended of these is LinkedIn, which has quickly become a great place to learn about not only a company but also its employees (Arms 2014), allowing prospective employees to decide whether or not they would mesh well with their future colleagues.

In order to research a job, the patron should first write a list of what they believe they can bring to a job, whether it is education, experience, or skill sets. This is especially useful if they have not been trained for a specific career but instead have varied work experience—it will help the patron see if he or she has overlapping skills from different employment. A premade résumé will help with if the patron has one, but this step can be completed without one, and the thoughtful reflection required might be useful to résumé writing, which in this series is Step Two. When this list has been compiled, the patron is ready to look at job listings, which they can do through approved sites that the library recommends, such as local posting websites that city or university entities run. A typical reasonable job listing should include the following: statement of the business and an indication of what sector the business falls under, clear and concise keywords that are easily identifiable, an objective for the job being listed, some indication of pay or benefits, and an explanation of how they will judge applicants (Taylor Christensen 2013). While one or more of these may be missing because of space constraints or other issues, a job listing that fails to contain a majority may not be worth the patron's time. Patrons should be taught to identify these parts of a job listing with examples from several different sources and employment areas. Experts on job searching incorporate these experiences into the concept of a job-search plan, in which the individual will "define your search objective, make a detailed list of prospective employers, and then write down your qualifications and rationale for each prospective employer" (Develder 2014). I advise the last step be done with the qualifications list created before the job search begins, because it will be easier for the patron to remember the various qualifications that they might have, especially those gained informally.

This first workshop can easily take between half an hour and an hour, depending on how much time the librarian would like to give patrons to spend looking at potential jobs. Each patron finding one or two appropriate listings, however, would be sufficient to give them a start on this part of the process and would prepare them for the next step in the job search.

STEP TWO: HOW TO WRITE A RÉSUMÉ AND COVER LETTER

Writing a résumé is an important step in the job-hunting experience, but it is one that most people tackle first, before they have considered a career path or looked at the job market, and this may be the wrong way to go about writing it. Many college classes have students write generic résumés that might not even be appropriate for the career they are pursuing, using instead a template designed for their major. It gives them experience with the process, but it may lead to a false sense of security, as students do not always get careers directly in line with their majors; employers may look at their educational accomplishments as evidence of hard work, accomplishment, and an ability to follow guidelines, rather than for the actual knowledge attained. In addition, many employers now screen prospective applicants with software that picks out keywords in their résumé and cover letters, rejecting those applications that do not explicitly state certain proficiencies. The patron may be rejected for a job that they are qualified for without their résumé ever being seen by a human being, because they did not do their research in the first step or did not properly apply it in this step. An example of this from the world of business is the concept of generally accepted accounting principles, often referred to as GAAP; the written out words would not necessarily trigger the robot to accept an application if the description listed the acronym, and vice versa (Arms 2014). Put the words in a résumé and cover letter exactly as they are written in the job description.

In addition, if one reads a job description carefully, one may find that he or she has even more to offer a business than the qualifications necessary. Develder writes of a law student who, upon reading a job description for a paralegal, found that the company needed more than that (2013). According to Develder, "She applied, using both her cover letter and interview to explain to the employer what she had to offer and to pitch the idea of them hiring a lawyer" (2013, 15). It took some negotiation on the applicant's part, but she made a job that was right for both her and her new employer, because she had spent time scrutinizing the job description and shaping her cover letter to match.

Résumé-writing workshops are commonplace among those who provide career help, so there is little need to dwell on the format of this step in the process. However, pay special attention to cover letter writing, which is something that many institutions do not teach. While sometimes optional, cover letters give the individual a more personal way to express their interest and qualifications for a job and may give them the necessary leg up against the competition.

STEP THREE: HOW TO PRESENT YOURSELF AT AN INTERVIEW

Many people, especially those who have attending college, have spent some time learning how to conduct themselves at an interview. For example, at Western Kentucky University, students have traditionally taken a communications class in which they give presentations (both informative and persuasive), write a résumé, and conduct mock interviews. In the past, a lot of time was devoted to how to dress and how to shake hands. However, the interview process for many jobs is much more than a one-time meeting in which a person sits face-to-face with a hiring manager. Especially when talking about more academically minded work, there may be a telephone interview or a video chat interview in addition to the one-time meeting—which may be longer than expected and involve a panel of people instead of just one person. The interview experience might include a meal—or more than one—with the prospective employer. All of these things deviate from the traditional expectation of the interview, especially for patrons whose prior work experience is lacking. Preparing for these other types of interviews is just as important as knowing not to wear more than five pieces of jewelry or to wear a well-tailored suit.

Despite it seeming that technology has complicated the interview process, some necessary interview preparations have actually become easier thanks to the plethora of information available on the Internet. An important step to being prepared for the interview is to have an idea of what kind of questions are going to be asked. While it is not wise to have an answer memorized, as it will make the interviewee sound stilted and robotic, it is important to have examples fresh in one's memory so that the interviewee is not struggling for the words when put on the spot. Haines explains that "answers to interview questions are usually enhanced when you can provide a relevant example from your own previous experience which demonstrates your understanding of an element of the role, or even examples of previously having done something similar in another job" (2013, 247). Not only will these more in-depth answers prove that the interviewee understands the question, but, provided they are appropriate and meaningful, they will stand out in an interviewer's mind long after they have seen other candidates. However, caution patrons not to oversell themselves. Common sense and the literature agree that a balance in all things is necessary in order to prevent alienating oneself from the interviewer (Bourne 2014).

Finally, the interview process typically ends with a question that is some variation of "Is there anything you would like to ask us?" This can be a great time for the interviewee to show just how much he or she knows about the company and how much they have thought about how their experience will help. The interviewee might ask about recent public news that he or she has read about the company, or something more personal about work the interviewer does (Haseltine and Gould 2013). Again, here it important to strike that balance between being interested and being too nosy; Philip Bourne writes, "I have also seen this overdone, leaving me with the awful impression the job candidate had been stalking me" (2014, 2).

In presenting these workshops, mock interviews are essential. There are many types of interviews, and rotating short sessions with each style helps patrons understand the differences while also giving them an opportunity to experience a difficult fact of interviews: they can be extremely draining. An information session prior to the mock interviews may also be necessary to communicate the basic interview information, so this particular workshop may need to be split into two sessions.

STEP FOUR: HOW TO GIVE A PRESENTATION

If the interviewee has to make a presentation as part of his or her interview process, this can prove daunting. Even if the interviewee has made presentations before as part of previous employment, there might be restrictions or expectations foran interview presentation that the interviewee will be unfamiliar with. Likewise, if the interviewee has never given a formal presentation, he or she may be clueless of what to expect. Though it is a common experience, giving a presentation in front of peers in a classroom setting is not the same as giving a presentation to strangers. Out of the workshop, this opportunity to present to strangers might be available at student or amateur-level conferences, and patrons should be provided with information about such events and encouraged to attend both as a presenter and as a spectator.

Technology should be a consideration when organizing a presentation. PowerPoint presentations are still a recent enough phenomenon that the interviewee may not have the luxury of using that software. However, if access to a computer, projector, and the Internet is available to the interviewee, there are a few free online solutions to that problem. There are, of course, guidelines to using presentation software. Slides should not be read from but used as cues—but neither should the presentation seem like it was memorized (Cardwell et al. 2014). In that same vein, slides should contain as few words as possible, exploring key concepts, dates, or definitions only. This is both so that the viewer does not get information overload before they hear what the presenter has to say, as well as to keep the viewer from being overly distracted by the slides (Mastrangeli 2014). Keeping in mind the concept of balance, it is also important to remember time constraints when building the presentation. A presentation that is too long will surely be cut off and will make the presenter look as though they cannot follow simple rules, while a presentation that is too short opens the door for embarrassing questions and the appearance of incompetence (Hites 2014).

For the workshop series, mock presentations and critiques from a group are most effective for patrons to learn from. There may be guidelines available prior to the session to allow patrons to make their presentations ahead of time, or time could be allowed during the workshop for them to create a short presentation, something that they could learn to give in five or ten minutes. Then the presentations would be critiqued using those guidelines.

STEP FIVE: THE MORE

Once an institution has mastered these four basic workshops for the job seeker, there are many ways to expand. One expansion that could prove popular is a workshop on how to keep a job once one has been found. It can be disorienting and daunting to be a new employee in an unfamiliar workplace. Workshops on how to go through the proper channels to find out work expectations might be appreciated, or institutions could present workshops on good workplace habits. Other presentations could include career advice from recently employed persons or their employers, information about trends in the labor market, or anything else your patrons might want. Another popular idea is to review common social media websites and show how public profiles can impact the patron's presentation of self. One pair of researchers developed several questions that could be asked during a peer critique of social media profiles:

- Who can find you online and where can they find you?
- What first impression do you create online?
- How do you use visual and verbal components to build your online presence?
- How professional and appropriate are such visual and verbal representations?
- What can you do to boost your online professional presence? (Ding and Ding 2013, 244)

These questions, among others, can start patrons thinking about the Internet as a public space, rather than a private one, which is essential for job seekers in the twenty-first century. To drive this point home, patrons should be asked to reflect on the information they found through online sources about the employer, and expect that the employer will be doing the same with them.

CONCLUSION

Hopefully, this chapter has provided a start to the organization process for workshops at various library institutions. Libraries can start with one or more of the workshops outlined and work their way up, creating more for different patron populations as the need arises. If the institution is looking for more ways to help their patrons, a quick survey at the end of the series might help guide new growth. Every patron population is different, and while the base four topics are fairly universal, there might be specific majors or employers who want something more. These four workshops as discussed, however, should get any patron on his or her way to a smoother job search, and a brighter future in the career of his or her choice.

REFERENCES

Aliprantis, Dionissi, Anne Chen, and Christopher Vecchio. 2014. "Job Search Before and After the Great Recession." *Economic Trends*, August 12, 13.

Arms, Doug. 2014. "How to Land the Job You Want." *Strategic Finance* 96 (9): 40–45.

Bourne, Philip E. 2014. "Ten Simple Rules for Approaching a New Job." *PLoS Computational Biology*, June, 1–3.

Cardwell, Michael S., J. Hector Aranda, Rene Hernandez, and Ho Hoi. 2014. "Empowering Your Presentation Skills." *Donald School Journal of Ultrasound in Obstetrics & Gynecology* 8 (1): 100–104.

Develder, Carla. 2014. "Job Searching Tips for Law Students and New Graduates." *Student Lawyer* 42 (5): 14–15.

Ding, Huiling, and Xin Ding. 2013. "360-Degree Rhetorical Analysis of Job Hunting: A Four-Part, Multimodal Project." *Business Communication Quarterly* 76 (2): 239–48.

Haines, Mark. 2013. "Career Opportunities: The Ones That Never Knock." *Legal Information Management* 13 (4): 240–51.

Haseltine, Derek, and James Gould. 2013. "Job-Search Basics: A Scientific Approach to Interviewing." *Nature Immunology* 14 (12): 1199–1201.

Hites, Ronald A. 2014. "How to Give a Scientific Talk, Present a Poster, and Write a Research Paper or Proposal." *Environmental Science & Technology* 48 (17): 9960–64.

Mastrangeli, Jeana. 2014. "PowerPoint Unveils Coordinate Confusion." *Journal of Humanistic Mathematics* 4 (1): 136–48.

Taylor Christensen, Stephanie. 2013. "Finding the Perfect Fit." *Managing People at Work* 377: 3.

Chapter Eighteen

Supporting Financial Literacy for Homebuyers

Jenny Brewer

PART 1: SERVICE NEEDS OF HOMEBUYERS

Financial literacy support from a public library can save library patrons significant amounts of money, time, and stress when it comes to home ownership. The library's role in supporting financial literacy for home-buying patrons is complex because, while buying a home can be a time-consuming process, it can also be extremely time sensitive. Many patrons will apply for a mortgage and get declined. They may then be in need of resources to correct the issues with their application. Other homebuyers may find themselves in the midst of a transaction and have issues with the title company or the tax office. These patrons will need ready reference material or databases that can quickly get them accurate information about their full range of options, which they may not be receiving from the parties they are dealing with, all of whom have investments in the transaction.

Basic reference librarian ethics should be assumed but are worth reiterating here because the stakes can be so high for the patrons. When providing financial information, it is very important that librarians only advise on the discovery and use of tools that will aid the patron's independent decision making. Librarians should never give the appearance of advocating for a specific choice, as there can be costly consequences if a patron follows a librarian's advice and does not achieve satisfactory results. It should be made very clear to the patron that a librarian's assistance is limited to getting the patron as much information as possible about options without giving an opinion on which option is best. Anything a librarian may happen to state as fact during a reference transaction ("mortgage rates are supposed to go down") should be followed with a source ("according to today's *Wall Street Journal*").

Purchasing a home can take anywhere from hours to years. Library patrons who set home ownership as a goal for themselves may need long-term support on this project. The first thing a library should reflect in its approach to this category of patrons is the reality that the process can be a journey, but a perfectly manageable one.

When planning library services for homebuyers, it could be most effective to orient your services toward buyers of a new or existing home with a conventional mortgage. This is overwhelmingly the most common type of transaction. In terms of the types of requests that may be made at the reference desk, these patrons can be divided into "best-case" and "unusual-case" buyers.

- The best-case buyers may not need much support beyond resources that will allow them to fact-check the information they are getting from the realtor and the bank.
- The unusual-case buyers, those who are purchasing a distressed property or who have long-term credit liabilities such as liens or bankruptcy, may be looking at a long road and are best served by case-by-case over-the-shoulder assistance.

Patrons who fall in between the best case and unusual case will most benefit from a thoughtfully selected slate of home-buying resources. The concerns facing these patrons fall into two categories:

- Property (choosing a home)
- Financing (getting a mortgage)

Choosing a Home

Many people begin the process far more worried about the money than the house, but may find these concerns reversed once they actually begin viewing properties. There can be additional issues beyond the basic challenge of finding a property in the right location, in acceptable condition, and with the desired number of bedrooms and bathrooms. Once the buyers find a home that meets their needs, there is a chance they could run into other property issues. There are any number of setbacks that can occur subsequent to making a selection:

- The buyer may be outbid by other buyers.
- The realtor may discover that property is owned by nonindividuals (heirs, bank, homeowner's association, government).

- The property may not appraise for the amount the sellers are asking.

Any of these issues can add a layer of complication to the process and may cause the buyer to consider passing on the home and starting over. Making this decision may require a trip to the library. Current, state-specific resources should be provided that can help the buyer independently confirm any information they get from the realtor or loan officer and which may contextualize the issue and support their decisions.

Getting a Mortgage

Although many buyers come to the process with a specific property already designated, such as renters who are offered the opportunity by a landlord seeking to divest herself of an asset, the best approach is to apply for a mortgage before choosing a house. Many real estate agents require a letter of preapproval from a lender before they will show houses.

The best place to start is with the patron's bank. Any lender is going to look at the following requirements:

Rental history. An applicant must be able to prove on-time rent payments for two years, ending with the current month. If the borrower lives in a commercially owned apartment complex, for example, the lender may simply send a verification form to be signed by the owner, manager, or agent. If the applicants have a private landlord, they may be required to provide twenty-four months of canceled rent checks, or a stamped and signed teller's printout of direct debits to their checking account.

Employment history. Buyers must prove that they have held the same position for two years. If they have not held the same position, they must have worked in the same field for two years with no gaps of longer than thirty days. A borrower who has transitioned from W-2 employment to 1099 or self-employment will not be able to get a home loan for two years after this transition.

Debt-to-income ratio. The total of a borrower's monthly minimum payment on all credit obligations, including the proposed mortgage (with taxes and insurance included) cannot be more than one-third or half of their monthly gross income. All income must have a two-year history—if a borrower decides to take on a part-time job in the evenings to reduce their debt-to-income ratio, they will have to hold that position a full two years before the lender will count that income toward their gross.

Credit score. A certain minimum credit score and level of past and current activity is required, depending on desired down payment.

Assets. A desired level of cash reserves will be verified. This will usually be at least two months' worth of mortgage payments, including taxes and insurance. (FHA 2015)

A large percentage of patrons who attempt to buy a home may find themselves declined for deficiencies in one of these categories. This is another situation where they may turn up at the library. Some of these deficiencies, such as rental history and employment history, can only be cured with time. It is very frustrating to find a house and apply for a loan, only to be told that you need to wait a whole twenty-four months to be eligible.

Borrowers who are declined for credit or assets, however, may have options they can exercise in the short term. Some credit scores can be improved in as little as ninety days, and cash reserves can begin to accumulate and season. The best way for the library to help cash- or credit-poor patrons to achieve the dream of home ownership is to simply provide materials and resources that advise readers on methods of building savings or credit.

For patrons who find themselves on the two-year clock, the best way for the library to help is to maintain awareness programs that increase the chances of patrons being aware of these issues long before they start looking for a home. Permanent displays, well-promoted pathfinders, or quarterly awareness programs can contribute to a level of community awareness that prevents declined applications down the road.

The first thing librarians can do to ensure that they are meeting their community's needs is to look at what their library is already doing and compare it to estimated community need. This will help the librarian target areas for improvement. Then, the librarian should look at what resources she has that she can apply to those needs. If she has more money than staff, she may prioritize materials over programming. If she has more daily foot traffic than program attendance, she may prioritize pathfinders and displays over classes. Finally, a librarian with a wealth of business community contacts may find it relatively easy to bring in outside consultants to lead programs. The Public Library Association's service response workbook for this service response has a thorough list of policy concerns that should be addressed by librarians choosing the last item.

PART 2: SERVICE RESPONSES TO HOMEBUYERS, A SAMPLE CASE STUDY

The Maple Glen Public Library has undertaken a community needs assessment based around the public library service responses (Anderson Public Library 2015). In preparation, library director Jane Smith has tasked the staff with evaluating their full spectrum of services against each service response and self-identifying areas where the library's offerings are inadequate. Staff will propose solutions for each area and may take action in areas where doing so would not unduly burden the staff or the budget. Proposals that will require a heavy investment will be evaluated against the results of the needs assessment and implemented where supported by the community, scaled to the level of that support.

Mrs. Smith has been focusing on the "Make Informed Choices" service response. She has assigned other librarians to "health" and "other life choices" and chose to evaluate "wealth" herself. She starts with mortgages because she worked as a loan officer while attending library school. She sets out to rate all service areas on their offerings for homebuyers, putting refinance, investment, and relocating aside to evaluate later. Here are the library service areas:

- Print collection
- Electronic collection
- Databases
- Technology
- Finding aids
- Awareness campaigns
- Programming
- Facilities
- Community partnerships

In anticipation of the many opportunities she expects to discover, she creates a "Make Informed Choices—Wealth" workbook with tabs for a wide array of financial literacy topics. On each tab she creates a matrix where she can track problem areas, proposals, and funding needs for each of her nine service areas.

She opens the workbook to "Mortgages" and sets out to examine her print collections. She runs a catalog search, limited to print books. She compares her results to the recommendations in *The Public Library Catalog* (Wyatt, Spires, and Toth 2015). She notes whether titles are "missing," "present," or "out of date." She finds that the 2007 version of *Nolo's Essential Guide to Buying Your First Home* is still on the shelf. She knows that many things changed after the 2008 global financial crisis and that retaining this edition could actually lead to negative results for her patrons. She weeds the book and creates a new cart with her wholesaler. She finds all of the titles she has marked against her recommended list as "missing" or "out of date" and adds them to her cart. She visually confirms that the titles marked as "present" are indeed on the shelf and then begins evaluating the order cart against her library's board-approved collection standards. When she is sure she has a book order that will fill gaps in the collection and bring it up to date, she checks the total.

She goes back to her spreadsheet and finds the "Problem Areas" column of the "Mortgages" tab and types into the cell next to "print collections":

"some titles are outdated, selection is incomplete." Under "Proposals" she types: "weed shelves" and "send Baker and Taylor cart 'Mortgages.'"

She repeats the process against a catalog search limited to e-books, creates an e-book cart, and updates the "electronic collections" row of her spreadsheet. She refers to Wilson's again to evaluate their periodical offerings and contacts her EBSCO representative to add a few titles.

Next, she goes to the library's website and checks her databases menu. Her "Databases by Subject" list has a "Business" heading but seems to assume that patrons will understand that consumer issues will also be covered. The databases under her "Business" heading include these:

- AtoZdatabases
- Business Abstracts with Full Text
- Business Source Complete
- Regional Business News
- Small Business Reference Center
- Thomas Register

She considers the impression this would make on a homebuyer. She does not feel that any of these databases would seem immediately relevant to this patron. She asks herself whether it is necessary to have a database offering in this service response and whether databases exist that could be useful to homebuyers. Because books can take years to publish, and real estate markets and lending guidelines change quickly, articles such as those found in databases can be necessary to supplement print and e-book collections (CQUniversity 2014.).

Ms. Smith decides that adding at least one consumer database would be a good idea. She looks at what is out there, finding that a great many public libraries are doing much better than she is. She assigns a staff member to generate a short list of databases they should look into and set up free trials. Her "Databases" column now reads "consumer databases lacking" under "Problem Areas," "add at least one consumer database" under "Proposals," and "pending" under "Funding Needs."

Under "Technology," she looks at computer software and computer hardware, peripherals, and other equipment, along with instruction in the same. Narrowing her focus to mortgages specifically, she can't think of any software that would be particularly useful, beyond standard office applications. Money management software provides useful forecasting and budgeting tools, but she does not want her patrons saving financial data on public computers. However, the recent emergence of online money management tools such as Mint would store patron data in the cloud and should be safe, assuming patrons consistently logged out after accessing their accounts. The electronic services librarian could conceivably teach an overview or "getting started" class.

On the equipment side, her library already provides public faxing and scanning services, which are both often needed to complete a mortgage application or to dispute credit inaccuracies. Should they look into replacing their typewriter? The library had owned two electric typewriters at the beginning of her tenure. Neither of them had been operational since 2012. It was conceivable that a patron would come in with paper applications they wanted to type onto, but annual requests for a typewriter had been in the single digits since the last one had broken. However, prices for typewriters had decreased drastically, starting at around one hundred dollars. It wasn't very much to spend to have one on hand just in case. She decides to tell the reference librarian that she can buy one if she wants to and only adds the proposal for "Mint class" to her spreadsheet.

She moves on to "Finding Aids." This is an easy one: they don't have one and should make one. However, it should probably wait until the new print materials arrive and the database decision has been made. She updates her spreadsheet accordingly and enters "no direct" under "Funding Needs" as the work can be done in-house and falls under the regular duties of the reference librarian.

"Awareness Campaigns": she likes this one, as it can be started immediately, and in-house too. However, there is a high degree of scalability in her options, ranging from bulletin boards to billboards. She realizes that her library's efforts to raise awareness should be based on community awareness needs. She makes a note to revisit this idea after the community needs assessment is complete. For now, though, they can at least do a bulletin board. She assigns a staff member to create a bulletin board detailing basic mortgage requirements.

She gets excited when she gets to "Programming." She has an idea! She quickly sketches out a proposal to bring in representatives from new home builders in the area for table displays at a Saturday program tentatively titled "Homebuyer Boot Camp." She outlines a presentation she can make later in the day based on what she has learned about mortgages.

She is aware of the risks of inviting commercial interests to present at the library, so she considers some preliminary guidelines for builder participation:

- They may not ask for patron contact information.
- They may hand out business cards.
- They may not negotiate prices.
- They may not dispense purchasing advice.
- They may display floor plans with price ranges indicated.

She sends these guidelines to the city attorney for further refinement. She is grateful that a recent renovation has expanded the library's classrooms and wonders if there are other considerations under the "Facilities" service area. She recalls Edge Initiative Benchmark 9.4: "Patron needs for privacy while conducting sensitive transactions are accommodated through at least one of the following":

- Installing privacy screens for computer monitors
- Placing computer monitors so they can't be viewed by other patrons
- Installing partitions between workstations
- Having public computers in private rooms (Edge Assessment 2015)

Her library has provided none of these options. She asks the electronic services librarian to price privacy screens and partitions.

She wonders how she will go about discovering new home builders who are active in her area and remembers Mr. Jones. Mr. Jones is a local real estate broker who participated in a series of focus groups the library held in previous years. She realizes she is activating "Community Partnerships" and begins listing other relevant contacts. She sat in on a United Way personal finance workshop: she finds the instructor's business card and adds him to her list. She further adds the president of the Chamber of Commerce, the director of economic development, the library's board president emeritus, and the broker who had held her loan officer license.

She considers the opportunities that could come out of potential partnerships with each list entry. The most obvious idea is to see if any of them have existing presentations they might like to repeat for a library audience. It occurs to her that she could do a quick informal survey of these contacts, though, collecting their opinions on the level of financial literacy in the community as they have encountered it in their various lines of work. She logs in to Constant Contact and creates a survey, with an introductory note alerting them to the upcoming service response needs assessment as well as potential roles for community leaders in the process. She concludes by asking them to recommend other contacts who might volunteer. She saves the campaign as a draft and prints it out to get feedback from the library staff and board, noting all steps taken in her spreadsheet and typing a question mark under "Funding Needs."

With the "Mortgages" tab of her "Make Informed Choices—Wealth" workbook all filled in, Mrs. Smith now has a set of proposals that add up to a comprehensive approach to services for homebuyers. She feels that staff can carry out most of her proposals, on a small scale at least, in the course of their regular duties. However, she looks forward to the opportunities that will come as a result of the community needs assessment.

REFERENCES

Anderson Public Library. 2015. "Long Range Plan: Anderson Public Library, 2015–2017." http://www.and.lib.in.us/long-range-plan/.

CQUniversity Library. 2014. "Evaluating Books, Journals, Journal Articles and Websites." http://libguides.library.cqu.edu.au/evaluating-resources.

Edge Assessment. 2015. "Devices and Bandwidth." http://www.libraryedge.org/benchmarks/organizational-management/devices-and-bandwidth.

FHA. 2015. "FHA Loan Requirements." http://www.fha.com/fha_loan_requirements.

Wyatt, Neal, Kendal Spires, and Gabriela Toth. 2015. *Public Library Core Collection: A Selection Guide to Reference Books and Adult Nonfiction.* New York: Grey House.

Chapter Nineteen

Teaching Career Information Literacy in the Academic Library

Frans Albarillo

An important role of the academic librarian is teaching career information literacy so that students can identify and assess their own information needs, create a strategy to find career information, and evaluate that information. This helps improve students' financial literacy by giving them authoritative information about potential professions or career paths so that they can make more informed financial choices as they move toward graduation. The work of librarians in this area complements the work of career counselors and career offices by approaching the subject from an information literacy perspective.

What librarians can offer students is the idea that career information, like any other field of information, is structured by professional associations and societies and is part of a larger domain of business and economics information; understanding these relationships will allow students to access a great variety of material ranging from labor force statistics such as salary and wage information to industry-specific trade journals and reports.

A good starting point for a librarian planning to teach career information is the Reference and User Services Association's (RUSA) report "Financial Literacy Education in Libraries: Guidelines and Best Practices for Service." The very first page clearly states that "career choices, education choices, and skills have a direct impact on income" (RUSA 2014, 1). Improving career and educational choices by teaching students how to navigate this information will have positive effects on their future as they select courses, decide on majors, and possibly consider professional or academic graduate work.

Students encounter career information in many different forms outside the library: as an element of first-year-experience programs, at the career center, or as part of their coursework. Within the library, career questions are frequently asked by students at the reference desk; resources related to these questions were covered in detail in chapter 14. In addition, it is common for professors to request instruction for their classes on some aspect of career information literacy. This chapter focuses on advice and general guidelines for teaching these sessions. At the author's institution, there is no formalized curriculum for career information literacy sessions. Requests come from a variety of departments ranging from English as a second language to business and precollege programs. The author has fulfilled requests for both single and multiple sessions in addition to piloting several workshops on career exploration using social media and business databases. The lesson framework discussed below developed from several years of teaching career information and can be adapted to a variety of teaching contexts. This plan is not a step-by-step guide or script; rather, the chapter can be thought of as a menu of themes and teaching strategies that a librarian teaching career information for the first time can adapt for a particular instruction need.

SESSION OUTLINE AND RESOURCES

Library instruction sessions for undergraduates generally last fifty or eighty minutes, giving time for one or two of the themes discussed below to be presented and explored. Crafting learning outcomes and objectives is essential in planning the lesson. The author provides some example outcomes, but these will vary according to librarian. Outcomes help librarians focus on the information literacy component of the career information. A key resource is the new Association of College & Research Libraries' (2015) "Framework for Information Literacy for Higher Education."

It's important to review the framework and make sure ideas in the framework guide the creation of library instruction outcomes. Other planning elements for an information literacy session include considering the major content areas and activities; the author's approach to teaching consists of a reduced lecture (taking from one-third to one-half of the time) that covers a particular theme. The remaining portion is allocated to a hands-on guided search activity. The session should conclude with a wrap-up portion that gives students the opportunity to ask questions. Lesson outcomes can also inform the creation of a formal or informal formative assessment to provide feedback on the success of the session. The general session outline follows:

- Introduction
- Pre-test (optional)
- Reduced lecture covering one or two resources (such as the Occupational Outlook Handbook or Business Source Complete)

- Guided search activity
- Answers to student questions that came from the activity
- Post-test (optional) or a one-minute paper (optional)
- Wrap-up

This session outline, and especially the guided search activity, assumes a computer classroom is available for the session, or that students will have laptop access. If there is no computer access for students and they are not able to do the guided search activity, there is the option of preparing a search activity in advance and emailing the exercise to students so they can complete it before the instruction session. Then the allocated activity time can be used to review search results, address questions, and demonstrate additional search strategies and techniques.

During the presentation, it is good to frame the lecture by providing an explanation of how you chose the resources you are presenting. This helps students understand that the librarian has curated a list of authoritative, unbiased, and current resources. It is also helpful to provide a larger list of additional resources students can choose to explore after the session.

A guided search activity is a preconstructed search that the student follows. These directions can be given as a handout or on a Google document. Elements of a guided search activity can include the following:

- Premade key words, including roots, thesaurus and controlled vocabulary, and natural-language phrases
- Key words from a variety of business vocabulary familiar to students, such as occupation titles, types, and company names
- Use of the same search terms for different databases

If the library session is short, the librarian can test the searches in advance because bad key terms often take a long time to correct. Additionally, when preparing to teach a particular theme, the author recommends the following:

- Test each resource and explore any additional content that is available when a user creates an account.
- Show students how to judge the quality and authority of the website before they create a user account and access additional services or input personal data.
- Identify free reports or access to newsletters.
- Alert students to paid résumé services offered by career websites like Quintcareers.com—students may often not be aware that information services and additional content cost money depending on a website's business model.

- Encourage students to check with the librarian for alternative ways to legally access any pay-per-view employment reports, salary surveys, and other business content.
- Create some examples that show students how to extract key words and terms from bibliographic database records.

An easy selection of key words in career domains are the "occupational groups" found in the *Occupational Outlook Handbook*. The author often uses "education," "training," and "library" as an example search. In the search activities the author makes explicit broad and narrow terms with narrow categories that refine to particular careers like archivists, librarians, and teachers, professors, which can be cross-referenced with topic facets like degrees, training, and salary. A simple upside-down pyramid can provide a good visual explanation when it is accompanied with a step-by-step demonstration of strategies for refining and narrowing searches (see figure 19.1).

This approach emphasizes the controlled-vocabulary nature of good websites and library databases that contain highly structured information. One fun way to demonstrate the differences in the databases being explored is to ask students to perform the same search using the same key words in different databases. This is very useful when you are teaching different databases from the same vendor. Creating a search activity that focuses on browsing content using menus and NAICS codes works well for sessions focusing on career exploration. A good activity can reinforce difficult concepts and lecture content in a short period of time.

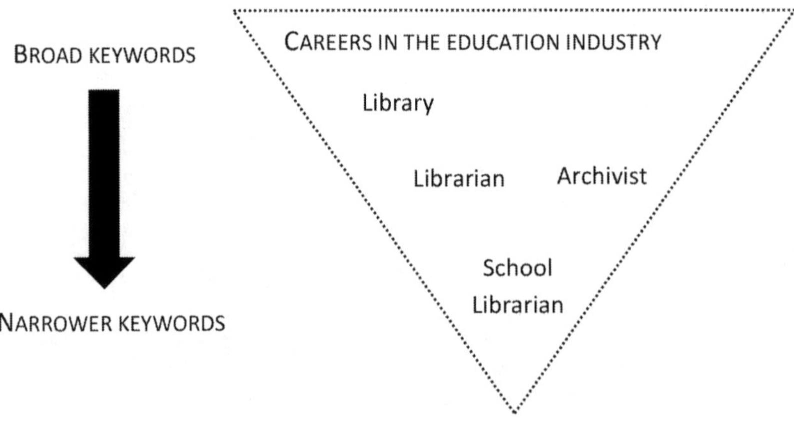

Figure 19.1. Narrowing Searches.

LESSON THEMES

This section focuses on ways of combining and presenting the resources and strategies for career information literacy discussed in chapter 14. These teachable content areas will be referred to as themes. These themes are not exhaustive, as there are many other ways to teach this material. These subscription sources are also not the only sources available, but the author chose them because they are often standard subscriptions for many undergraduate institutions and some public libraries. Teaching government resources in combination with one subscription source that gives access to trade publications, newspapers, and basic company and industry information exposes the student to the variety of structured business information, such as searching using NAICS codes and controlled occupational vocabulary. A teaching session can be devoted to one of the following three themes:

- Exploring career information
- Job hunting and interviewing
- Company and industry information

It is possible to combine all three themes into one session, which is a typical library instruction request at the author's institution, but this is not ideal because it is a lot of information to convey in one session—the result would be insufficient time for the search activity, which is critical to reinforcing and contextualizing the content of the session. An alternative, depending on the nature of the instruction request, might be to assign a guided search activity either before or after the session, to allow students to explore the resources on their own.

Typically, a session on *exploring career information* is useful earlier in a student's undergraduate experience, as this is when students can benefit the most from a career exploration class that orients them to career paths and how those connect with their major, so that they can make a good career choice based on a wide variety of information. Key resources for career exploration and planning include the following:

- Occupational Outlook Handbook (OOH)
- Occupational Information Network (O*NET)
- Library catalog

OOH can help students linking career interests to academic qualifications, while O*NET allows students to explore which skills match best with particular careers. While the information in OOH and O*NET is projected at a national level, the librarian may want to show city-level or state-level employment and workforce data. Additionally, the librarian can refer students to the Milken Institute, which has data on wage, job growth, and industry at a city level. Local states also have their own workforce statistics and employment resources. These government websites can be challenging to use, so they are often a good resource to show in a classroom setting where a librarian can help students navigate the website. Knowing local employment state or city trends can be a critical factor in a student's career exploration. Relocating for a job or career has costs associated with it including moving expenses, time invested in relocating, and emotional costs (when a student leaves behind a support or professional network). Geographic search terms are good filters that students can use to narrow their searches for career information or company and industry news so that results are limited to particular regions, states, cities, or counties.

The library catalog should always be taught as a place to look for classic career-focused books, such as *What Color Is My Parachute* or the College Board's *Book of Majors 2015*, focusing on techniques that allow students to identify areas where they can physically browse through books. This is important because subject headings can be confusing and students may not be aware that career books are shelved in completely different places. Here are some useful subject headings:

- College majors -- United States -- Handbooks, manuals, etc.
- College students -- Vocational guidance -- United States -- Handbooks, manuals, etc.
- Women -- Vocational guidance
- Career development
- Mass media -- Vocational guidance
- Medical personnel -- Vocational guidance

The librarian will want to craft information literacy learning outcomes that might resemble the following for a career exploration session:

- Identify and locate authoritative information on training and qualifications required for a career.
- Find cost-of-living information and job trends in a particular geographic area.
- Identify call numbers where students can browse circulating books.

While exploring salary, training, and occupational outlook data, students can get a rough estimate of their degree's return on investment by using the salary and occupational outlook data alongside student loan repayment calculators. The *New York Times* and the office of Federal Student Aid (within the Federal Department of Education) have online loan repayment calculators for student loans.

A session on *job hunting and interviewing* is best given to classes that have juniors or seniors. Again, this can be part of a library-led workshop or in partnership with the local career office. Key outcomes are the following:

- Locate, identify, and understand relevant associations, qualifications, and association publication outlets.
- Familiarize students with local professional associations and any professional networking, internship, and employment opportunities.
- Orient students to nonassociation (third-party) information about a particular profession, company, or industry for a balanced viewpoint.
- Learn some industry-specific vocabulary for interviews and résumé writing.

Local, national, and international associations can be identified in the following ways:

- Searching Google by using terms such as "association," "society," and "union" (adding geographic key words such as "national," "northeast," or "New York" can identify local associations)
- Using the Occupational Outlook Handbook's lists of national associations
- Browsing trade and industry journals for association conferences and events

Once a local association is identified, students are usually very interested in finding calendar events, contact information, and employment resources. Associations are a great way students can learn more about a profession. Some associations also have job banks and Listservs and provide student memberships or mentoring opportunities. Often a national association will have some publication or be associated with a trade journal—these are useful for salary surveys and information about trends in the profession.

Students should also look for career discussions in local business magazines, newspapers, or blogs that are not related to or published by an association. Professional associations will present their profession in the best light, so looking at third-party discussions of a particular industry or profession can give the student a deeper understanding of how professions operate and are perceived by the business community. Trade and business journals also have articles on outstanding professionals who can serve as an inspiration for desirable job candidates. Leaders are often asked how they got their start in the profession. Even if the student is not a business major, local business magazines can have articles on workplace culture or regional industry practices. A very useful local business journal database is Bizjournals.com. It has regional business newspapers and provides a publication, the *Book of Lists*, with annual rankings of best companies to work for by city and industry.

Nonbusiness majors will find these rankings very useful, and they can be a good place to start looking for internships and job openings. Trade and professional journals can also be found in databases like EBSCO's Business Source and Gale Business Insights: Essentials.

By using information found in association websites and publications, student are exposed to professional vocabulary that can contribute to their interview skills. A job hunting and interviewing session can also focus on social media topics, such as who to follow on Twitter, LinkedIn, and Facebook. Managing online reputation and personal branding are very important topics, and librarians can find many good articles on online career blogs and sites such as LinkedIn. It's not difficult to find this information by searching reputable career websites, university career centers, and social media outlets. As social media continues to grow, it will be difficult to find books and printed material that can keep up with the latest social media job hunting and employment trends. The role of the librarian is critical in helping students find and evaluate reputable and authoritative blogs and Twitter feeds.

Librarians might also want to show students how to locate and identify online résumé and cover letter templates. Students can access online cover letter templates for Microsoft Office, Google Docs, or LibreOffice. Locating templates, searching the catalog (for résumé and cover letter books), and using O*NET are great activities that combines searching and résumé writing.

A session focused on the theme of *company and industry information* generally emphasizes learning how to search using the North American Industry Codes (NAICS). Most business databases such as Gale Business Insights: Essentials and EBSCO Business Source allow users to search by company name and industry code. The librarian will want to compare and evaluate the following information during a company/industry instruction session:

- Company webpage
- News sources reporting on a company
- Third-party company reports
- Third-party business reports
- Trade and industry journal articles about a company or industry

It's critical to frame career information using company and industry business databases because these sources represent a third-party analysis. Students often research the company website without looking at other publications. The librarian will want to emphasize the importance of knowing how to identify the bias that often appears on company websites. EBSCO's Business Source, Gale Business Insights, or LexisNexis Academic are three popular subscription databases where trade journals and third-party reports can be found. Finding paid content in these databases, like reports or salary surveys, through library or university subscriptions, at no cost to the student, can be an empowering way to show students the high value of business information. The librarian can show how much a particular report would cost outside of the library, and afterward guide the students to the report or show how they can request it through interlibrary loan. The librarian can also show students how to access public library electronic databases to reinforce the idea that the student's search should not end with the university library; rather, the university library is a portal to a system of libraries both academic and public.

Career information literacy exposes students to other sources, including trade and association journals (which often have salary surveys) and professional business reports (which introduce students to the technical jargon of a specific profession and gives broader background information on key companies and industry trends). Students who know how to access such information can better understand the career and industry they are targeting, make more informed decisions, and become knowledgeable interview candidates. To summarize, company and industry information is often complementary to job hunting and interviewing, so pairing both themes to create a longer workshop works well, especially for a three-hour session. Career exploration using OOH and O*NET combined with trade journals, professional associations, current news sources, and state and local government sites makes another great three-hour session.

EVALUATING THE SESSION

There are many books on how to assess an information literacy session. Some quick summative assessments include the following:

- One-minute paper
- One-sentence summary
- Asking students to paraphrase one concept that was either new or difficult
- Pre- and post-testing

In the one-minute paper, the librarian asks the student to reflect on what the student liked and what the student found challenging in the session. The one-sentence summary asks students to summarize the entire session in one sentence. Both techniques are very useful when you analyze the data at the classroom level to see if there is agreement across students on a particular aspect of the class. Asking students to paraphrase a concept is a good assessment when you are trying to evaluate how a concept like key word searching or Boolean logic was understood. Pre- and post-tests are more formal assessments of the effectiveness of a session, and there are many articles available on this topic in the library literature. Here are ways to get student feedback online:

- Create a survey on Google Docs.
- Embed an assessment in your LibGuide, web page, or handout.
- Use the free version of Poll Everywhere to run short assessments for small classes.

It's important to receive feedback on your examples and see if your formative assessments match your intended learning outcomes. Gathering data using informal and formal assessments is the key to building and improving your content as well as keeping your content relevant to academic library patrons.

CONCLUSION

There are many ways to teach career and business information; this chapter is by no means the definitive way to teach this subject, but it is a good place to start with a framework that can be adjusted to a variety of academic library settings and resources. This chapter emphasizes thinking about outcomes including when in the student's education it makes sense to teach different themes within career information literacy content. The resources here will probably change. At the time of writing, the Association of College & Research Libraries adopted new standards for information literacy; this will undoubtedly shape our future practices. The themes provided in this chapter should stay consistent and are a helpful way to group different kinds of career and business information into a teaching program that emphasizes students acting on good information to make the best possible financial choice when deciding on their major and career goals during their undergraduate years.

REFERENCES

Association of College & Research Libraries. 2015. "Framework for Information Literacy for Higher Education." http://www.ala.org/acrl/standards/ilframework.

Jagman, Heather, Krystal Lewis, Brent Nunn, and Scott Walter. 2014. "Financial Literacy across the Curriculum (and Beyond): Opportunities for Academic Libraries." *College & Research Libraries News* 75 (5): 254–57.

RUSA. 2014. "Financial Literacy Education in Libraries: Guidelines and Best Practices for Service." http://www.ala.org/rusa/financial-literacy-education-libraries.

Roggenkamp, John. 2014. "Financial Literacy and Community Colleges: How Libraries Can Get Involved." *College & Research Libraries News* 75 (3): 142–43.

Sheley, Christina. 2014. "Get Hired! Academic Library Outreach for Student Job Seekers." *Indiana Libraries* 33 (2): 71–72.

Chapter Twenty

Quick Tip Guides on Student Financial Aid

Jennifer Wright Joe

For legal as well as ethical reasons, librarians might want to turn away financial aid questions and direct their patrons to better, more helpful sources. If a question leads you to that conclusion, by all means, follow your instinct. A correct answer that takes longer to find is better than an incorrect answer immediately. However, it is important that students get answers to these questions in as timely a manner as possible, and it is every institutional representative's duty to know either the answer or where the student can find the answer.

Receiving financial aid, and, by proxy, receiving helpful, timely, and accurate information about financial aid, has been positively linked to institutional enrollment and retention (Park, Denson, and Johnson 2014). With enrollment numbers fluctuating as the economy tries to recover from the Great Recession, recruitment and retention has become everyone's responsibility (Kalsbeek and Zucker 2013), and library staff being able to answer these questions competently will produce better recruitment and retention outcomes. Findings by Dowd, Pak, and Bensimon (2013, 3) show that positive interactions with employees of the university help students better accept and process information, such as that of financial aid. Therefore, it would stand to reason that a student who has already had a positive reaction with a reference librarian, either through class instruction or at the desk, will hold that person's advice in higher esteem and be more likely to follow it and follow up with individuals that the librarian suggests they contact, even if the student has never interacted with them before.

What questions, then, can a librarian answer faithfully and without fear of repercussion? Information-seeking questions that do not require intimate knowledge of the student's account, which is privileged information, are the only acceptable questions to answer at the reference desk, but that category covers a wide array of information. Among the questions the librarian can answer are those about contacting the financial aid office, the average cost of attendance for their institution, the FAFSA (Free Application for Student Aid) process, institutional deadlines, and scholarship opportunities. The university financial aid office's website is a good place to start finding the answers to these questions, but some answers might be found in the library's own catalog. Academic libraries often have many resources for scholarship and aid information that they can use to assist patrons who are looking for ways to pay for college.

CONTACT INFORMATION FOR THE FINANCIAL AID OFFICE

The first piece of information that any librarian should know is the contact information for the financial aid office. This information is typically found on the university website, already gathered for the librarian. For ease of access, the web page containing this information should be bookmarked on every reference computer. If the library has a list of helpful numbers that the faculty and staff regularly use, the financial aid office should be on the list. Librarians should also know or know where to find the physical location of the financial aid office as well as the mailing address of the office, which depending on the size and structure of the university may be different locations. Some financial aid offices also have generic e-mail addresses for certain types of questions, and these should also be readily available to the reference librarian. Also note the preferred method of contact the office employs; depending on staffing, they may prefer different contact methods depending on the student's needs, whether it is a question, a complain, or the need for an appointment.

Another thing that librarians should know, which does not come up often, is whether or not the building that houses the financial aid office (as well as other major departments on campus) is undergoing any kind of renovation or construction. These announcements are often made just one time through an administrative memo or a university-wide e-mail, but notes should be made about any location changes or accessibility issues that should arise so that students can be assisted more efficiently. Students with disabilities might need assistance in reaching these areas while construction is happening. Though the financial aid office was not involved, we had a similar situation arise during construction at our university, and we were able to accommodate students with assistance from the library to help them reach their destination because there was a chart of the various areas of construction and relocation.

Finally, the librarian should know the hours of operation for the financial aid office, including any special hours because of holidays or university closures. If the librarian is at a branch campus, keeping these hours straight might be slightly more difficult because the financial aid representative might have fluctuating hours over the course of the semester. Check with the campus administrative office for an up-to-date schedule and keep it posted at the reference desk for staff.

AVERAGE COST OF ATTENDANCE

Average cost of attendance is an important number for students to know, especially if tuition costs have changed, as the maximum amount of financial aid allowed to students through the government is limited based on status as well as need, regardless of the institutional costs. Students seeking this information will also most likely be interested in alternative forms of aid, covered later in the chapter. Librarians are in a good position to help with this question in particular, and it is important that they do so because for first-year students, the higher the amount of unmet cost, the less likely students are to finish their degree where they started (Jones-White et al. 2014, 344). The first step to realizing the unmet need and attempting to meet it is to find out the cost of attendance and compare that with known aid amounts.

Average cost of attendance is calculated by the university and may be available on the student's account. If the institution does this, librarians should be able to give students direction on how to access it, as that calculation will be most relevant to the student; it will more than likely take in different types of tuition (in-state, out-of-state, tuition incentive programs) as well as estimates of extraneous costs, such as room and board and textbook purchases. However, if the institution does not provide these more personalized estimates, a good estimation of cost should still be available on the website, and the amounts, rounded to make memorization easier, should be listed in a reference guide for the most typical student situations. Going one step further, the librarian should also be able to access more specific information, either on the website or obtained from the administration. While a librarian cannot advise the student on financial matters such as cost cutting, he or she should be able to give the students any facts that are available, so the students can make a more informed choice about the help they will need going forward.

FAFSA: THE PROCESS

The FAFSA (Free Application for Federal Student Aid) process is clearly outlined on most university financial aid websites as well as the FAFSA website (http://www.fafsa.ed.gov), but librarians should still be able to explain the basic process to students in a concise manner fitting with the length of typical reference interactions. If they require more detail, patrons should be directed either to the financial aid department at the university or to the government's website for more thorough information. Dynarski and Scott-Clayton note that "complexity, delay, and lack of transparency in the aid process mean that students and their families have little idea how much aid they will receive until after they have applied to college" (2013, 76). If a student has gone through a family status change, they may not be able even to estimate the amount of aid they will get for the new year and could be anxious about finding out how much money they may receive.

In addition to this, it important to be able to clearly explain the FAFSA process to students because while the official deadline to file is late in the year, filing early may result in Pell Grants or other need-based monies that are dispersed on a first-come, first-served basis. This above all else should be stressed when talking to a student so that, if they are still confused about any part of the process or hit a roadblock later on, they will know to seek help from the university's financial aid office immediately. Though the students coming to the reference desk will have already gone through the FAFSA process once, assuming that they are currently enrolled at the university, they may have had help from high school guidance counselors or their parents, and filing the paperwork for their sophomore year might be the first time they have done it alone. Furthermore, while this chapter has been mainly focused on four-year institutions, studies show that community college students in particular are less likely to file a FAFSA and that this negatively impacts retention even in the second semester of their first year (McKinney and Novak 2013). Institutions that counsel community college students through two-plus-two programs should be especially aware of this fact because the students coming to them for their remaining years may never have filled out a FAFSA and community colleges are less well staffed than four-year institutions by their very nature.

INSTITUTIONAL DEADLINES

Institutional deadlines are a common question both for the financial aid office and the reference desk, and an easy one for librarians to answer, provided that they know where to look for this information. Unfortunately, unlike other information on the university website, this information may be scattered. At my institution, administrative staff receive a paper copy of the administrative and financial calendar for the school year in August. This includes the academic calendar, with term beginnings, term endings, and school closures, withdrawal deadlines, tuition and fees deadlines, and more.

This calendar is also in the registration guide, the contents of which advise students on more than just registration; there is a section on tuition and financial aid as well. If one does not know where to look, however, the title of this publication might fool the viewer into missing a plethora of information. Our university's registration guide is now only available electronically, but a printed version kept at the reference desk might be easier to access than the digital document, depending on how technologically savvy the staff is and how easily searchable the university's website is.

If the institution does not have this type of document publically available, a representative from the library should contact the pertinent administrative offices (admissions, financial aid, and bursar) and compile a master list of dates for the reference desk to use. This will prove much easier than attempting to find it with the patron right in front of them. However, because the institution may make changes to the calendar after it has been compiled, be sure that someone is in charge of making sure the list is up to date and accurate so that patrons are not misled or confused.

FINANCIAL AID OPPORTUNITIES

Librarians should be able to explain different types of financial aid to students in order to guide them to the resources they need to apply. In addition to traditional federal loans, of which there are several subtypes, there are also private loans, grants, scholarships, assistantships, fellowships, and more. Librarians can become particularly adept at showing students financial aid opportunities that are not loans, and this could mean great things for the patrons. A study has shown that loans "are potentially detrimental to a student's educational goals" (Jones-White et al. 2014, 348), depending on the percentage of the financial aid package that is made up of loans. At the very least, a large amount of loans might set them up for future financial trouble. Librarians can help point students to loans they may qualify for that most people have not even heard of.

Libraries typically have well-stocked shelves of the latest catalogs of scholarships and grants available to students in various disciplines. Directing students to those reference sources should be no different than directing them to any other resource in the library, though with how quickly things can change, some information should be confirmed through Internet resources, if possible. However, scholarships are not just handed out at the federal or state level; also of interest to a librarian should be the financial assistance available from the university, only for students attending that university. While these types of aid can still be highly competitive, the odds are still better for the student applying because they are competing against a limited pool of applicants. Not only that, but in addition to helping the student fund college, more regionally specific aid can help student success, with a study finding that "state/local grants and institutional grants were associated with greater gains in teamwork and leadership, respectively" (Park, Denson, and Johnson 2014, 790) than their federal counterparts. Librarians being well versed in the types and amounts of grants and scholarships available is also good for the university; while the governing body for these endowments will no doubt make an effort to publicize the available money, most institutions will have more separate accounts than can be advertised; it is then up to the departments to inform students of what opportunities there are. An inquisitive librarian might even find that their library system offers student scholarships; the Friends of WKU Libraries recently began giving out the Western Kentucky University Library Student Assistant Scholarship, a scholarship bestowed yearly upon a qualified library student worker.

Student work is also a type of financial aid, albeit a type that is often overlooked or misunderstood. In order to qualify for the Federal Work Study Program, analysis of FAFSA must prove a student's financial need. If a student does not qualify, however, there may be off-campus options for employment that are as flexible in their hours as student work often is. Students should be cautioned in this case, as anecdotal evidence shows that inflexible positions off campus might be detrimental to a student's well-being (Case 2013). Whichever the student prefers, librarians should be able to guide them to available jobs, either on or off campus.

CREATING THE QUICK GUIDE

Some of the information covered in this chapter is available on the institution's website and can be found with relative ease. However, if an institution's information seems scattered or is difficult to access, reference services may consider creating a "Quick Guide" to financial aid questions that could be available either as an internal-access web page or as a PDF on the reference desk computers. The example reference guide in table 20.1 has some universal answers filled in. For all other questions, a generic summary of information has been provided.

This guide is by no means an exhaustive list, and reference librarians are encourage to adapt it or add to it as they see fit. It should be updated frequently, either on a yearly or semester basis, with some information, such as Internet links, checked even more often. While many reference librarians may find it unnecessary, it does help in training new staff who are unfamiliar with the university or student workers who may not take the same time and care as faculty and staff in answering questions.

Table 20.1. Quick Guide Example

Question	Answer
Where and when do I fill out my FAFSA for the upcoming school year?	http://www.fafsa.ed.gov , any time after January 1.
How do I contact the financial aid office?	Phone number, mailing address, and hours of operation.
Who do I call about . . . ?	Bursar number, registrar number, admissions number.
What is the average cost of attendance or how can it be calculated?	Average costs, if provided by the university; location of tuition costs as available.
How can I find my cost of attendance?	Directions if available at the institution.
What types of financial aid are available?	Federal loans, private loans, grants, scholarships, assistantships, fellowships, work study options.
What are the institutional deadlines for financial aid?	These include registration, tuition and fee deadlines, as well as the academic calendar.
What are some important websites to know?	http://www.financialaidtoolkit.ed.gov/tk/ https://studentloans.gov/ Institutional financial aid website

CONCLUSION

The examples listed here are for use in answering questions about financial aid at the librarian's institution that are about the library's institution. However, librarians should be prepared also to answer questions about financial aid processes and information at other colleges and universities; students may be dual enrolled, such as in a two-plus-two program, where general education requirements are fulfilled at a community college and upper-class credits are earned at a university, or they may be seeking information about financial aid at an institution they are thinking about attending for an advanced degree. Using the information here about where to find what information (financial aid, the bursar, the registrar, or other campus entities), the savvy librarian should also be able to locate most of the information on unfamiliar institution's website. Of course, when in doubt, provide the student with contact information for the appropriate department at the other institution.

This guide will get librarians thinking more about the functional questions of attending a university, in addition to the study questions they typically receive. With a quick reference guide as assistance, librarians should be able to make themselves more familiar with the answers to these questions and improve response times without overstepping the bounds of their position. The quick guide is also important if the library typically has student workers staff the reference desk at low-traffic times; students may be more likely to ask someone that they identify with, rather than faculty or staff. Finally, if librarians are interested in learning more about the financial aid process, they should visit the Federal Student Aid Financial Aid Toolkit to learn more about governmental financial aid. It exists as a resource for anyone who might be in a position to counsel, mentor, or advise students about financial aid.

REFERENCES

Case, Joe Paul. 2013. "Implications of Financial Aid: What College Counselors Should Know." *Journal of College Student Psychotherapy* 27 (2): 159–73.

Dowd, Alicia C., Jenny H. Pak, and Estela Mara Bensimon. 2013. "The Role of Institutional Agents in Promoting Transfer Access." *Education Policy Analysis Archives* 21 (15).

Dynarski, Susan, and Judith Scott-Clayton. 2013. "Financial Aid Policy: Lessons from Research." *Future of Children* 23 (1): 67–91.

Jones-White, Daniel R., Peter M. Radcliffe, Linda M. Lorenz, and Krista M. Soria. 2014. "Priced Out? The Influence of Financial Aid on the Educational Trajectories of First-Year Students Starting College at a Large Research University." *Research in Higher Education* 55 (4): 329–50.

Kalsbeek, David H., and Brian Zucker. 2013. "Reframing Retention Strategy: A Focus on Profile." *New Directions for Higher Education* 161:15–25.

McKinney, Lyle, and Heather Novak. 2013. "The Relationship between FAFSA Filing and Persistence among First-Year Community College Students." *Community College Review* 41 (1): 63–85.

Park, Julie J, Nida Denson, and Matthew Johnson. 2014. "Examining a Financial Climate of Support: How Institutional-Level Financial Aid Relates to Teamwork, Leadership, and Critical Thinking." *Journal of College Student Development* 55 (8): 779–94.

Chapter Twenty-One

United States Government Resources on Financial Literacy

Karen Evans

This chapter will provide a wealth of information on financial literacy, starting with defining the term of financial literacy and discussing why people should care about being in control of their finances. The website DailyFinance.com illustrates why people should understand the importance of financial literacy and work toward being financially literate. According to the website, "only 40 percent of adults keep a budget and track their spending. Three-fourths of American families say they live paycheck to paycheck. More than one-fourth of American families have no savings at all" (Bera 2014). This information paints a grim picture of American families and their finances. Living paycheck to paycheck often means that families are struggling to pay for basic necessities; adding funds for emergencies, vacations, or educational opportunities for their children are often impossible. Hopefully, learning about finances and the tools available to track personal finances can provide positive ways for people to increase their financial security.

Financial literacy is defined as "the ability to use knowledge and skills to manage one's financial resources effectively for a lifetime of financial security" (Jump$tart! 2015). Being literate about your money encompasses many different areas of life:

- Budgets
- Credit scores
- School loans
- Bankruptcy
- Savings
- Retirement

Finances can be a very private and personal issue, but there are also less private areas of finance that are just as important for your well-being; these areas include knowing how to spot a scam or a Ponzi scheme, thereby saving a savvy person thousands of dollars.

Understanding financial matters and being knowledgeable about personal and family finances allows the development of financial security and plans for the future. Without a plan to be fiscally fit or the knowledge to create budgets, savings, or retirement strategies, it is very difficult to develop a sound personal financial life. The websites profiled in this chapter can provide the information you need to create a sound financial life for yourself or your family.

Several tools are available from the federal government to increase comprehension about finances; these tools are available for children, adolescents, and adults. The U.S. government publishes a wealth of free electronic information and resources on finances and financial literacy. This chapter explores the variety of items available for various age groups and varying financial situations to assist users in becoming financially literate and financially stable. The resources are listed alphabetically and provide information on the contents of the website, the intended age groups if listed, and the possibility of translating the website into another language.

UNITED STATES GOVERNMENT RESOURCES

Consumer Financial Protection Bureau: http://www.consumerfinance.gov/learnmore/

This consumer financial site provides information on many different areas:

- Checking accounts
- Disaster checklist for finances
- Credit reports
- Identity theft
- Mortgages

Another section of the website is devoted to student education; information on student loans and banking is presented. Students can compare offers of financial aid to determine which is best for their needs; schools can be compared three at a time. There are resources on repaying student loans offers and suggestions for students on repaying federal and nonfederal loans. Specific financial information is available for students, older persons, service members, and veterans. The site also provides access to filing a complaint and checking the status of your complaint. Complaints can be filed for many types of loans or about products and services. Some resources are available in several languages; content can be translated using tools located at the top of the pages.

FDIC: Financial Education and Literacy: http://www.fdic.gov/consumers/education

Seven links on this site provide resources and information on financial literacy for consumers, teachers, caregivers, and youth. Money Smart: A Financial Education Program offers programs for adults, older adults, youth, and small businesses. It is the official website of the United States federal government for financial education. Many of the modules in Money Smart cover the following financial areas:

- Banking
- Borrowing monies
- Checking accounts
- Credit and saving
- Loans
- Home ownership
- Recovering from a financial setback

The section for students covers paying for higher education, setting financial goals, and credit cards. Modules for small businesses cover time and financial management, record keeping, credit reporting, insurance, and taxes. This site also provides training resources for those who want to provide instruction on money issues. Online videos are available for trainers along with information on workshops. Podcasts and computer-based instruction are available for some topics. Many of the brochures are free and available in several languages.

The Teacher Online Resource Center is another section of the FDIC financial literacy website. Many topics are covered, from consumer news to paying for college. An electronic newsletter is available highlighting tips and updates on financial education along with success stories from financial educators. Resources about financial literacy are available for teachers to use with K–12 students.

The Parents and Caregiver Resource Page offers resources for pre-K to two years of age, age three to middle school, and high school and young adult. Each site contains a Q&A for parents and a book list with titles about buying, saving, budgeting, credit cards, and checking accounts. Resources are available for age-specific groups; the pre-K site includes a *Sesame Street* production about saving and spending; financial games are presented to the age-three-to-middle-school group; and the high school students have access to career exploration, understanding taxes, and consumer news. The site also provides parents and caregivers with a guide to being money smart for children pre-K through age two.

MyMoney.gov: http://www.mymoney.gov/Pages/default.aspx

MyMoney.gov is a creation of the Congressionally Chartered Federal Financial Literacy and Education Commission and was established by the Financial Literacy and Education Improvement Act, Title V of the Fair and Accurate Credit Transactions Act of 2003. The commission is made up of more than twenty federal units, including the Consumer Financial Protection Bureau, the Department of Defense, the Federal Trade Commission, the National Credit Union Administration, and the Department of Health and Human Services. The site provides five key building blocks to financial literacy:

- Spend
- Earn
- Save and invest
- Protect
- Borrow

Each building block has a page devoted to it; often including actions you can take, hints and tips, and spotlight resources. The pages on the five building blocks include basic tips and resources and ideas to assist the user in achieving that particular topic. Additional resources cover kids and advertising, where kids can play the game Admongo and learn how different facets of advertising affect their spending. The game provides information and resources for parents and educators. Another section covers financial aid, including preparing for college, what types of aid are available, how students qualify, how to apply, and how to manage the loans. Each section of financial aid contains links to additional resources. The section on preparing for college includes exploring careers, choosing a school, applying to a school, and a get-ready checklist. The site also includes information on financial scams and how to avoid them. MyMoney.gov has specific resources for youth, teachers and educators, and researchers. The youth section contains financial games, websites, cartoons, coins and medals, mint history, and information for parents. The teachers and educators section can locate curricula, classroom resources, handouts, and guides on aspects of financial literacy. Materials are specifically created to work with a variety of students, from children to older adolescents. Among the available items are the Money Smart for Adults Curriculum, High School Fed Challenge, and the Federal Reserve System's Resources for Educators. Researchers can search the Financial Literacy and Education Commission's Financial Capability Research Clearinghouse. They have access to over four hundred reports and articles from federally supported research, with data sets that are available for use in new research on financial capability topics. Life events (new child, home ownership, education), tools (budget worksheets), and money quizzes (borrowing, saving, protecting) are also available.

Federal Trade Commission: Consumer.gov: http://www.consumer.gov

Available in English and Spanish, the Federal Trade Commission site has three sections on managing your money, credit loans and debt, and scams and identity theft that provide solid information for consumers. Sections often begin by explaining the topic (what is a budget, what is a debit card). Additional sections provide basic information on the topic; the section on managing your money covers opening a bank account, using debit cards, and renting an apartment or house. The help section links resources on managing your money, help for immigrant communities, and scams and identity theft. Several of the resources are available as videos on YouTube.

Federal Trade Commission: Consumer Information: http://www.consumer.ftc.gov

The Consumer Information site of the Federal Trade Commission has coverage on the following areas:

- Money and credit
- Homes and mortgages
- Health and fitness
- Jobs and marketing
- Privacy and identity

Clicking on each topic leads the user to a series of links on information about each topic. Clicking on money and credit provides know-how on shopping and saving, buying and owning a car, credit and loan, dealing with debt, and solving consumer problems. A section of the website highlights scams, and you can sign up for e-mail alerts concerning scams. The site can also be viewed in Spanish.

Institute of Museum and Library Services: https://www.imls.gov/issues/national-initiatives/financial-literacy

The Institute of Museum and Library Services and the Consumer Financial Protection Bureau joined together to create financial education resources for public libraries. The goal is to have free resources available for librarians to promote information literacy to their patrons. More than twenty free publications are available, and librarians can sign up for free monthly e-mails that suggest programming ideas.

Internal Revenue Service: http://www.irs.gov/Help-&-Resources

Taxes are an important part of being financially responsible, and the IRS has provided several resources for individuals and businesses. Individuals can receive information on filing and refunds, fraud, identity theft, phishing, payments, refunds, and records. Businesses can find resources on an employee identification number (EIN) and the tax calendar. One can also access the Taxpayer Bill of Rights and sign up for free e-mails from the IRS. Links from the home page provide information on a variety of topics, including charities and nonprofits, online tools, and tax codes and regulations.

MyCreditUnion.gov: http://www.mycreditunion.gov/Pages/highlights.aspx

MyCreditUnion.gov provides facts about credit unions, including the history of credit unions, the differences between banks and credit unions, determining if a credit union is the right option for you, and joining a credit union. A link on protecting your finances allows users to retrieve information on consumer protection, credit reports and scores, identity theft, tips for young adults, and Pocket Cents. Pocket Cents links to resources for several groups and situations:

- Youth
- Teens and tweens
- Young adults
- Parents
- Educators
- Seniors
- Marriage and family members
- Service members

Each section contains pertinent information for that particular group on debt and credit, prepare and save, protect and prevent, life events, education, and resources and activities. Financial tools and resources include a college scorecard, a glossary of terms, calculators on mortgages loans and savings and retirement, and personal budget worksheets.

Planet Youth: Native American Youth Connection: http://www.hud.gov/offices/pih/ih/codetalk/planet/learn_financialliteracy.html

Planet Youth provides resources for American Indian, Alaskan Native, and Native Hawaiian adolescents. Financial information covers scholarships and colleges for Native Americans, including tribal colleges and universities, internship, fellowships, and college preparation. Programs (Money Matters: Make It Count), websites (Native Financial Education Coalition, Native American Community Development Corporation), games (Mad Money, Practical Money Skills for Life), and videos ("Four Things You Can Do with Money," "Elders Perspective on Money") complete the site.

Office of the Comptroller of the Currency: http://www.occ.gov/topics/community-affairs/resource-directories/financial-literacy/index-financial-literacy.html

The Office of the Comptroller of the Currency provides information on the office's mission, strategic plan, and annual reports. Resources are available by topic (credit, consumer protection, international banking), key resources, top tasks, and what's popular. News and issuances, tools and forms (bankers, job seekers, consumers), and publications (news releases, bulletins, and alerts) provide a wealth of substantive material for viewers.

United States Courts: Bankruptcy: http://www.uscourts.gov/FederalCourts/Bankruptcy.aspx

Unsure how bankruptcy will change your life? The United States Federal Court site will provide answers to many of your questions. Bankruptcy Basics explains the bankruptcy process and the different types of bankruptcy known as chapters (7, 9, 10, 11, 12, 13); a glossary of terms and bankruptcy forms are available to view. A quick links section leads to forms, rules, resources, case policies, and administrators.

United States Department of Labor: *Savings Fitness: A Guide to Your Money and Your Financial Future*: http://www.dol.gov/ebsa/pdf/savingsfitness.pdf

Saving Fitness: A Guide to Your Money and Your Financial Future is a thirteen-chapter electronic book with a fitness theme focusing on finances. Topics include "A Financial Warm Up," "How's Your Financial Fitness," "Strengthening Your Financial Fitness," "Financial Fitness for the Self-Employed," and "Maximizing Your Workout Potential." Resources and worksheets complete the illustrated, easy-to-read book.

United States Department of Labor: Taking the Mystery Out of Retirement Planning: http://www.dol.gov/ebsa/publications/nearretirement.html

This resource provides seven chapters in English or Spanish, plus a resource section, providing users admittance to a site with a diverse selection of help tools to figure out a successful retirement. Chapters cover tracking your money for retirement, comparing income and expenses, five ways to close the gap, and making your money last. Resources consist of calculators for retirement savings, investing, and saving and tools for getting help. Users can download the sixty-two-page illustrated guide or order copies via telephone. The online version has worksheets one can complete for each chapter.

United States Department of Veterans Affairs: Retirement and Financial Literacy Program: http://www.va.gov/ohrm/worklifebenefits/rflep.asp

The U.S. Department of Veterans Affairs offers the Retirement and Financial Literacy Program (RFLEP) for those interested in budgeting, retirement, and savings. The site highlights the responsibility federal employers have toward making sure their employees are aware of resources on retirement and financial literacy, and the responsibilities the employees have toward themselves and their financial status. The site also provides calculators for debt payoff, savings, student loan repayment, IRS withholding, and mortgage comparison. Other tools include a savings bond wizard, money tips, and new credit card rules. Links give users access to additional financial literacy resources; most of them are links to other U.S. government agencies, including the Federal Deposit Insurance Corporation, Federal Reserve, and Securities and Exchange Commission.

United States Mint: Financial Literacy: http://www.usmint.gov/kids/teachers/financialliteracy/

The U.S. Mint has many activities for adolescents and younger children, including Alexander's Coin Conundrum and Money Hungry Piggy Bank. A section of the website is devoted to educators and contains lesson plans (K–12). The site advises that all lesson plans were written by teachers and meet national standards. Lesson plans are broken into several sections:

- Age groups
- Coin program (one cent, nickel, quarter)
- Random lesson plans
- Teacher features (classroom ideas for social studies, language arts, technology)

- Unit plans (ancient and modern coins, creative coin combinations)

Under "Lessons for K–12" and "By Coin Program," educators have the ability to use a lesson plan finder. The educator clicks on the grade, the subject, coin type, and coin program to determine which programs meet their criteria. One can also sign up for e-mails and updates concerning the website.

United States Securities and Exchange Commission: http://www.sec.gov/

One of the duties of the Securities and Exchange Commission (SEC) is to protect investors. Their website promotes resources for investors, brokers/dealers, accountants, small businesses, and international financial issues. A section titled Spotlight provides insight on many topics, including financial reports, strategic plans, money market funds, and the Foreign Corrupt Practices Act. Links provide access and information on enforcement, education, filings, and regulations involving the Securities and Exchange Commission.

United States Social Security Administration: http://www.ssa.gov/

The Social Security Administration provides many useful tools, from the ability to check on your Social Security statement and manage your benefits to using the online list of services. One can create an account to track and verify benefits and earnings, or one can track benefits, receive a Social Security statement, appeal a decision, or perform several other duties using online resources. If you need to change your name or apply for a Social Security card for a child, the website provides the steps to perform these actions. Whether you are concerned about benefits for yourself, your spouse, or disabled children, this site can provide the answers. Living outside the United States or recently released from incarceration? Social Security has you covered and can provide the information you need via this website. The section titled Information For includes resources for same-sex couples, Native Americans, the blind or visually impaired, wounded warriors, and several other groups. This site has a treasure trove of information concerning Social Security and the many questions about who can obtain benefits and when.

United States Social Security Administration, Women: http://www.ssa.gov/people/women/

The Social Security office has created a page specifically for women and their retirement. Available electronic publications include "What Every Woman Should Know," "Understanding the Benefits," and "New Numbers for Domestic Violence Victims." An assortment of information is available for women in many scenarios:

- Working women
- New mothers
- Brides
- Divorcees
- Caregivers
- Widows

Each link provides relevant information for that particular status. This site provides excellent information for women and their social security benefits.

United States Treasury: Ready.Save.Grow: http://www.treasurydirect.gov/readysavegrow/readysavegrow.htm

Created by the U.S. Treasury to help people save and become financially secure, this program provides resources on treasury saving programs. The site provides "Top Ten Questions and Answers" about using the treasury site for financial goals. A video library provides access on how to set up an account, buying bonds online and as gifts, and payroll savings. This site provides information on purchasing bonds and treasury securities.

USA.gov: Retirement: http://www.usa.gov/Topics/Seniors/Retirement.shtml

Available in English and Spanish, this site offers a list of links to items on retirement. Numerous topics are covered, including cash balance pension plans, individual retirement plans (IRAs), ways to prepare for retirement, and working after retirement. Although women are not mentioned on the home page of the website, clicking on ways to prepare for retirement will provide a link to a web page prepared specifically for women and retirement savings.

CONCLUSION

The websites described in this chapter illustrate the resources available from the U.S. federal government on different aspects of financial literacy. Whatever your age or financial status, the federal government has electronic resources that can provide greater understanding concerning financial issues and lead you to a more solvent and secure financial future.

REFERENCES

Bera, Sophia. 2014. "The Scary State of Financial Literacy in America." Daily Finance, April 18. http://www.dailyfinance.com/2014/04/18/the-scary-state-of-financial-literacy-in-america/ .

Jump$tart! 2015. "National Standards in K-12 Personal Finance Education." http://www.jumpstart.org/assets/files/2015_NationalStandardsBook.pdf.

Part Three

Case Studies

Chapter Twenty-Two

Case Study of Financial Literacy Instruction in the Library

Jeri Weinkrantz Cohen

In 2012–2013, the Patchogue-Medford Library Teen Services Department in Patchogue, New York, was selected to receive a grant from Capital One Bank and participate in the bank's Financial Literacy Challenge initiative. With five thousand dollars, we created a series of programs aimed at teens and their parents. Our program was so successful that the bank gave us an additional grant of fifteen thousand dollars to repeat and grow the program in 2013–2014. In a highly diverse community like ours, where English is the second language for many and almost 50 percent of the school population receives free or reduced lunch, financial knowledge is necessary for all our students and their families to succeed and prosper. Knowing how to make sound financial decisions and deal with financial institutions can make a huge difference and help families in our community reach their goals. For our service district's large immigrant population, basic financial education about banking, saving, managing money, and financial planning in the United States is even more necessary. Especially for teens and immigrant families, lack of knowledge about financial options can have serious consequences, affecting educational opportunities and financing, savings, day-to-day spending, credit ratings, indebtedness, and avoidance of hoaxes and scams. Financial awareness improves not only their lives, but also the community we share. The Capital One Bank Financial Literacy Challenge helped us bring this important knowledge to the community.

Our Financial Literacy Challenge programs taught important financial concepts to teens and parents in our community. We offered workshops both inside and outside the library, extending our outreach efforts. We structured our classes to have the greatest impact possible in our community. We have many teens who are graduating high school and thinking of college or employment, but who have little or no knowledge of even basic money management. We knew that many families have difficulty discussing financial matters and wanted to help facilitate that. We decided to schedule workshops that would separate teens and their parents and offer simultaneous classes for each group, with opportunities for them to get together and discuss what they had learned. The presence of a large Spanish-speaking immigrant population required that we arrange for bilingual instructors to properly serve the community. Since the immigrant population must understand the banking terms in English, we decided that the classes would be taught primarily in English, with explanation in Spanish where needed.

We also offered a series of two-hour workshops taught by a college professor on topics of interest that were open to everyone. In the second year of the grant, we reprised the original workshops and used the additional money to buy iPads and tablets that we loaded with financial and budgeting applications. This enabled us to take the program out of the library, to the high school and a local residential program for homeless teen girls. The programs are designed to be replicable, and we look forward to continuing them, especially the outreach in the community.

Our programming for the Financial Literacy Challenge was based on the free BankIt program for teenagers and parents provided by Capital One. The BankIt program was developed by Capital One in partnerships with the Search Institute. We decided to cover the following topics combined into four units:

- Basic banking and budgeting
- Setting financial goals and credit
- Earning, spending, and saving
- Moving forward with money

Our teen programs at the library are always developed to expand outreach efforts to the underserved and to complement what is offered in school. Our programs for parents of teens are aimed at expanding outreach and availability of information to all segments of our very diverse community. Capital One's BankIt program was a very good match with the teen and teen parenting programs we run at the Patchogue-Medford Library since we consider the Search Institute's "40 Developmental Assets for Adolescents" when planning. The availability of program materials in both English and Spanish and the inclusion of the Search Institute's developmental assets made this program a perfect fit for our community and aided greatly in its success.

The full-day programs were scheduled on two Saturdays, for five hours each day. Our plan was to start both days with breakfast, split up the teens and adults and teach a unit, have lunch together, teach a unit in the afternoon, and end the day with discussion and snacks.

We included meals in the day for several reasons. First, it saved time. Second, it kept the group together, rather than having them leave in the middle. Third, and most importantly, it gave us a forum for bringing the teens and adults together for unstructured conversations about what they were learning.

We decided to hold the workshops on Saturdays since we hoped this would enable the most people to participate. Since parents work and the teens are in school, we felt evening meetings might be harder for them to attend. We decided to run the workshop over two Saturdays and limit the attendance for the two-day workshop to twenty to twenty-five parents and teens so that the teachers could give each participant individualized attention. Sign-up started slowly but went well; seventeen people preregistered for the first workshop. On the days the workshop ran, additional people, not preregistered, showed up, so we had a total of about twenty-five people. In some cases, both parents came with a teen. In one case, the parent came without the teen because the teen was working. In another case, the family had seven children and brought only one of their teens; the others stayed with their younger siblings. We had one participant who usually works Saturdays and took two days off work to come to the workshop with his wife and daughter.

For all the full-day workshops, the library's large meeting room was divided and set up as two classrooms. The adults were in one half of the room for most of the day, and the teens in the other. When the students arrived, food and coffee were set up on the adults' side of the room so we could get to know each other comfortably. Each room had a display of books, handouts, and other materials about personal finance suited to the age groups.

The workshop tables were set up with calculators, notebooks, pens, and pencils for each participant. The teens received check registers so they could learn to track transactions. The adults received household budgeting books to help them design budgets and track their income and spending. The adults also received flash drives loaded with information from the lessons so they could refer back to it later. Information on applying for college financial aid was available and distributed.

Our teachers were prepared with handouts and lesson plans for each unit. Each lesson included evaluations (written or oral) and interactive activities to help the students understand and retain the learning objectives. In the final lesson, the teens played a bingo game where they had to show that they recognized the financial terms and concepts that had been introduced, and the winner received a twenty-five-dollar Visa gift card.

At the end of the workshop, adults and teens who had completed the entire ten hours were awarded certificates of participation.

In the second year, with the larger grant amount, additional gift cards were raffled to encourage participation in activities, and one participant was selected to win a five-hundred-dollar scholarship based on financial changes she made.

In both years, a college professor presented four two-hour evening sessions on financial topics: budgeting, dealing with financial institutions, paying for college, and using credit. These topics were selected because patrons had requested information in these areas and the classes were open to both teens and adults. Classes were small, and people received individual attention. Individual investment options were not addressed; the workshops and all classes focused on basic budgeting, planning, and good use of credit.

Tablets purchased through the grant in the second year enabled us to move beyond the library and reach parts of our service population that may have trouble coming to the library or dedicating a full day to workshops. Our staff taught financial literacy topics to a business class at the Patchogue-Medford High School and basic budgeting to girls at a local shelter. The girls are required to live on a budget, and we gave them calculators and budget calendars to help them meet their goals. We were glad to make these connections and will continue to serve these parts of the community.

Our Financial Literacy Challenge program was extremely successful in reaching our community and in teaching financial concepts to teens and their families. It brought families in our community together to seriously think about money and open a dialogue about how they can improve their financial positions. Using the Capital One grant and the BankIt learning program they supplied, we were able to give workshop participants the tools to help them budget better, plan their spending and saving for the future, implement or reinforce good savings and spending habits, and plan for the future with a basic understanding of investments. The participants, many of whom struggle financially, are now better equipped with the tools they need to manage their finances, bills, expenses, and savings so that they can be more confident, in control, and plan for the future.

Our stated goals for the grant were the following:

1. Improve the financial literacy of participating parents and teens, as evidenced in participant comments and evaluations.
2. Help families become more aware of the financial options available to them by describing various services available and ensuring that participants understand the differences.
3. Help parents and teens be more comfortable discussing finances, as encouraged and demonstrated during class discussions.
4. Help teens develop money management strategies and articulate financial goals, as shown by their comments and evaluations.

5. Help teens develop personal financial decision-making processes by introducing them to a variety of financial concepts, ensuring that they are able to undertake basic financial activities and that they understand how planning can help their future.

In the process of meeting all our goals, our classes brought together people from all parts of our multiethnic community. People who in usual circumstances might never have met learned about the issues and viewpoints of different groups, often making for interesting conversations and information exchanges. They had an opportunity learn from each other and discovered both differences and similarities in their situations.

Detailed planning helped ensure the success of our workshops. The availability of bilingual instructors, providing suitable tools and learning environment, providing enough preparation time for the instructors and the availability of the comprehensive BankIt program all contributed to our success. We tailored the BankIt materials based on our instructors' knowledge of the community and made extensive use of the program's bilingual materials. Our teacher for the adults, Gilda Ramos, was born in Peru. She has been employed at the Patchogue-Medford Library since 2005, starting as a clerk, then as a Spanish-speaking library assistant, and now as library assistant. Gilda loves teaching. She has taught computer classes in Spanish, English as a second language (ESL), and Spanish conversation classes. Rita Alfano, a bilingual young adult librarian employed at the library since 2008, taught our teens. At the time, Rita also worked for Capital One as a teller in our local branch and is extremely familiar with the financial issues many of our residents face on a daily basis.

Using the Bankit program, our instructors selected topics of interest to the community, considering what could be covered in ten hours and what seemed to be most needed for both groups, the adults and the teens. They determined their specific learning objectives for each topic, created a schedule allowing for ample coverage of each objective, and planned how each objective should be presented. Time was scheduled for discussion and interactive activities for both groups to keep them engaged. The teens learned to write checks and maintain a check register. They played a bingo game to ensure that they understood the financial terms introduced in the classes. They created sample budgets. The adults received household budget books, and did exercises in budgeting, saving, investing, and dealing with stressful money situations, as well as some interactive online activities.

Assessment tools were developed to ensure that the students were grasping the main concepts. Written pre- and post-tests were not used for every topic due to time constraints but were given at the beginning and end of the workshop. Much of the follow-up to each topic was oral and interactive to keep the students engaged and enable them to learn from each other. Although not all students completed the written evaluations, participants showed a good grasp of the material, and an increase in knowledge was demonstrated in all of the topics tested. We also solicited oral and written feedback from all the participants and received very positive responses. Adults were asked for free-form comments; the teens were asked to list three things they learned.

Our major challenges in putting together our financial literacy program involved publicity, scheduling, weather, and ordering delays.

We went through many different routes to publicize our financial literacy workshops. We knew the topics being covered were very important to our community, and wanted to fill the class. However, we found it was difficult to convince people to give up their free time to attend a class like this even when the subject matter is as important as personal finance. We publicized as widely as possible, describing the workshop as interesting and fun as well as educational. We used our usual methods of publicity, including our newsletter and flyers in the library. The flyers were in Spanish and English, as were the blurbs in the library's newsletter. Additionally, we posted the classes to the calendar of our local Patch (http://patchogue.patch.com). To reach more people, especially in the Spanish-speaking community, we made sure flyers got to several local businesses and organizations, and that the class was featured on our Spanish Facebook page and mentioned in the local Spanish newspaper and radio station. We talked the program up as much as possible in every venue we could.

Scheduling programs in our building is often difficult because we have limited meeting space. We wanted to cover eight to ten of the topics in the BankIt program. First, we thought of having a series of two-hour classes, but we realized that having two longer sessions would work better for a variety of reasons. First, in our community, adults might have difficulty in coming to evening classes, either because it was right after work or because they work evenings. Second, reserving the meeting room for so many days was a logistical problem. Saturdays seemed like a logical solution to these problems—the room is usually available for teen programming that day. We could schedule two five-hour days, cover the material we wanted to, and hope that adults and teens would be willing to give up their day off to learn about this very important topic. We decided to make it more attractive by offering a continental breakfast and lunch as part of the program. We scheduled the program for two Saturdays, from ten a.m. to three p.m. The meeting room was available, as were our two very busy instructors.

Both of our instructors have very full schedules, so it is difficult to schedule them to be in the building at the same time on the same day. Gilda Ramos, our teacher for the adults, worked full-time as a library assistant in our Reference and Adult Services Department during the grant period. She was also completing her master's degree in library and information science.

Rita Alfano, our teacher for the teens, is a part-time librarian in our Teen and Media Services Department. She also works part-time as a reference librarian at another library, and during the grant period she held a third job as a teller at the Capital One bank next to the library. We not only needed them to be available for the program itself but for preparation time since it was very important that they coordinate their lessons for the teens and parents. Both were very accommodating, rearranging their hours to get the work done.

We planned, but winter on Long Island is unpredictable. On February 9, 2013, which was to have been the second day of the first-year workshop, the library's service area was struggling with three feet of snow from Winter Storm Nemo, and we had to cancel the program. In many ways, this set us back to square one—we needed to find a day when the meeting rooms, our teachers, and as many of our participants as possible would be available. The second half of the program was rescheduled for Saturday, February 23, from noon to five p.m. Some of the original participants did not make the second class, but additional people who had heard of the program came.

In the second grant year, scheduling our workshops outside the library added an additional layer of complexity. At the high school, even though we had the complete support of the business teacher and the school administration, required testing and snow days made it difficult to find days that worked for everyone. Even finding open evenings at the girls' shelter was difficult since the residents are required to have jobs and are not all available at the same time.

Another challenge we faced the first year was the delayed receipt of the interactive whiteboard we planned to use in presenting our workshops. Using grant funds, we ordered our whiteboard in November, with the idea that it would be available and ready to go by our first workshops, scheduled in mid-January. We encountered two issues: First, the interactive whiteboard could not be mounted in the meeting room we planned to use because of technical issues with the screen currently in the room. We had to purchase a mobile cart on which the whiteboard would be placed. The cost of the cart was almost double the amount of the actual board, and we needed to seek additional funding to pay for the mobile cart. Fortunately, we received an unrestricted grant from New York State Congressman Lee Zeldin, which covered most of the additional cost. Second, after assuring us of a two-week turnaround time for delivery and assembly of the whiteboard and mobile cart, the vendor discovered that the company they had been contracting with to supply the cart had discontinued the item. Our vendor was unable to immediately find a suitable replacement. When the vendor finally found a new stand and had it delivered and assembled, we had already held our 2013 full-day workshops using our existing technology (laptops, projectors, and screens). The interactive whiteboard was available for use for our 2013 short classes and for all of our 2014 programs. Learning from this experience, in the future we will leave more time to order any necessary technology or equipment needed for the workshop, or plan programming based on available, existing technologies rather than newly purchased items.

We designed our financial literacy programming so that it could be run again and again at our library and around our community. Our instructors are library employees who are ready to teach similar material as needed. The addition of our interactive whiteboard will allow us to use more interactive technology and continue to enhance the course. The purchase of the tablets and the availability of many inexpensive and free mobile applications and online programs will allow us to replicate and improve these important programs. The success of the program and the positive feedback we received from participants not only validated the need we saw in the community but also allowed us really to hear and learn about specific financial challenges our community is facing. We look forward to offering future classes that respond directly to the community's needs.

Providing this educational opportunity helped the library fulfill its mission: "to provide educational, cultural and recreational opportunities for the community, and to facilitate and support the informational needs of every community member."

Chapter Twenty-Three

Collaboration Fits the Bill for Best Practices in Programming for Public Housing Residents

Roland Barksdale-Hall

Quinby Street Resource Center Library of the Mercer County Housing Authority promotes quality community life through education, job training, and culture. As is the case for most special libraries, the resource center provides (1) support to its agency and its resident services in fulfillment of the agency's mission, strategic plan, and goals, and (2) information delivery to its administration, staff, and customers, in this particular case, the public housing residents and people who resided in areas served by public housing. Mercer County Housing Authority offers clean and affordable public housing for approximately 670 moderate- to low-income households, reaching 600 minors spread out over a vast geographical area with limited public transportation.

In 2012, I was hired as a library director at the Quinby Street Resource Center Library, located in Sharon, Mercer County, Pennsylvania. The Mercer County Housing Authority, which is one of approximately 3,300 public housing authorities in the United States, secured a grant from the Shenango Valley Foundation to support financial literacy. The public housing agency was in the implementation phase of a planning process that involved completion of a five-year strategic plan. *The Mercer County Housing Authority Strategic 5 Year Plan, 2013–2018* identified the following objectives:

- Increase the number of working families
- Increase programming at center
- Establish a newsletter to market and inform community
- Improve resident-supportive services

Figure 23.1. Quinby Street Resource Center Library. Photo by Roland Barksdale-Hall.

The housing authority established as part of its goal to enhance the quality of life for families who need affordable, safe housing choices and supportive services in well-maintained neighborhoods. After more than a decade of service to the community, the Quinby Street Resource Center branch of the Shenango Valley Community Public Library was closing. The anticipated closure was due to the public library's loss of funding. The housing authority stepped in to assume full operating responsibility for what became an independent library.

Research placed the library and organization in context. The Quinby Street Resource Center Library collection consisted of four thousand books and one hundred multimedia materials along with six computers and a multiservice meeting room. Earlier studies identified several service factors: poverty, underemployment, and limited access to public transportation for residents in the area served by the Quinby Street Resource Center branch library. A record of crime and low education test scores were identified as factors. During a ten-year period, the Quinby Street Resource Center, located in the Malleable Housing area of Sharon, made significant inroads in the reduction of crime in what was considered an intractable problem neighborhood. A 2014 study by the Annie E. Casey Foundation reported Pennsylvania as worse in regard to educational outcomes for African American children than the average nationwide. The Quinby Street Resource Center library collection served the surrounding community, where local school districts reported failing scores on standardized reading and writing scores.

Marketing strategies targeted to underserved population in the community were developed. Building a relationship of trust was a goal. Residents received a flyer with an introduction to the new librarian. Information provided his family connection to the neighborhood. Under the heading "Information Solutions That Work for Your Community," the flyer marketed the following information services:

- Employment—find a better job, plan an exciting career
- Career planning—help in applying to college or technical schools
- Computer training—assistance in using computers, writing letters
- Community programs—various enrichment options, from courses about cooking to workshops about tracing your roots

A combination of emails to site managers, announcements in newsletters and a monthly calendar, door-to-door distribution, telephone calls, and posting on the Resource Center Community Bulletin Board have provided results. Word of mouth and telephone calls have proved most effective. Program goals identified were the following:

- To promote financial literacy
- To promote marketable job skills and identify employment opportunities
- To promote cultural enrichment and life skills
- To undergird leadership role of residents in public housing

ROLE OF COLLABORATION

The Quinby Street Resource Center Library has collaborated in promoting financial literacy. Speakers from several agencies were tapped for program offerings, which are described below.

Collaboration between the housing authority, Penn State University Cooperative Extension, and Greenville Literacy Council made possible the first program, "Creative Holiday Spending." Flyers billed the six-week program as a how-to on putting more stretch in your dollar, giving gifts and not going broke, and cooking holiday meals with demonstrations. Each time residents attended a program their name was entered into a raffle. Residents showed good attendance and responded favorable to the incentive of a twenty-dollar Walmart gift card at the end of the program.

The Greenville Literacy Council was contracted for several classes on getting a GED, résumé writing, and computer training. When the Greenville

Literacy Council closed, new partnerships to get GED classes back in the center were explored.

"Bank on That" was a one-day program. A branch manager from First National Bank talked to residents on the importance of budgeting, keeping tabs on your finances, and building the confidence to make right financial decisions.

An employment specialist from the local Urban League affiliate discussed résumé preparation and employment resources available at the Urban League.

"Start Smart: Immediate Hire with Manpower" was a one-day program. Residents responded favorably to the flyer on employment opportunities available through temporary employment agencies. The buzz was immediate and resulted in residents being hired for positions. The program was well attended. Residents filled out the online application for Manpower immediately following the presentation.

Pennsylvania Work Wear representative presented a statewide program that provides work clothing.

Collaboration between the Quinby Street Resource Center Library, the Community Library of Shenango Valley, and other library team members focused on increasing technological access to employment resources through an Innovative Librarians Explore, Apply and Discover the 21st Century technology proposal. Service on a Section III Committee focused on job training for both underemployed and employed. According to the Housing and Urban Development website, Section III established legal provision for hiring of public housing residents for public housing projects. A four-session training program consisted of an introduction, résumé writing, dos and don'ts, mock interviews, and interviews with a temp agency, electrical contractors awarded contracts, and job trainers for electrical engineering.

ROLE OF CULTURE

William F. Strickland, author of *Make the Impossible Possible: One Man's Crusade to Inspire Others to Dream Bigger and Achieve the Extraordinary*, has recognized the role of the arts and culture in empowering low-income communities. He is a recipient of a MacArthur Genius Award and director of the Manchester Bidwell Corporation and its subsidiaries, Manchester Craftsman Guild and Bidwell Training Center, based in Pittsburgh. He played a significant role in developing the plan for the learning center with emphasis on targeted job training. In 2014, Pennsylvania Governor Tom Corbett announced a $2.6 million Economic Growth Initiative Grant for the local learning center based on Strickland's concept plan in Sharon, Pennsylvania. The Community Foundation of Western Pennsylvania and Eastern Ohio committed to matching funds. Other project supporters included the local chamber of commerce and a commercial business development group.

The literature has showed the great importance of extended family networks in some minority communities. Residents of public housing responded favorable to the role of culture in increased programming. Communidades Latinas Unidas En Servicio (CLUES) identified a connection between financial literacy and mental health. Feedback from a key resident contact person supported the need for a mental health piece. Respondents to a survey on critical issues identified the following needs: employment, care for family members (both children and adults), and transportation. Responses to what other type of programs they would like to see included ethnic cooking demonstrations.

"Souper Tuesday" targeted unemployed, underemployed, retired, and other residents who go through periods of the winter blues. An Expanded Food and Nutrition Education (EFNEP) nutrition educator from the Penn State Cooperative Extension showed how to make tasty soups, from white chili to chicken noodle soup. A nurse from a hospice service gave free informational presentations on mental health. Topics ranged from winter wellness to depression, anxiety, and stress. The program had one of the highest attendance rates overall.

"Celebrating Multiethnic Heritage: Searching Our Roots" was designed to recognize the important role of extended family networks. Residents responded favorable to discussion about family reunions and life lessons learned from family elders. In the past, participation dropped during the winter between programs. The program overlapped with "Souper Tuesday" to maintain participation.

"Family Literacy Programming": This collaboration between the Quinby Street Resource Center Library and Barnes and Noble Books recognized the role of community leadership. Both a resident and person in the neighborhood were presented with an excellence award in recognition of their contributions to a local history book, *African Americans in Mercer County*.

REFERENCE QUESTIONS

Can I use the library's telephone number as a call back number? Residents did not have a reliable telephone number. Research discovered free cell phones with a certain amount of minutes every month for individuals and families who meet eligibility requirements through the Federal Lifeline Assistance Program Q Link Wireless website.

Where can I get a part for this model of car? Residents searched online for mail-order auto parts. Transportation was a significant factor in job satisfaction.

Do you know where I can get a chair and couch? The resident was renting their furniture. He questioned the wisdom of rental furniture as a fixed monthly expense. The search into used furniture and various purchasing operations were explored. Referrals were made to several social service agencies as well.

How do I effectively communicate the personal responsibility of finding a job and keeping a job? Mandy, a job seeker, got the free phone with minutes. She gave the phone to her teenage son, who used all the minutes. She asked to use the library as a call back number. The librarian explained the library did not offer message services and did not agree to take calls from her prospective employers. Mandy learned that a telephone is a tool for job searching and personal emergencies. She used a friend's phone number on applications.

What are the best websites? Popular websites with residents included Indeed, Monster, and Snag a Job. Handouts included Job Searching Websites with topics. Topic headings include "State Career Service Center," "Career Service/Federal," "Career One Stop," "National Job Search Sites," "Small Business Development Centers," "Newspapers," "Industrial Specific Search Sites," "Disability—Work Accommodations/Education," "Veteran's Education/Employment," "Education," "Regional PHEAA Office," "Ohio Employment," and "Labor Marketing Information."

What is my password? Some residents forgot passwords, did not know when they worked at previous jobs, and expressed frustration in filling out an application online. Residents were encouraged to keep the same password. Residents also were told to keep a written record of passwords.

How am I to remember when I worked there? Residents were encouraged to think back to how old their child was at the time and then calculate the year.

Can you be my reference? Some residents were not aware that they needed the names of three references who are not family members, along with their addresses, telephone numbers, and emails, for job applications. References needed to be aware of their current status.

What is a prefix or suffix for a name? In numerous cases, residents experienced frustration in not being able to move on to the next screen in online applications until applications were completely filled out. Something as simple as clicking on Ms., Mr., or Dr. challenged progress.

How many cups go into a gallon? This was a question for a cooking position at a donut shop. Residents sometimes exhibited puzzlement over tests and online assessments for available positions. In some cases literacy was a factor; in other cases residents lacked the required job skills.

Why do I have to go to the job career center? Some residents were required to go to the job career center when they showed a preference for Quinby Street Resource Center Library. Residents cited transportation and one-on-one assistance as factors. Some residents negotiated with agencies to stay closer to their home. Some received permission to print out or keep track of applications in lieu of visiting the job career center. Others were not successful in negotiations. They were required to make weekly visits to the job career center.

NEWSLETTER PUBLICATION

What went wrong? The new librarian launched the Quinby Street Resource Center newsletter. The newsletter contained a letter from the property manager, staff profiles, program highlights, and a calendar. Residents had two columns with cleaning tips and a children's corner. The newsletter had been published bimonthly for two years when the resident leadership expressed dissatisfaction with the material in the publication and the paper's color. Residents expressed a need for more listings of referral agencies, community news, and spotlights on resident leaders. Residents produced several issues of their own community newsletter *In-the-Know* before reaching a compromise.

Collaboration between the resource center librarian and the resident leadership resulted in an improved Quinby Street Resource Center newsletter and increased readership. The newsletter has continued to be printed on the same white paper. However, the content has changed. The recent issue carried empowering stories along with photos of two high school graduates in caps and gowns. Both graduates discussed plans to continue their education. The Sharon School graduate worked at Dairy Queen. She served in the National Guard and planned to study art in college. The Farrell High graduate was homecoming king. He planned to attend a college. The issue included the academic achievements of those on the academic achievers and honor roll. The featured heroine of the month told of her lifelong struggle as a resident leader to eradicate drugs, promote education, and build better housing. An announcement about the AmeriCorps summer program rounded out the issue. This issue received positive feedback from residents of public housing, the community, housing authority staff, and administration. Resident leaders, housing administration, and the librarian teamed up to distribute this issue of the newsletter. The new and improved Quinby Street Resource Center newsletter has achieved the target goals: market success stories and inform readership of leadership, community news, and social service agencies. Collaboration between the library and key resident leaders turned the situation around and into a win-win situation.

TIPS FOR PLANNING A FINANCIAL LITERACY PROGRAM

- Identify the target audience and conduct a community analysis: For the best results, decide on your target audience and do a community analysis at least four to five months in advance. I identified key resident contact persons in target groups. I worked with youth, adult males, adult females, caretakers with infants to eighteen, and those fifty-five and older.
- Identify the stakeholders and build trust relationships: It is important to build trust with residents. This included members of the Residents Activities Council and local resource centers.
- Identify the specific need and available services: Residents run short on food and need assistance with heating and utilities. They identified nutrition, budgeting, and cooking demonstrations as needs. They preferred hands-on cooking demonstrations to basic talks about cooking.
- Plan a budget: The budget included meals, demonstrations, incentives (twenty-dollar Walmart card), marketing, and more. Weigh staffing time that goes into event planning and facility use as costs. As resources dwindled, the library cut back on incentives and refreshments for programming.
- Consider collaboration and suitable venues: Collaboration between a service organization and a women's shelter funded by a grant from First National Bank offered a six-week financial literacy course. Several public housing residents signed up for the course, which targeted women. The lesson plans covered finding a job, the essentials of credit, creating a budget, building credit history, and knowing your credit history. Residents received an incentive at each session they attended. Due to the number of public housing residents registered, the course was held on the public housing site.
- Make appropriate referrals: A phone survey of residents showed a six-week nutrition and budget course offering by the Prince of Peace, a religious charitable social service agency. Respondents were asked what programming provided by other agencies has benefited them. Public housing residents who completed the program received a hundred-dollar home heating voucher. Residents have found the heating voucher beneficial in reducing service shutoff notices and building good credit history. The library compiled a list of referral agencies for publication in the Quinby Street Resource Center newsletter.

CASE STUDIES

One-on-one assistance produced results. Residents sometimes did not ask questions in a group setting. In some instance, the librarian provided decision-making tips in one-on-one settings. Residents benefited from a simple decision-making worksheet. It contained space to formulate a list of musts, wants, and desires to use in weighing choices.

Marjorie was a fiftysomething female. She had a prior work history. She possessed a college degree. She had not been in the job market for over three years. She had a vehicle with which she did not feel safe in traveling out of town to work. She applied at many places in her field but was unable to locate employment. She worked in AmeriCorps but had more substantive experience than many of the youth who volunteered. She found employment as a manager in a senior service employment program. She assisted fifty-five-year-olds from low-income households and rural communities in identifying employment opportunities. Her challenge looking for a job provided experience for her new job. She now assists her peer group in getting back in the workforce. The majority of fifty-five-year-olds know what type of work they do not want to do. This can be beneficial in focusing the job search.

Tamika was a twentysomething single mother. She was enrolled in higher education. She received a call that a temporary position was available. She went to the interview and found she had to take a test. She did not take the test. She had not made plans for childcare for more than an hour. She rescheduled her interview and was hired.

Ramos was a thirtysomething male and single parent. He had prior work experience as a shipping and receiving manager. He had skilled certifications in an industrial field. He faced a reduction in his hours and pay in his temporary job. He was unable to cover the cost of gas and related expenses. He possessed a license and no vehicle. He did not apply at certain places. He did not like working where there were other people he knew. He felt the employers did not hire minorities. He had anxiety about using a computer. He forgot his username and password. He applied online to Walmart and other retailers. He posted his skills online and was hired by an employer within two miles of his home. He had full benefits and was going to ride a bike to work. He expressed appreciation to the librarian for encouragement in posting his résumé online.

Lola was a fiftysomething female. She had previously worked for ten years at one fast food restaraunt. She had worked thirty miles away and experienced car problems and quit her last job. She sought employment in retail or fast food somewhere within a fifteen-mile radius. She wanted Sundays off. She identified variable costs. She reduced costs on her car insurance to the minimum. She kept track of the minutes on her free phone. She used her cell phone for important business. She came in three times a week and spent two to three hours applying for jobs. She had interviews with a retailer. She would have been hired, but she did not check that she would work in the apparel department and needed to update her application. She could not remember her password, so she told the interviewers she would update the application later. She came to the center and tried several passwords she might have used. She finally got the right one. I told her she needed to keep a written record of each password used for a job application for each employer. She contacted the retailer and the position had been filled. The librarian worked with her to expand her radius to twenty miles. She found a fast food position. She has weekends off. The workers at her new job value her contribution.

CONCLUSION

As a librarian, job satisfaction has ranked high at the Quinby Street Resource Center. A job benefit has been to hear success stories and thank-yous from residents in public housing for improvements in their quality of life. A former resident in public housing, Lynne did the work to repair damaged credit and purchased a home through a program cosponsored by the Mercer County Authority program designed to promote home ownership. The number of families working has increased through support provided by a grant from the Shenango Valley Foundation for financial literacy. The Mercer County Housing Authority's Quinby Street Resource Center Library, located in the vicinity of the Sharon/Farrell Weed and Seed, a state revitalization program, has improved the quality of services to residents in public housing. Collaboration between the housing authority, libraries, and other agencies has enhanced community choices. Thank you for support and encouragement to Karen Lemmons, Jason Alston, Nannette Livadas, Holly Campbell, Beth Burkhart, Charles Fleet, and Sheila White.

REFERENCES

Business Journal. 2014. "Pa. Awards Grant for $5.6M Training Center in Sharon." October 10. http://archive.businessjournaldaily.com/economic-development/pa-awards-grant-56m-training-center-sharon-2014-10-10.

Communidades Latinas Unidas En Servicio. 2014. *My Family, My Self: The Latino Guide to Emotional Well-Being*. Center City, MN: Hazelden.

Echols, S. Michele. 2014. "I Could Tell You Stories: Am I a Librarian or Social Service Provider?" *BCALA News* 41 (4): 30–31

———. 2015. "I Could Tell You Stories Part II: Stories to Tell." *BCALA News* 42 (2): 54–55.

Klaric, Melissa. 2015. "Returning to a Program That Works: Sharon Police Reopen Substation in Malleable Heights, Aim to Build Trust." *Sharon (PA) Herald*, May 30.

Strickland, Bill, with Vince Rause. 2007. *Make the Impossible Possible: One Man's Crusade to Inspire Others to Dream Bigger and Achieve the Extraordinary*. New York: Broadway Books.

Chapter Twenty-Four

Fraud Alert

How Libraries Can Help Patrons Recognize Fraudulent Schemes

Linda Burkey Wade

When money gets tight, patrons utilize the library and its resources to help build their résumés, find a job, and sign up for health care and many other state and federal services. During a bad economy, scams and con artists appear more frequently, though they always seem to be around trying to take someone else's hard-earned money or savings. This article discusses how crooks tend to target their victims and the role any library can play in helping all ages recognize scams. Though the elderly are the most targeted demographic, all ages are vulnerable to financial scams. Also, this chapter contains resources and ideas that librarians can utilize to help patrons avoid becoming victims of con artists.

TARGETING THE MARK: CON ARTISTS PLAY NAUGHTY OR NICE

Crooks tend to target seniors because they are available, likely to have money, most likely to talk with them on the phone, and tend to be polite. Additionally, older adults probably won't report the crime or may not be able to remember the details if they do tell authorities. Older adults are often afraid that their families won't let them live alone once they have become a victim of fraud. Also, they may not know who to report the fraud to. Finally, senior citizens may fall for product scams more easily than younger adults. Due to the various types of frauds, including online scams, telemarketing fraud, bill scamming, imposter scams, and job scams, not just the elderly are at risk.

Someone at any age can become a victim to financial predators. Even Rosa Maymi from American Association of Retired Person (AARP), who teaches regular programs about all types of scams, has fallen prey to a phony email that looked like it was from her bank. She clicked on the link and was directed to a suspicious form asking for information her bank already knew; she did not fill out the form (Maymi, Leach, and Schifferle 2014).

Con artists are good at getting to know their victim and making even an educated person feel comfortable enough to let down their guard, giving information to a stranger. Whether the crook gains a person's trust or bullies the victim into sending money, it's time for librarians to help patrons recognize and protect themselves against these crafty thieves.

PROGRAMMING: HELP PATRONS RECOGNIZE AND AVOID RIP-OFFS

As with any good library programing, marketing and finding out about your target audience are important keys to providing presentations your customers and community will attend. You will need to find out the types of scams in your area and what your community is interested in learning about. Like most libraries, you may not have a budget for additional programs, but you can still provide quality informational sessions on fraud prevention. The good news is most of the work and materials have already been done for you and are free from the Federal Trade Commission (FTC), AARP, and the FBI. Links to these materials are provided later in this chapter.

According to the Financial Fraud Research Center (FFRC), an estimated 25.6 million people fall prey to various financial scams yearly (FFRC 2014). However, the FFRC states that the total number of victims is underestimated because many individuals do not report these types of crimes. Consumers who have been victimized often will not share information because they lack confidence in law enforcement, don't know who to report the scam to, or may feel ashamed or guilty for being tricked. One way victims can overcome these obstacles is to talk about these topics with others, which will embolden them to report fraudulent crimes to authorities.

The library, being a trusted community resource, can help local consumers by providing programs that discuss popular scams and scam evasion strategies. You, as the librarian, can be the presenter or moderator of any of the following presentation ideas:

- Invite a local law enforcement officer to talk about scams going on in your library's county, town, or area. Make sure to include tactics to reject the scam/scammer and how to report the fraud.

- Bring in a local attorney to discuss options for reporting and pursuing legal recourse after various scams. They could also cover the steps and laws for recovering from identify theft.
- Moderate a discussion group called "Share Your Story." For this program, have patrons talk about their own experiences. This may be difficult for some people to do as they may feel embarrassed at having been a victim. Emphasize how important it is to share their experiences to help others.
- Provide programs detailing various types of fraud and how to avoid them. This could include an overview of all types of scams and their avoidance, or be about specific types of scams. The focus might be on schemes targeting specific age groups or one type of fraud, such as identity theft, bill scramming, imposter fraud, lottery scams, or product/health-care fraud.
- Host webinars from well-known organizations, such as AARP and the FTC. Webinars are readily available on preventing fraud, and the director or another staff member could host a discussion after viewing the programs as a group.
- Other library sessions or programs could focus on teaching the details of smart investing, safe and secure online purchasing, product scrutiny strategies, and financial literacy programs.

Be flexible; even the best-planned program may turn into a "Share Your Story" session. Remember, talking about previous fraud experience is as important to get the word out as what you had planned and often makes the problem more real to listeners because they can put a face to the issue. This is especially true when patrons can see that even their respected peers have become the prey of these criminals. Good advice for patrons is to always take precautions, check out the information from another source/person, or return a phone call to a known number. One should never be in a rush to answer questions, click on a link, or pay for any deal that sounds too good to be true. Scammers are in a rush and want the victim to "act now." When presenting or leading discussions, be respectful and empower your audience; don't humiliate them or belittle their experience. Your information should be quick and to the point as you don't have time to waste and neither does your audience.

DON'T BE FOOLED: THERE ARE FREE TOOLS AND RESOURCES AVAILABLE

As mentioned earlier, AARP has the Fraud Watch Network, which can be found by searching using your favorite search engine. Another source for material is the Federal Trade Commission's website, with their material located by searching "FTC fraud." Additionally, the Federal Bureau of Investigations has resources you can find by searching "FBI scams." These organizations have a wealth of information on their websites available to you and your patrons. They have free materials, various media files, and articles providing information on how to report fraud. Additionally, these establishments write blogs on current scams, let victims share their stories, have forms for reporting scams, help people get access to their credit reports, and provide phone numbers for identifying fraud. These agencies have done all the work for you, so you can simply help your patrons navigate these vast resources to the information and answers they need about scams. Following are listed some of the best resources from the AARP, FTC, and FBI websites:

Free printed materials. The FTC provides free handouts for your patrons at https://bulkorder.ftc.gov/. Be sure to select "Pass It On" publications. Materials from the FTC include tear sheet pads/flyers, booklets, and bookmarks. Also available is a "Pass It On Sample Folder" to get conversations started with people who may need more information. Anyone can order these; however, the minimum orders are geared toward libraries and other organizations so that the materials can be handed out.

Webinars and videos. At http://www.consumer.ftc.gov/media the FTC has over one hundred videos, webinars, and other media on fraud, scams, and help tips to avoid fraud. This website also has several games to test one's knowledge about rip-offs.

Phone numbers and online reporting of fraud. AARP provides a Fraud Watch Hotline, which allows a person to call and talk to a fraud expert. This person will help the caller determine if they are possibly being defrauded and who to contact if it is in fact a scam. The hotline number can be found on the Fraud Watch Network homepage or by searching for "Fraud Watch Hotline."

Blogs, Facebook, and news feeds. The Watchdog Alerts news feed is available from AARP even if you are not a member; simply look for the "Get Watchdog Alerts" button. The FTC provides and maintains a blog on current scams at http://www.consumer.ftc.gov/scam-alerts.

Fraud Alert Map. AARP has a "Fight Fraud in Your State" option by selecting "Spot a scam? Tell us about it" from the main Fraud Watch Network homepage. This web feature allows consumers to share their fraud story online. The map allows viewers to look at law enforcement scam alerts as well as the rip-offs others have reported.

Articles. AARP's main Fraud Watch Network page includes links to popular articles on getting to know con artists, such as "Meet the Con Artist." Also provided on the main page are links to news stories on the latest scams and crooks who have been caught.

These agencies have created Facebook and Twitter accounts to help get information out to consumers. The Consumer Financial Protection Bureau (CFPB) at http://www.consumerfinance.gov/ is another online resource tool for reporting financial product frauds. Both the CFPB and the FTC have Spanish versions of their articles and materials for those libraries and patrons needing them. Furthermore, don't forget to utilize your library's print and online collections for articles on fraud.

OPTING OUT IS EASY: OTHER TOOLS AND IDEAS TO HELP PATRONS AVOID RIP-OFFS

Another way to help patrons avoid fraud is to choose to opt out. Are patrons tired of receiving insurance and credit card offers? OptOutPrescreen.com is the official consumer website authorized by Equifax, Experian, Innovis, and TransUnion for consumers to opt out of credit and insurance offers. The site offers a five-year or permanent opt-out option. A patron can fill out the online form for the temporary five-year option or print out the form and mail it to the Opt-Out Department to permanently stop receiving insurance and credit card offers. Though the credit reporting agencies remove consumers from the offer lists within five days of receiving the request, it can take up to thirty days before consumers stop receiving offers because their name may have been given out prior to filling out the form. If your patron changes their mind, they can opt back in on the same website by filling out the online form. This stops the credit reporting companies from adding a person's name to company offers when they ask for a list of people with good credit ratings.

Patrons signing up for the Do Not Call Registry will aid in cutting down the number of businesses that can call their phone. It won't stop scammers, but it can cut down on legitimate product offer calls and telemarketing. However, one new trick illegitimate telemarketers are using is falsifying their call number to look like a local call. New technology is enabling criminals to make calls from anywhere and misrepresent their number with caller ID so that they can conceal who they are and where they really are located.

At https://www.dmachoice.org/ a patron may "opt in" to direct marketing by only selecting mail they wish to receive. The Direct Marketing Association's (DMA) website is for use by customers to create an account and select the mail they do want to receive. The site organizes direct mail into four categories: credit offers, catalogs, magazine offers, and other mail offers. On this site individuals may request to start or stop receiving mail from individual companies within each category—or from an entire category at once. The DMA has 3,600 business members and leaders in direct marketing. Founded in 1917, DMA gives the consumer power and know-how to manage mail preferences. You can be sure that they value any personal information you provide, and it will only be used to put your selections into effect.

Another helpful free service is Nomorobo, which blocks "robo calls," calls made automatically using a computer that delivers a recorded message.

Nomorobo is a free service that will hang up on robo calls after one ring so your patron will never receive it. However, some phone companies and services aren't allowing their customers to sign up. A patron would need to go to the site and answer questions about whether they have a land line or cell phone and the carrier or type of phone service it is (i.e., choose carrier or other phone service, such as Internet VoIP). Unfortunately, if a customer's carrier isn't on the list, they probably won't be able to use this service. Here is a summary of these options:

- Opt out of credit and insurance offers provided by consumer credit companies at OptOutPrescreen.com.
- Sign up for the Dot Not Call Registry at DoNotCall.gov.
- Select your mail preferences with Direct Mail Association Choice at DMAChoice.org.
- Sign up for Nomorobo, a free robo call blocking service at Nomorobo.com.

OTHER NON-INTERNET TIPS FOR PATRONS

Now for some things your patrons can do to avoid scams that don't involve the Internet.

Calls. Hang up right away, keep your number to yourself, tell companies you do not do business over the phone and not to call anymore, and do not answer calls from numbers you do not recognize.

Call blocking devices or a phone with call blocking lists. Another way to stop robo calls is by using a number blocking device. Some newer phones provide a call block list with a limited the number of calls that can be blocked (e.g., some phones only block thirty numbers), while newer phones will let an owner block one hundred to three hundred numbers. Usually, these blockers work by letting the phone ring once and then hanging up on a blocked caller. Separate blocking devices are available for use to route calls through, but note that some blocker devices draw their power from the phone line, in which case the device may not work if too much power is being used. That tends to happen in assisted living and apartment buildings, so a patron may wish to find a blocker with a separate power cord.

Check those bills and read each entry. Scammers add service fees and annual "membership" charges to bills, trying to collect money. Patrons need to be on the alert to make sure there aren't any services or fees added to a bill that were not approved or agreed to by them.

Stop mail delivery. It is always a good idea to stop mail and other materials from being delivered to a home when on vacation or away for extended periods of time.

Lock your mail box. Purchasing a locking mail box is a simple way for patrons to protect themselves from credit card scamming or having crooks obtain other account information.

HOW LIBRARIES CAN HELP PATRONS

According to a congressional hearing on fraud on the elderly (House of Representatives Energy and Commerce Committee 2013), the education of consumers and a massive public awareness campaign are the best ways to combat financial fraud. Libraries are great tools to disseminate information and can assist the public in learning about financial exploitation and how to avoid it.

We as librarians must be understanding and approachable. Therefore, don't be condescending or say you told them so. Encourage them to report the crime and help them find the appropriate authorities to report the fraud to. Many of those options have been discussed throughout this chapter, and here is a quick recap:

- Call the AARP Fraud Watch Hotline.
- Fill out a form on the FTC website or utilize their article on who to contact.
- For financial and product scams, contact the CFPB and local police.
- Encourage patrons to share their stories when it becomes appropriate to help others.

To help make your customer successful at identifying and avoiding fraud, your program should do the following:

- Be relevant to your audience (i.e., age, interest, types of fraud for various age groups)
- Be brief and to the point
- Be empowering and respectful, not demeaning
- Provide resources and tools
- Enable and encourage them to share their knowledge with others

Be flexible: sometimes your outreach programs will turn into discussion sessions on the various types of schemes people have experienced. That's okay, as sharing those stories will help another person not fall prey to those scams. The ultimate goal is to help your patrons share their knowledge with others. It is likely they already know about scams whether by first hand as a victim or through avoiding the scam. What your customers may not know is that they are a trusted source to help others avoid fraud. Provide them with the tools to have conversations with their friends, family, and other groups. Crooks tend to target seniors, though anyone of any age can be vulnerable to a scam. The library is not just helping patrons avoid fraudulent schemes; it is helping the entire community.

REFERENCES

AARP. 2014. "Fraud Watch Network." http://www.aarp.org/money/scams-fraud/fraud-watch-network/.

Ballenger, Brandon. 2015. "8 Tips to Stop Annoying Robo Calls." *MoneyTalksNews*, January 15. http://www.cbsnews.com/news/8-tips-to-stop-annoying-robocalls/.

FBI. 2015. "Fraud Target: Senior Citizens." http://www.fbi.gov/scams-safety/fraud/seniors.

Federal Trade Commission. 2014. "Pass It On." http://www.consumer.ftc.gov/features/feature-0030-pass-it-on.

FFRC. 2014. "The True Impact of Fraud: A Round Table of Experts." Conference Proceedings, Washington, DC, April 30–May 1. http://fraudresearchcenter.org/wp-content/uploads/2014/06/The-True-Impact-of-Fraud-Proceedings-Final.pdf.

Hazel, Denice. 2015. "Financial Literacy." *Library Journal* 140 (1): 1.

House of Representatives Energy and Commerce Committee. 2013. "Fraud on the Elderly: A Growing Concern for a Growing Population, Serial No. 113-41 on Elderly Fraud." 113th Congress, May 16.

Maymi, Rosa, Jennifer Leach, and Lisa Schifferle. 2014. "How to Spot Frauds and Scams" AARP Webinar, December 10.

Kirchheimer, Sid. 2013. "Con Artists Use Scare Tactics to Take Your Money." *AARP Bulletin*, September. http://www.aarp.org/money/scams-fraud/info-08-2013/con-artists-use-fear-to-intimidate.html.

Small, Bridget. 2013. "Fraud Affects 25 Million People: Recognize Anyone You Know?" *FTC Consumer Information Blog*, April 22. http://www.consumer.ftc.gov/blog/fraud-affects-25-million-people-recognize-anyone-you-know.

Chapter Twenty-Five

Getting the Patron to Yes

The Academic Librarian's Role in Supporting Salary Negotiations

Aliqae Geraci, Daniel Hickey, and Kelly LaVoice

As is the case with many financial literacy topics, salary negotiation is a skill for which only a limited number of students receive practical instruction and coaching. Being armed with a strategy is key, as is having the reliable information needed to persuade the other party and reach an amicable consensus. As the cost and value of higher education is hotly debated, institutions are increasingly accountable for student career outcomes, including quality of placement and compensation. Academic librarians are uniquely positioned to assist patrons in salary negotiations, connecting students at all levels with the information they need to secure competitive salary and benefits packages. However, little has been written about this opportunity in the library literature. This chapter highlights salary research resources, related library services, strategies for implementation, and the importance of collaborating with campus partners to maximize resource and service offerings.

SOURCES OF WAGE DATA

Identifying reliable, relevant, and current sources for salary and wage data can be challenging for students and librarians. Having accurate data for evaluating a salary offer is key, as is the ability to locate oneself within a given salary range based on geography, skill set, experience, or institution type. The following section reviews various salary data sources and discusses their applicability in order for the patron and librarian to evaluate each source according to their needs and priorities.

In order to provide effective reference support for salary negotiation beyond what patrons can self-source online, librarians must be able to assess the various sources of compensation data in order to match resources to patron's needs, explain data gaps, and assist in selection of the best data points. Variables to consider include methodology and data source (either sourced from employers or individual employees) and scope (geographical or institution specific), as well as precision (standard occupational classification [SOC] or job title) and the perennial evaluative criteria of currency, data transparency, and accuracy. Organization-level data will be the most difficult to obtain, as a rule, unless the organization is required to disclose this as a public entity or through some type of filing requirements, or chooses to publicly disclose data. In addition, identifying salary data alone will be insufficient for a patron seeking to navigate and evaluate an employment offer that is likely to include a number of nonsalary compensation factors such as benefits, flexibility of scheduling, or professional development support.

The United States federal government collects salary and wage data through a number of national programs, primarily the U.S. Census Bureau and the Department of Labor's Bureau of Labor Statistics. Most career centers and job help services have a copy of the government-produced Occupational Outlook Handbook on hand or will direct clients to the online edition (U.S. Bureau of Labor Statistics 2014). Median salary figures cited in the handbook are derived from the Bureau of Labor Statistics' Occupational Employment Statistics (OES) program, which generates annual estimates for a range of occupations. Over eight hundred OES occupational profiles, organized within major groups, feature national wage estimates as a well as state- and city-level average hourly and annual wages and employment counts. Occupational income data is also collected by the federal government as part of the U.S. Census, which can be searched with great geographic precision, albeit with much broader and fewer occupational categories than available in

Table 25.1. A Compensation Data Matrix

Source/ Scope	Geographic	Institutional
Employer	• ERI Salary Assessor • Occupational Employment Statistics (OES) data • ALA-APA Salary Survey • Salary.com	• ARL Salary Survey • Public-sector data
Individual	• Census-based income data • AALL Salary Survey • Payscale.com • Glassdoor.com	• Glassdoor.com • Proprietary institutional database

the OES data. The American FactFinder interface allows users to select topics related to People (Employment: Occupations and Income/Earnings: Individual) and then specify desired geography (U.S. Census Bureau n.d.). This query returns occupation by sex and median earnings in the past twelve months, derived from American Community Survey five-year estimates, organized by broad occupational categories and then gender.

For patrons seeking state or local public-sector salary data, access varies depending on the state. Many state and local governments mandate the release of compensation data of public-sector employees on request, and while some share the data preemptively, independent organizations may also organize and provide access to the information. For example, the California State Comptroller developed a salary database that allows users to search by position, agency, and department, with data current to 2013 (California State Controller's Office n.d.). A similar database is maintained by the State of New Jersey Transparency Center (State of New Jersey n.d.). While the New York State government does not provide its own platform, a number of other organizations have developed their own tools. SeeThroughNY.net is comprehensive and browseable by employer type (City of New York, villages, public authorities, schools, and more), but the position field is largely unpopulated, requiring users to rely on agency designations or knowledge of individual assignments (Empire Center n.d.). Ultimately, the comprehensiveness, currency, and relevance of public-sector salary data available depend on the state.

Many professional organizations and industry groups maintain occupation- and industry-specific salary surveys that serve as a more in-depth benchmark for salaries, as a resource for employers and employees alike in addition to maintaining a longitudinal knowledge base. Often survey data is available as part of a membership benefit and not readily accessible online, so students may be surprised to learn that reports are often available through a university library or interlibrary loan.

When patrons search Google for salary data, they inevitably stumble upon a few free, commercially maintained resources. Differentiating between the top three—Salary.com, Payscale.com, and Glassdoor.com—may be a challenge initially, especially as the free data largely serves as a teaser for services or products, but there are a couple of important points of divergence.

Salary.com is a website that provides free salary data and career guidance in addition to marketing HR and compensation software. Their SalaryWizard is searchable by job title and location, or browseable by industry, occupational category, and salary range, and then location. The basic profile includes national or local employer size, educational level and years of experience, as well as salary and benefits values ranges. Full occupational or customized reports can be purchased. Salary data is available for the United States and Canada, and an enhanced subscription is available to businesses. Salary data is derived from employer surveys, but viewable data are not linked to specific institutions.

Payscale.com similarly features free salary data while marketing subscription content and services, but it differs from Salary.com in a key aspect: data source. The salary data marketed is generated through individual employee surveys ("over 40 million people"). Users seeking salary data are prompted to answer demographic and career questions about their location, years of experience, skills, employment status, or job offer—essentially populating the database. Users are then directed to a "Full Salary Report" that includes local and regional hourly median wage and salary data, with some variables like certification or degree.

Like Payscale.com, the salary data available at Glassdoor.com is crowdsourced from individuals. An initial search for a salary by position title and location results in national and locational averages within a tenth-to-ninetieth-percentile range along with the last date of update. Users are prompted to contribute additional information (either a salary number for a job, or a review of an organization, for either a current or former employer) in order to access institution-level salary data and reviews, a feature that differentiates the site from Salary.com. As with Payscale.com and Salary.com, users are also directed to job postings, and ultimately, the product at hand is the suite of services being marketed to employers.

In higher education, universities are developing proprietary institutional databases or subscribing to platforms that facilitate the collection and tracking of alumni salary data. One company offering this type of solution is 12Twenty. Platforms are typically purchased and maintained by schools (although alumni and career departments often lead implementation) and branded to conform to the school's identity. Data is frequently limited in scope to self-reported offers and entry-level salaries. Successful implementations employ concepts from behavioral economics (incentives, competition) to increase reporting and grow the data set. These databases can include other information germane to recruiting: other forms of compensation, number and themes of hiring manager's questions, and so on. Librarians without strong preexisting ties to their career centers may find it challenging to access such databases.

Locating trustworthy and current *nonsalary* compensation information about an organization is even more challenging than identifying position-level salary data. The precise makeup of benefits packages are generally specific to the organizational context as opposed to an industry norm and unless shared on a public website are likely inaccessible outside of the interview process. Relying solely on "Top 100 Companies" or "Best Places to Work"–type articles, which favor large organizations as best examples of family leave or other benefits policies, can be problematic when interviewing in a smaller organizational context, although they can be quite useful in facilitating patron exploration of potential job and career preferences and in identifying cultural attributes of an organization beyond compensation. Augmenting found salary ranges with standard company/organizational research sources like Hoover's, Guidestar, or ESG Manager, as well as crowdsourced information from websites like Glassdoor.com, can provide the patron with a broader sense of organizational culture and policy to guide them through the initial application, interview, and negotiation process, until more specific information is provided by the potential employer. Ultimately, the additional information can assist the patron in selecting between multiple comparable offers, while building an awareness of resources to support future choices.

Enterprise solutions can be deployed within the library information environment with broad appeal. ERI Platform Library's Salary Assessor is a subscription database developed by the Economic Research Institute and is used by many companies. Cornell University's Martin P. Catherwood Library maintains single-point access that is used by a range of patrons, including students, faculty, community members, and administrative staff. Salary data is sourced from employer surveys and public records and augmented by internal job analysis, and is searchable for over six thousand position titles in over seven thousand cities in North America and the United Kingdom (Economic Research Institute 2015). Base salary and total compensation ranges are available in median and percentiles (adjustable) and by years of experience (customizable). Users can also generate a set of geographic comparables that include the ERI mean as well as cost of living for a specific occupation. Salary Assessor access and training is publicized through Cornell University Library research guides serving the hospitality, management, and labor relations schools, as well as through library-level relationships with individual career services offices and in library instruction sessions.

Comprehensive career support tools are not the exclusive purview of the academic library. Cornell University provides student access to Vault.com's Career Insider, which in addition to organizational, occupational, and industry overviews, features some basic salary ranges for positions. However, library liaisons can serve as access points for navigating and contextualizing the information while suggesting additional compensation resources specific to the discipline, industry, or occupation.

Library research guides are ideal reference and instructional vehicles for showcasing the broad range of data sources, outlining research strategies, and directing students to more in-depth liaison assistance. The University of Pittsburgh Library's Career Resources @ Pitt provides a tightly curated list of salary negotiation resources and links to federal and industry salary data (University of Pittsburgh Library 2015), while Simmons College Library's Salary Data guide is broad, with multiple tabs directing to resources for national and industry data as well as negotiation advice and strategies (Simmons Library 2014). Cornell University research guides that target communities within the schools of Industrial Relations and Hotel Administration are tightly aligned to disciplinary resources and reflect close collaboration with the career services offices of the respective schools.

LIBRARY SERVICES AND SERVICE MODELS

For students seeking assistance in their job hunt, librarians can help them make sense of an often complex and fragmented career service and resource landscape. It is important to be able to articulate the library's service ethos for finding job and salary information to manage patron expectations. Librarians should be careful to explain the scope of their assistance, and refer patrons when the need for coaching or strategy goes beyond librarian expertise.

Understanding how patrons envision their preferred career trajectory and their "plan B" alternative can guide librarians when considering what types of information to seek and what resources to consult. An undergraduate with military experience seeking his or her first civilian job approaches sources of salary data in a different way than a graduate student embarking on an academic career or an alumnus making a midcareer transition.

The following are a few points to take into consideration when helping patrons: the patron's experience and standing in the academy, the job function they intend to pursue, the potential employer's sector (public, private, NGO/not-for-profit) and industry, geographic preferences, desired salary range, and preferences for organizational culture or size.

Establishing a strategic framework for supporting career research is key for reference work focused on career and salary information. The service should be user centered, scalable to a targeted user base, and sensitive to the confidentiality of the hiring and negotiation HR process. Librarians have to determine what service levels they offer to different patron groups (undergraduates, graduates, alumni, etc.) and be prepared to justify those distinctions.

Librarians must assess their career and salary-related work. One method to determine what is most important to measure is to ask, "Why is this service valuable to my patrons? What proves this? How do I go about collecting this proof?" Depending on the library environment, a quantitative measure of consultations might be most appropriate. In another, anecdotal testimonials may be the most persuasive. Ideal measures of outcomes (as opposed to perceptions), such as placement data for all students helped or measures of future fluency with salary information, may be beyond the ability of the individual librarian to collect.

STRATEGIES FOR IMPLEMENTATION

Libraries have both the resources and services to assist students with aspects of career support and salary negotiation; however, students receive the most relevant and meaningful support when librarians step outside of the library and partner with other campus stakeholders with relevant expertise. For academic libraries, career services departments are natural partners with similar goals: assist students with finding job placements. Career services provide key assistance, such as résumé reviews and interview preparation. While the value of potential collaborations has been discussed in library literature, most studies have found that career services staff and librarians believe greater impact could come from deeper collaboration.

Abel (1992) found that these units were not cooperating meaningfully or frequently. A 2003 follow-up study by Quenoy and Oregeron found less than 40 percent of the career services representatives and library staff responders surveyed collaborated with their counterparts (Quenoy and Orgeron 2003). The examples given included career services advertising library collections and services and using library resources within their own sessions. The study found that while library career sessions were presented jointly with career services 78 percent of the time, career services presentations only included a library presence 20 percent of the time. When surveyed about prioritizing collaboration, less than 10 percent of career professionals felt that this was a priority. To optimize the student experience, librarians need to market themselves to career services, highlighting their value as partners in the career support arena. It is important to acknowledge that career services providers may have limited experiences with and expectations of the library. They may be unaware of the resources purchased and the workshops and consultations provided by the library. In addition to communicating the library's value to career services and related campus departments, it is necessary to set expectations for partnerships. The availability of library staff and needs of students help dictate the necessary time commitments and frequency of offerings.

In most universities, a small number of career services staff are responsible for assisting large and diverse student populations. According to the National Association of Colleges and Employers, the average student to career services professional was 1 to 1,889 students. While the 2014 fiscal year was the first overall financial increase in career services operating budgets since the recession, the median operating budget is still lower than it was at the height of the recession. Recognizing the constraints on career services offices helps librarians frame their potential value: Market collaborations with the library as meaningful strategies for saving time and increasing student success. Clearly articulate librarian strengths, as well as areas that career services can provide valuable information. For example, highlight resources that help students identify themselves in a salary range; then connect students to career services staff that are better trained to assist with the protocol for initiating and guiding negotiation strategy. It is critical to emphasize the importance of networking with professionals in the same field. While career services staff and librarians can recommend networking outlets, job seekers must ultimately find and form long-term connections within their industry to gain insight or advantageous benefits from these relationships. In addition to career services, other potential partners for collaboration include subject librarian colleagues, academic advisors, alumni affairs officers, and professional organizations.

Campus collaborations look different at each institution, but library literature is sparse on specific examples of innovative collaborations. In 2013, Wake Forest University hosted the Rethinking Success Conference to discuss how helping students develop careers and succeed in the professional world must be prioritized for academic institutions (Chan and Derry 2013). The conference included representatives from seventy-four academic institutions, with attendance by career services officers, university presidents, deans, faculty members, and professional employers. Their mission was to develop new methods for integrating career services support into all aspects of the student experience, involving partnerships with senior administration, faculty, career services, alumni relations, and others. The result was "A Roadmap for Transforming the College-to-Career Experience." While the library is only mentioned once, the framework of developing new strategic partnerships represents an opportunity for librarians to join university-wide efforts.

CORNELL UNIVERSITY CASE STUDY

The Johnson Graduate School of Management at Cornell University has about 550 two-year MBA students. The professional nature of this degree program makes career placement support a priority. Johnson has a prominent Career Management Center with academic advisors for each student concentration. Johnson also has an on-location Management Library, with four librarians responsible for connecting with faculty and academic staff. In 2013, an opportunity for collaboration emerged when a librarian, academic advisor, and career services staff member held joint consultations with each student in the Sustainable Global Enterprise track who had not received a full-time job offer by the spring semester. This allowed the librarian to gain a further understanding of the personal and physical resources available through these related departments, while simultaneously enhancing both the student and partners' understanding of the library. Librarians assisted students with gathering information needed to prepare for interviews and information on salary ranges for similar positions in the geographic area. Academic advisors and Career Management Center staff were able to connect students to alumni in similar positions, who provided advice and potential job opportunities. The Career Management Center provided access to in-house yearly employment reports that included extremely valuable placement data and salary information for alumni. Students gained the benefit of having three unique perspectives in one consultation and were able to better understand the unique yet valuable roles of each contributor. While individual consultations for all two-year students was not realistic, identifying target student populations and committing to pilot programs can lead to exciting new opportunities for the library to interact with patrons.

After establishing which partners would be both willing and able to collaborate on providing career support services, examine ways these groups can meaningfully come together to work with students. Potential outlets for collaboration, workshops, consultations, webinars, learning tools, and the like are endless. Examples of best practices for collaborations include the following:

- Gathering patron data: Before students attend a workshop or consultation, provide an online or paper registration form that asks students to briefly describe their particular career need. This allows all partners in the session to prepare or determine if the student's immediate need would be best addressed by another campus partner.
- Host programs in nonlibrary spaces: While students may be frequent library visitors, an event in the career services center may draw a more varied audience.
- Embed library resources into preexisting career services websites.
- Host office hours in the career services department.
- Subscribe to local and national Listservs and organizations: Determine what organizations the university subscribes to that could provide valued insight, such as the National Association of College and Employers and the National Career Development Association.
- Professional development for career services providers: While the intended audience may be career services staff or academic advisors, these opportunities can impart valuable skills that enhance librarians' ability to provide meaningful research assistance.

It is critical that the library connect with campus partners to provide students with the wide range of career-related support they need to navigate the job market and negotiate offers to gain employment after graduation. The best collaborations can begin organically, on a small scale, and grow as demand and success stories proliferate. Librarians must clearly communicate realistic expectations, both of services and sources they can provide as well as the extent to which the job seeker must take an active role in the process. Marketing offerings by collaborating with existing networks, such as advisors, alumni, and LinkedIn, allows students to gain perspectives from professionals with a wide range of expertise.

IMPLICATIONS AND FUTURE RESEARCH

There is still much work to do to examine the impact of services and collaborations related to compensation-themed reference interactions. Future research may begin by gauging customer satisfaction and perceptions of efficacy. Ideally, a study measuring salary negotiation outcomes, including those with information-based interventions, would better illuminate the real-world impact of services. A challenging but valuable study would be surveying hiring managers, looking at the information used in negotiations from a prospective employer's viewpoint.

As academic libraries seek to further align their work with the goals and priorities of the university, librarians must ensure that their work dovetails with the institution's top-level measures of success. While student academic output in the form of grades has been a primary focus, an examination of the economic success of students postgraduation pervades the popular discourse about the value of higher education. The resources and strategies discussed in this chapter are a first step toward libraries contributing to that goal. By collaborating with career service providers, librarians arm students and alumni with information that enables the use of negotiation strategies to secure desirable jobs and competitive salaries. Doing so strongly links the value of library service providers to an emergent measure of student success.

REFERENCES

Abel, Charlene. 1992. "A Survey of Cooperative Activities between Career Planning Departments and Academic Libraries." *Reference Librarian* 16 (36): 51–60.

California State Controller's Office. n.d. *Government Compensation in California.* http://publicpay.ca.gov/.

Chan, Andy, and Tommy Derry. 2013. "A Roadmap for Transforming the College-to-Career Experience." Rethinking Success, May. http://rethinkingsuccess.wfu.edu/files/2013/05/A-Roadmap-for-Transforming-The-College-to-Career-Experience.pdf.

Economic Research Institute. 2015. "Salary Assessor Methodology/Disclaimer." June 23.

Empire Center. n.d. "SeeThroughNY." http://seethroughny.net/.

Glassdoor.com. n.d. http://www.glassdoor.com/index.htm.

PayScale.com. n.d. http://www.payscale.com/.

Quenoy, Paula, and Elizabeth Orgeron. 2003. "Working with Wisdom: Collaboration between Career Services and University Libraries." Association of College & Research Libraries 11th National Conference, Charlotte, NC.

Salary.com. n.d. http://www.salary.com/.

Simmons Library. 2014. "Salary Data." June 16. http://simmons.libguides.com/Salary.

State of New Jersey. n.d. "Public Payroll." http://www.yourmoney.nj.gov/transparency/payroll/.

U.S. Bureau of Labor Statistics. 2014. "Occupational Outlook Handbook." January 8. http://www.bls.gov/ooh/.

U.S. Census Bureau. n.d. "American FactFinder." http://factfinder.census.gov/.
University of Pittsburgh Library. 2015. "Career Resources @ Pitt: Salary." June 22. http://pitt.libguides.com/c.php?g=12095&p=64648.

Chapter Twenty-Six

Marketing Planning for Library-Based Financial Education Programs

Mary Jo Ryan and Kit Keller

TELLING THE STORY

Having the greatest financial resources, programs, and workshops available in your library is pretty much irrelevant if no one knows about them. Successful library-based financial education programs incorporate marketing planning as a component of program planning. As with all planning activities, marketing planning is intentional and inclusive. Marketing planning helps library staff and volunteers stay focused on the target audience, and it helps ensure that communication messages lead with the customer needs—not with what the library has and does. The process evolves through predictable stages. It is circular in nature since we are always learning from the outcome of our communication activities and adapting the next communication effort to what we learned, as shown in figure 26.1.

ASSEMBLE A MARKETING TEAM AND TRAIN THEM

The investment of time spent building a local library marketing team to plan and implement an effective marketing strategy pays dividends in library customer engagement and community awareness. Library staff and volunteers on the marketing team can use a simple marketing planning template to make decisions about how to best reach their target audience. The marketing template can help the team schedule and implement communication efforts that will influence that audience and connect them with financial education resources to help solve financial problems unique to their financial life stage. Communication materials will be customized for that target audience. These

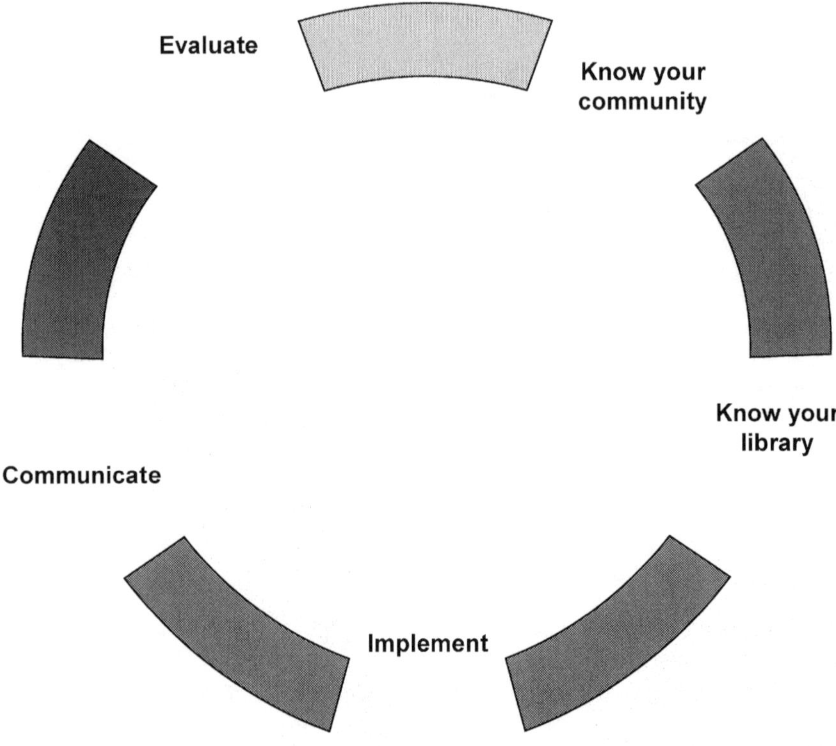

Figure 26.1. Communication Is a Planning Process.

materials will also build community buzz around financial education activities available in the library and online—amplifying word-of-mouth marketing through outreach, social networking, and trusted intermediaries to help spread the word.

Marketing is not a skill taught in most library schools. Recent research shows that librarians need to be exposed to marketing concepts in order to maintain their central position as information providers, communicating through traditional tools as well as new and emerging technology. The techniques and tools used in Smart investing@your library grant projects serve as models for librarians as effective communication practices that can be applied to new and existing library programs and services.

Marketing training resources for library staff and volunteers are readily available. For example, see materials developed through ALA/FINRA Smart Investing@your library grants, including the "Media Training Guide for Smart investing@your library Project Leaders" (http://smartinvesting.ala.org/wp-content/uploads/2011/08/How-to-Work-with-the-Media-2.0-

Training-Guide.pdf) and the webinars "Taking a Blended Approach to PR" (http://smartinvesting.ala.org/pr-webinar/) and Smart investing@your library Builds Nebraska Communities' "Marketing Customer Training @ Your Library" (http://nlc.nebraska.gov/grants/finra/webinars.aspx). Marketing training gives the marketing team confidence in their ability to communicate with members of the target audience about the educational resources that will help address their financial concerns. The training can be conducted in an informal setting—be sure to bring the popcorn when watching the webinars in a group.

SELECT A TARGET AUDIENCE

The first step of the marketing planning process, "Know Your Community," jump-starts target audience selection and segmentation. When it comes to marketing library-based financial education programs, one size does *not* fit all. This is clearly demonstrated by recipients of Smart investing@your library (SIYL) grants. As part of the application process, all libraries completed a community needs assessment in the area of financial literacy topics—investing, saving, budgeting, financial planning, earning, spending, credit, and so on. There is a wide variety of topics that could address local needs, and levels of content within each topic, from the very basic to the more complex. Community assessment, often overlooked in program development and communication efforts, can be critical to successful communication about and implementation of the activity.

Increasingly, libraries serve as connectors, joining community organizations with people who need their services and connecting both people and organizations with authoritative information resources to meet shared needs. Knowing one's community is a key factor in the successful completion of this community role. Successful program delivery is accomplished when libraries use community assessment to better understand and respond to changing community needs, and build communication efforts around those needs.

Assessing community financial education needs is an important first step. The library marketing team researches community demographics and reaches out to others in the community for information on specific target audiences. Since financial education needs differ dramatically based on the particular financial issues library customers are facing, community demographics play a key role in marketing planning. The National Financial Capability Study (FINRA 2012) is a good starting point. This study provides state-level data about "indicators of financial capability and evaluate[s] how these indicators vary with underlying demographic, behavioral, attitudinal and financial literacy characteristics" (FINRA 2014).

Additional assessment tools are available from the SIYL website, including sample survey instruments, Gen X pre- and post-survey instruments, and other tips and successful techniques for learning about specific community needs related to financial education.

Schaumburg Township District Library in Illinois conducted a community assessment and learned that approximately fourteen thousand individuals in the community were unemployed at the time of the library's SIYL grant application. They identified the primary target audience as Schaumburg residents twenty-five to fifty years of age who were nonlibrary users and who were struggling financially. One critical strategy was to train local employment counselors and social service providers to serve as intermediaries by providing basic financial information and resources and referring clients to the library for assistance. Their understanding of the needs of their target audience informed the communication process.

Once the marketing team circles in on the potential target audience, it's very important to involve key informants—individuals at organizations that serve the target audience. Listening to these key informants can generate a wealth of information about the target audience: their financial problems to be solved, challenges to be overcome, and worries to be alleviated. Focusing on the specific audience reminds the marketing team that "it's not us, it's them." Consulting with trusted friends and intermediaries who represent and work with that audience keeps the customer in front of us as we develop marketing messages. The initial marketing exercise should be carried out by the marketing team, as shown in textbox 26.1. Consult the two worksheets provided in the appendix to this chapter as aids for this exercise. This is a great activity to do over coffee, and it solidifies the outward focus of the marketing team.

The second step of the marketing planning process, "Know Your Library," helps the marketing team accurately assess the library in order to ensure that marketing messages present the library in a way that connects with the target audience. Library staff and volunteers know their own libraries pretty well, but the marketing team can learn something new by taking a systematic look at the library. Marketing teams are encouraged to select from the following exercises to get to know the library in a different way.

KNOW YOUR LIBRARY EXERCISES FOR MARKETING TEAMS

Brainstorm

Brainstorm the first words that come to mind when answering the following questions:

Value: What is the library value to the community?

Values: What are the core values of the library's service to the community?

Voice: What is the tone or personality to be projected in communication about this educational opportunity?

The marketing team can use the words generated by this brainstorm in marketing messages to remind the community of the value and values of the library—and to ensure that the message has the right voice and tone.

Textbox 26.1
Know Your Community Exercise for Marketing Teams

Brainstorm ten questions a potential partner might ask about the library educational opportunity, and make a list of seven to ten organizations (clubs, agencies, groups, businesses, etc.) that are potential library partners or represent potential library customers in the target audience for the training.

Use your local newspaper, telephone directory, or other appropriate resources for this activity. Contact local churches, social service organizations, and senior centers, and ask staff for recommendations of community groups. A simple Google search for "community groups" in your area can provide a list of potential partner groups. For each of the organizations listed, provide the following information:

- Name, address, email, and telephone number for a contact person in the organization
- Connection between library financial education activities, services, and products—and the benefit to their organization
- Possible activities that would communicate—or market—the library's services and products to the organization (e.g., offsite demonstrations or training, speaking engagements, etc.)
- Ways a partnership with this organization would benefit the library (it's not an accident that this is the last prompt; the marketing team is training itself to think about the customer need and the partner organization first—and the library benefit last)

Guided Visualization

Try to approach this with a fresh eye. Turn down the lights. Sit with eyes closed. Ask the marketing team to pretend that they are members of the target group, a person with no experience with the library. Put yourself in their shoes and ask a recorder to chart the marketing team's observations as they pretend to walk up the sidewalk to the library, pass through the door, and move throughout the library. Start at the street or in the parking lot. Notice the exterior signage and condition of your library. How are customers greeted when they enter the library? Is the library arrangement convenient, easily accessible? Is your library signage easy to read? Is it easy to spot library staff? Are the staff members approachable? What barriers to the library's staff and materials do library customers face?

Photo Safari

One way to really get to know your library is to try to see it through the eyes of a stranger by studying photographs of the library. Work with the marketing team to take photographs of your library. Take the photographs from the point of view of the customer. Go outside and enter the library through the door that library customers use. Look at everything you see with fresh eyes and take pictures from the perspective of someone who has never been in the library before. As much as possible, analyze the photos from the point of view of someone who is not familiar with the library. Try to involve representatives of the partner organizations and members of the target audience in this analysis, especially if they are not current library customers.

Mystery Customers

Ask representatives of the partner organizations and members of the target audience to "mystery shop" the library. Mystery customers are asked to look for information to help solve their financial problems and share their assessment of existing library services and products to meet their financial education needs with the marketing team.

The marketing team can use the observations generated by the guided visualization, photo safari, and mystery customers exercises to inform communication messages and reform the library space prior to initiating financial education activities. These exercises can help the marketing team assess the curriculum, the physical facility, and the collection to determine how they will meet the needs of the target audience and what needs to be communicated about the library resources to sell the product (training and resources) to the target audience.

To initiate the next step, "Implement Communication Strategies," the marketing team can use the Worksheet Strategy Menu provided in this chapter's appendix to determine the mix of communication strategies that will be used, who will be responsible, and when they will be implemented. This mix of communication strategies is critically important for successful project implementation. When SIYL grant participants were surveyed about their most successful promotional activities, the responses included a mix of both old and new methods. The chart in figure 26.2 shows communication activities that were ranked by respondents as either moderately effective or very effective for promoting grant activities.

Interestingly, old-fashioned word-of-mouth activities ranked for three successive years by grant participants as highly successful marketing methods. As we discuss later in this chapter, libraries are encouraged to initiate activities that build word-of-mouth marketing—not just wait around for it to happen. In-library displays were another popular means of getting materials into the hands of community members. However, many participants also explored nontraditional marketing techniques, often in an effort to reach nonlibrary users and community members who traditionally do not walk through the library's front door.

Orange County Library System in Florida implemented two successful SIYL grants in which they partnered with the Graduate School of Business at Rollins College to serve the financial and investor education needs of lower-income and Spanish-speaking residents, especially wage earners in the region's hospitality industry. Library staff implemented effective marketing and outreach activities that resulted in increased awareness among this target audience. These included colorful ads placed on buses, creative videos targeting the hospitality trade, and other nontraditional methods that were de-

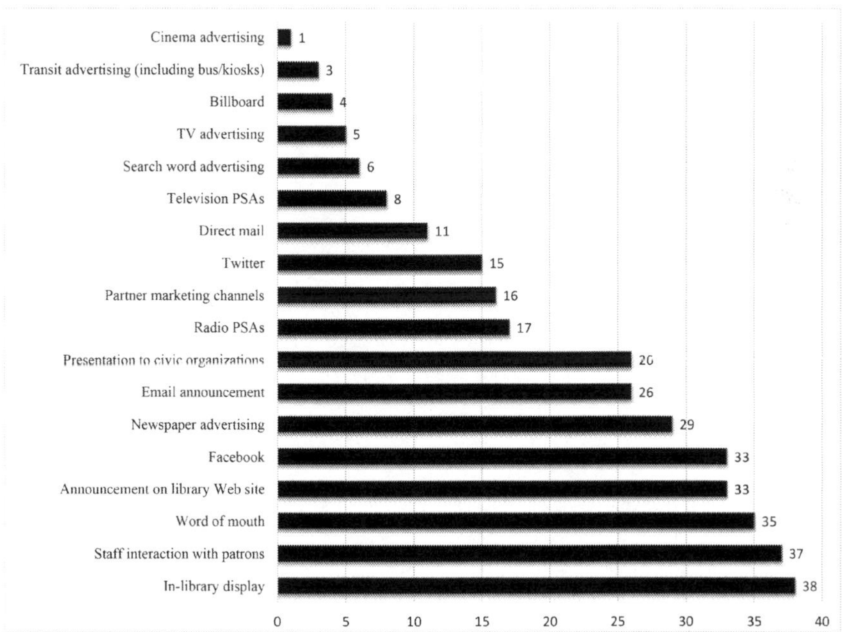

Figure 26.2. Communication Methods Ranked by Their Degree of Success in Promoting Grant Activities.

veloped following analysis of their target market. The project manager noted, "The marketing we did promoting the workshops had quite an impact because we got quite a few people coming into the library who'd never been to there before and really just came because they saw one of the bus ads for the workshop. So when they said, 'I'm here for the workshop,' we responded, 'Welcome to the library.' We showed them what else we had to offer, and we got new cardholders as a result." Also, they created videos specifically targeted at people who work in the service industry, employing the largest percentage of people in the area (see, e.g., "Money Tips," https://www.youtube.com/watch?v=4DD-0dx2eKs).

Richland Library in Columbia, South Carolina, sought to improve the financial literacy of low- to moderate-income residents, with a special focus on the African American community. The library partnered with Lunch Money, a children's band that "brings indie-rock to family audiences," to write a children's song about money, earning, and saving for the future ("Shake, Shake, My Piggy-Bank": https://www.youtube.com/watch?v=X7HZoZbhiSY). They integrated performances into the library's story-time programs and other events for young children. The library also worked with Columbia College and local schools to engage teens in creating performances and games that teach younger children financial basics.

MIX THE OLD WITH THE NEW

Brooklyn Public Library developed its highly popular Teen Virtual Investment Club as part of their second SIYL grant. The club is a competitive financial literacy program for teens. Volunteers (ages fourteen to nineteen) attend free training from experienced financial educators to learn how to make smart investment choices and work closely with each other and educators to manage an online virtual stock portfolio while building personal finance knowledge and skills. The original club was expanded to engage more teens in the library's branches. Teens were encouraged to recruit their peers, and they used social media to enhance their learning. Peer recruiting proved very effective and resulted in the unintended consequence of empowering the teen recruiters, who adopted the role of representing both the program and the library, demonstrating a sense of ownership and becoming loyal, informed library representatives among their peer population.

Greenville County Library System in South Carolina created a multifaceted marketing theme to reach their target audience of low-income women. In a needs assessment survey, these women had used words like "dread," "nervous," and "indifferent" to describe their attitudes toward managing money. The campaign used relatable terms such as "dreams," "success," and "empowerment." It was called "Your Recipe for Success: Become Master

Chef of Your Financial Future." Along with the approachable, nonthreatening tone, Greenville identified opportunities to intersect with the target audience:

- Created bus ads
- Engaged Spanish-language media and placed local cable television ads on the Lifetime channel, Food Network, Oxygen, and A&E
- Distributed twelve thousand newsletters at grocery stores

The images and metaphors in this project turned personal finance assumptions into changed attitudes, changed attitudes into changed behaviors, and changed behaviors into changed financial habits.

As the marketing team determines the marketing mix, the focus should be telling the story of this educational opportunity, who the potential learner is, and how they will be helped by the experience. With each communication strategy, the team also asks who can *help* tell the story using this strategy—identifying ambassadors who can help create word-of-mouth marketing (like Brooklyn's teen recruiters). Events inside and outside the library can raise awareness of financial education curriculum and other resources. The event planning form provided in the appendix will be a helpful guide (figure 26.03, Know Your Community Worksheet).

When crafting marketing messages, personalize the message and lead with the concerns of the target audience. Answer their question, "What's in this for me?," before it gets asked. An example of this can be seen if, instead of this message—"The library has financial education materials available, workshops scheduled . . ."—the marketing team uses this message—"Money for college or to buy a home? Take a free, online, self-paced class to improve your skills at money management and help you meet your goals."

One way to personalize the message is to "storify" it—tell a story (protecting confidentiality) of someone who represents the target audience and uses the educational opportunity to solve a financial problem, overcome a challenge, or alleviate worries and fears. Including a testimonial in the message can be a good way to "storify" the message—something like, "Susan L. lives in rural Nebraska. She says her family lives 'paycheck to paycheck' and worries that they won't be able to buy a home. She's not alone. In Nebraska, 19 percent of individuals reported that over the past year, their household spent more than their income (National Financial Capability Study 2012). Susan learned about credit scores, home mortgages, incentives for first-time homebuyers, and more at the Communityville Public Library."

This story is a good hook. It leads with the customer and mentions what the library can do about her concerns. It appeals to the heart and to the head. But what's missing? Always include a call to action in every communication message. A call to action is something like, "Call the library at 444-555-1234 to register for next month's homebuyer's workshop, or email the library at moneyforyou@communityvillelibrary.org to get your login password for the online home ownership class offered by the Communityville Public Library."

Evaluation of the effectiveness of the communication effort is critical to crafting the next message. Feedback is essential to inform new communication efforts. Ask customers, "How did you hear about the program/resources/curriculum?" Ask the partners and intermediaries what they observed and if there is any buzz in the community. Accepting feedback with an open mind and an open heart is essential to the marketing process.

Planning for the marketing aspect of your financial education program is a critical piece of a successful program. When well executed, the planning process facilitates reaching the target audience and sending a message that motivates participation.

APPENDIX

Communication:

Getting the Word Out about Customer Training

Know Your Community – Exercise for Marketing Teams

Brainstorm ten questions that a potential partner might ask about the library educational opportunity.

1. ______________________________

2. ______________________________

3. ______________________________

4. ______________________________

5. ______________________________

6. ______________________________

7. ______________________________

8. ______________________________

9. ______________________________

10. ______________________________

Know Your Community Worksheet.

Organization:			
Name:	Phone:	Address:	Email:
Connection:	Activities:		
The benefit to them:	The benefit to the Library:		

Organization:		
Name:	Phone:	Address:
Connection:	Activities:	
The benefit to them:	The benefit to the Library:	

Organization:		
Name:	Phone:	Address:
Connection:	Activities:	
The benefit to them:	The benefit to the Library:	

Organization:		
Name:	Phone:	Address:
Connection:	Activities:	
The benefit to them:	The benefit to the Library:	

Organization:		
Name:	Phone:	Address:
Connection:	Activities:	
The benefit to them:	The benefit to the Library:	

Organization:		
Name:	Phone:	Address:
Connection:	Activities:	
The benefit to them:	The benefit to the Library:	

Organization:		
Name:	Phone:	Address:
Connection:	Activities:	
The benefit to them:	The benefit to the Library:	

Organization:		
Name:	Phone:	Address:
Connection:	Activities:	
The benefit to them:	The benefit to the Library:	

Know Your Community Index Cards.

Strategy	Library Customer Target	Ideas for Our Library	Target Date	Person Responsible	Results
Outreach: **Share the message directly.** **Go where the customers are.** **Partner with organizations.** Speaking engagements Interview shows Sponsorship of community events/activities Offsite seminars Offsite workshops Service club membership Other club memberships Offsite delivery of library services Offsite demonstrations Offsite displays Other					

Build Word of Mouth

Strategy	Library Customer Target	Ideas for Our Library	Target Date	Person Responsible	Results
Print: **Customize. Call to Action.** · Newspaper · Magazines · "Shoppers" (free or classified ad magazines) · Yellow Pages · Special directories (regional, seasonal, Chamber) · Trade or industry directories (e.g., *Thomas' Register*) · Cooperative ad support from your library vendors · Flyers · Posters · Handouts Other **Paid Advertising** **Professional Assistance.** Radio Television Outdoor billboards Other					

Build Word of Mouth

Worksheet Strategy Menu.

Strategy	Library Customer Target	Ideas for Our Library	Target Date	Person Responsible	Results
Specialty Advertising Matchbooks, keychains, other novelties Calendars Datebooks Bookmarks Other					
One-On-One Selling Presentation materials Storytelling. Elevator Speech. Personal letters Customized proposals Telemarketing Library personnel training Other					

Build Word of Mouth

Strategy	Library Customer Target	Ideas for Our Library	Target Date	Person Responsible	Results
Telemarketing Inquiry handling/reference Direct marketing by phone Service: customer complaints, follow-up, special offers Other					
Facilities Site location and shared advertising Signage (inside and outside) Window displays Point-of-use displays Fixtures and layout of library Lighting Other					
Other Promotion Electronic techniques: · Web site · E-mail · Social Networking Blimps and balloons Sandwich boards Temporary Signs Other					

Build Word of Mouth

Worksheet Strategy Menu, *continued.*

Event			**Date**
Location		**Staff Contact**	
Planned Attendance	General Public	Stakeholders/Partners	

Program			
Performers/Speakers Involved		Cost	In-kind Services
		Contract Signed?	
Performer Contact Info:	Phone	Email	
Room Set-up:	Tables/Chairs/Etc.	Format	

Technical What is needed?	Sound equip. needed	Who will provide and operate?	Cost
	Projector/Laptop/Screen	Who will provide and operate?	Cost
	Other	Who will provide and operate?	Cost

Publicity/Advertising Who will create and distribute?	Poster		Cost
	Newspaper	Date Sent	Cost
	Library Website	Date Sent	
	Radio	Date Sent	Cost
	Other		Cost

Refreshments What is needed?	Food	Who will provide?	Cost
	Drinks	Who will provide?	Cost
	Napkins/plates/tableware/etc.	Who will provide?	Cost

Supplies	Special program needs	Who will provide?	Cost

Final Attendance	General Public	Stakeholders/Partners	**Total Cost**	

Follow Up With Partners/ Stakeholders & Speakers	Thank you:	Discuss opportunities for partnering:
	☐ Note ☐ Call ☐ E-mail	☐ Volunteer ☐ Training ☐ Funding ☐ Other

Event Planning Form.

REFERENCES

FINRA. 2012. "National Financial Capability Study." http://www.usfinancialcapability.org/results.php?region=NE.

———. 2014. "About the National Financial Capability Study." http://www.usfinancialcapability.org/about.php.

Chapter Twenty-Seven

MoneyFitness

One Academic Library's Experience of Building a Financial Literacy Program at a Small Liberal Arts College

Kate Moody

In the spring of 2015, Lane Library at Ripon College, a small, residential liberal arts college, began offering the financial literacy workshop MoneyFitness. The course was six weeks long, meeting once a week with two-hour sessions between four and six o'clock at night. The first hour focused on personal money management and the second hour on finding and winning scholarships. Students received no credit for attending, yet in the first semester it was offered, sixteen students, 2 percent of the population of Ripon College, completed MoneyFitness.

HOW MONEYFITNESS CAME INTO BEING

Recently, student loan debt became the second largest form of consumer debt after home mortgages, surpassing credit cards (Chopra 2013). While there are good arguments for why a liberal arts school is not responsible for teaching life skills like financial literacy, we felt that we could not ignore the fact that we are increasingly graduating students with unprecedented debt, which will have a lasting and potentially negative effect on their lives. If we believe that such a debt burden is worth incurring, we should at least give students the tools to manage its effects on their finances appropriately.

Data show that college students are not just bad with money; a majority are functionally financially illiterate (Inceptia 2013). On our campus, in speaking with students who had taken out student loans, we found that only a small minority knew the difference between a subsidized and an unsubsidized loan; just one student was able to explain how credit cards make money. These are anecdotal examples but indicative of a common problem and suggested a need among the students for exposure to basic financial concepts. Lastly, the recent initiative by Association of College & Research Libraries (ACRL) President Trevor Dawes to bring financial literacy to academic libraries highlighted precedent and the need for us to get involved.

USING OUR STRENGTHS

We began brainstorming what our financial literacy program would look like by reviewing programs at other schools by searching online and reading through the 2013–2014 *College & Research Library News* series on financial literacy. The programs we found tended to be based out of either financial aid or student services or were their own department. Some schools even offer financial literacy courses for credit. They are supported by multiple grants from national and state organizations. They have full-time staff dedicated to financial literacy. While we did not have the resources of the other schools, we did have the determination to create a successful program.

To make our size work for us, we leveraged the advantages of being part of a small school—little bureaucracy and a close relationship with the students. The program was given the green light after a short discussion with the chair of the library. We created the logo and all advertisements, physical and digital, ourselves. To communicate to all students at once, librarians at Ripon can send an all-student email at any time. This accommodating environment reduced the amount of time and effort it took to get the project up and running. Because of the tight-knit community, students came to the librarians in person to learn more about the program and librarians could promote the workshop to students they knew on an individual basis.

DETERMINING PATRON NEED

One of our main concerns was getting students who most needed financial literacy training to join a class that offered no credit. To involve students who would otherwise never come to a financial literacy program, we paired it with a scholarship workshop. We got this idea from Roggenkamp (2014). To assess student interest we sent out a "one-minute survey" that asked students for the following:

- Demographic information
- If they had taken out loans for school

- If they needed help paying for school
- How many scholarships they had applied for
- How many they planned on applying for
- If they were interested in taking a scholarship workshop

There were 141 respondents, 18 percent of the student body. Nearly all needed help paying for school. About one-third had applied for more than nine scholarships, and one-third were planning to apply for more than nine scholarships. Twenty percent did not know what kind of student loans they had. Fifty-four percent were very interested in taking a scholarship workshop, and only 7 percent professed no interest. We already knew that there was a need for financial literacy on campus; now we had our proof that there was a market for a scholarship workshop.

COLLABORATORS

In 2014, at a speaking event at Marquette University, Trevor Dawes, former president of the ACRL, discussed the need for libraries to make connections across campus to support financial literacy. These connections could aid in promotion, bringing in speakers, and getting students involved. When asked who in particular we should collaborate with on campus, the answer was essentially everyone who will have you.

To identify collaborators, we listed all the departments and offices on campus that might be interested in working with us and contacted them. We had hoped to involve the Financial Aid Office and Student Support Services, but both of these offices were satisfied with their existing offerings, which touch on aspects of financial literacy. Ripon's Center for Social Responsibility, an organization dedicated to reducing injustice and guiding students into leadership roles to engage and support local area organizations, was our most enthusiastic supporter, offering to connect us with downtown businesses. We joined meetings of RC Hawk, a student life organization made up of representatives from departments improving any of six aspects of student wellness, including financial wellness. This forum provided contact with departments working closely with students' needs. They were very helpful in getting word out about MoneyFitness to students and employees alike.

Alumni Affairs and Career Services offered to have a panel discussion with recent graduates who were working in the financial industry to talk about life after school and what they thought was most important for students to know about money before graduation. Admissions was supportive as they saw it as a good enticement for prospective students; however, they needed outcomes before they could throw any weight behind our initiative. Our most successful collaboration was with the student business club, Enactus. Their president, Taihua Li, a passionate advocate for personal finance, became a cofounder of the MoneyFitness program. He helped teach the workshop, created curriculum, and designed the advertisements.

Our overall experience in trying to collaborate with other departments was a mixed bag. Mr. Dawes's advice, to get as many collaborators as you can, was wise as otherwise we would have only contacted the two departments who ended up turning us down. We ultimately drew on our flexibility as educators and decided to teach the workshop ourselves, with the help of Mr. Li. Our library staff is already comfortable with the idea of teaching outside our areas of expertise and crafting programming for an uninitiated audience since we have been running a MakerSpace workshop series for years, which requires librarians to teach basic skills in software, design, and other digital humanities media. If we could not find anyone else to teach the workshop, we would do it ourselves.

RESOURCE EVALUATION

To teach our own classes, we needed to get informed on the topic and be able to point students to solid resources when they wanted to learn more. There is an avalanche of information on financial literacy available online and in print. The quality and reliability of these sources varies widely. Many banks and credit institutions have resources that can be very useful. But buyer beware! While the majority of the information they present is accurate, they tend to show bias and present information that is in their own, rather than the consumer's, interest.

Federal and state government financial literacy materials are far better sources, as they are not trying to sell products or perpetuate debt-incurring consumer behavior. However, occasionally they can be hard to navigate and show all the signs of having been written by a committee. Here are a few of the sites we relied on to educate ourselves and our students:

- For creating class content, the FDIC Teacher Online Resource Center: https://www.fdic.gov/consumers/education/teachers.html.
- The Consumer Financial Protection Bureau has a section of its website dedicated to helping librarians spread financial literacy. They also offer online training and digital and print materials: http://www.consumerfinance.gov/library-resources/.
- MyCreditUnion.gov has great resources and tools for consumers and educators, as well as useful links to other government websites: http://www.mycreditunion.gov/.
- MyMoney.gov breaks down financial literacy into five main categories. Helpful for coming up with curriculum: http://www.mymoney.gov/.

- The ALA provides a short bibliography of resources from FINRA (the Financial Industry Regulatory Authority) that covers points other sites missed: http://smartinvesting.ala.org/reliable-content/.

MARKETING

An important step in marketing a financial literacy program to college students, we believe, is to call it anything but "financial literacy." To the average nineteen-year-old, that term sounds official, intimidating, and indefinable. When explaining the program to our students, we prefer terms like "money management" and sometimes "personal finance." This is why we chose to call our program MoneyFitness and consciously left "financial literacy" off all of our materials. The title incorporates ideas students are already familiar and comfortable with. Students know and like money. They also know that fitness is a good thing, even if they may not practice it themselves.

We found that when we approached students to see if they would be interested in taking part in "MoneyFitness, a money management workshop," we got a positive reaction. They listened courteously, were open to the idea, and thought it would be an important course to take. The response was notably different when they were asked if they would be interested in a financial literacy workshop. In that situation, they would often get a little tense, fumble with their words, admit ignorance when it came to money issues, and say they should take it but probably would not.

We began advertising at the end of the fall semester. The workshop was to start in the second week of the next semester. Throughout campus we put up posters designed to garner interest. The posters said things like, "in small text] If you win one $500 scholarship, that will be the same as earning [large text] $35.71 an hour" and "6 weeks of free money, coming soon." The bottom of both posters were lined with small images of one-hundred-dollar bills, just like phone numbers to be torn off and taken home. Our goal was not to explain what the workshop was but simply to plant a seed in the students' minds that something new and big would be coming to campus.

We used the basic economic principle of supply and demand to increase the number of students who wanted to take the workshop. Unlike most library classes open to the community, MoneyFitness was not a drop-in workshop. The classroom it was held in easily holds twenty students, but we only made twelve spots available. To be considered for one of these spots, students had to compete with each other by filling out a short application asking them about their loans, if they could define a set of financial terms, what they knew about personal finance, and finally, why they wanted to get into the program. The application was embedded into an email, making it easy to fill out. By creating scarcity and competition for the workshop, we increased student demand.

We had a very positive response to the email. Many students came to us to find out more. We offered two sessions of MoneyFitness in the spring semester, we had a total of thirty-five students apply for only twenty-four spots. We chose who would get in based on their enthusiasm, reason for applying, and student standing. Of the students admitted, we had a 66 percent retention rate.

CONTROLLING COSTS

There are many free resources for curriculum building. The FDIC offers teachers a free CD-ROM of financial literacy lessons and PowerPoint presentations targeted to students. Banks sent free brochures on financial literacy, which were, mostly, useful. The government websites such as those listed above and sites like YouTube provided the rest of the course content.

As with so many projects, MoneyFitness was run on a shoestring budget. We bought a few financial literacy and scholarship books to add to the collection from our general book fund. We contacted various parties on campus for support and managed to get the Dean of Students to pay for pizza, once. We used the leftover snacks purchased for finals to have during our breaks. We met in the library's computer lab and used library equipment such as whiteboards, projectors, and computers—all free of cost. The one item purchased that was not library related was some play money we used during the budgeting and credit card exercises. Six thousand dollars of play money cost us roughly twenty dollars in real money. Printouts, the few made, were done with regular library funds.

CURRICULUM

We tried to base our curriculum on the data we collected from our students and on various studies of college students' financial knowledge. From all this data, we came to the conclusion that our workshop needed to start with money management basics and cover things we are all expected to know but are rarely formally educated on. After brainstorming possible class topics with Mr. Li, we came up with the following six-week financial literacy curriculum (the scholarship workshop curriculum is omitted):

1. Importance of money management, overview of workshop, budgeting basics
2. Budgeting and building emergency savings

3. Credit score (including finding out what yours is) and credit card basics
4. Student loans (types, payback options) and credit cards (interest rates, types, how to choose one, how to use it responsibly)
5. Financial institutions (banks and credit unions) and products (CDs, money market accounts, stocks, bonds, mutual funds)
6. Taxes (the progressive tax system and the difference between marginal and average tax rate) and saving for retirement (options and the importance of starting early)

Working with a student was tremendously helpful in determining what students needed to learn. He had valuable insights into student finances, and during class the other students were able to relate to him.

In trying to get the students engaged and make the subject matter applicable to their lives, we incorporated an interactive exercise into each class. Class began with a quick recap of what we had gone over during the last class. When we needed to emphasize the reason a week's topic was important, we began with an interactive exercise to highlight what happens if money is mismanaged. For example, we have a budget role-playing game in which one student plays "The Banker" and the other plays "Jane Dough." The Banker gives and takes money as Jane gets paid and spends it but does not explain what the money is being spent on. After about five minutes, the students go through the same process, except Jane is told what she has spent her money on. It is a succinct illustration of why budgeting is vital to proper money management, and led to productive, sometimes heated, class discussions. No matter the interactive exercise we began with, it was followed by a short lecture on the topic, and students worked together or individually to apply the topic to their own lives.

If we did not need to "sell" the subject, we would start with a lecture and possibly a short YouTube video, then move on to an exercise and class discussion. We found videos kept students' interest, legitimized what we taught, and reinforced our lessons. The combination of lecture and video helped cement the information in our students' understanding.

OUTCOMES

We were very pleased with the success of MoneyFitness. All students had to take a pre- and post-MoneyFitness assessment, a short series mostly of true-and-false questions. The postworkshop test also included a section evaluating the workshop itself.

- The average entrance score was 57.5 percent; the exit score was 80.0 percent.
- When asked if they would recommend this workshop to other students, on a scale of 1 (I would not recommend it) to 5 (I would recommend it to everyone), students rated MoneyFitness a 4.6.
- 93 percent of students said they did change or planned to change the way they manage their money.
- 86 percent of students felt they had a better grasp on money management.

PROGRAM REVISIONS

The first session of MoneyFitness went well, but we identified several things we could improve upon for subsequent sessions.

Greater Focus on Less Information

Classes must be tightly focused to achieve our goals. We had to triage what we had time to teach, what was essential to cover, and what should be built into a separate class or left out entirely. For example, the first time we discussed budgets, we tried to include converting expense categories into percentages. Explaining the mathematics took up too much of our limited time, rushed the rest of the lesson, and confused and sidetracked students' attention. When we ran the budgeting class in the second session, we simplified the lesson by concentrating our efforts on getting students to understand why budgeting is necessary and empowering, how to build a budget, and building a budget for themselves. Greater focus on less information was more successful. We provided additional resources if students wanted to go deeper with the topic.

Class Time and More Food

Having taught this twice, we plan to shorten the length of each class from two hours to one, and to focus each session on either money management or scholarships, but not both. From a teaching perspective, two hours is ideal for covering two discrete topics, but it is a lot to ask of students. Student feedback suggested that we would receive more applications if the time commitment were shorter. And, to no one's surprise, they also said we would get more involvement if we regularly provided pizza.

Do Not Give Out a Syllabus

Some students do not understand why certain topics are important, or they believe they already know enough, so there is no reason to come to class. If they know the topic well, we want them in class so they can help explain it to their peers. If they think they know the topic but only have a partial or incorrect understanding, we can correct those errors. We found it best for attendance to let the next class topic be unveiled at the next class.

Take Attendance

Taking attendance discourages skipping class, keeps track of student engagement, and helped us learn their names.

Classroom Camaraderie Is Essential

We increased the amount of time spent on role-playing activities and class discussions, as these built a positive classroom dynamic. The more the students got to know each other, the more likely they were to open up, offer advice, ask questions, request help, and be willing to take risks. They also tended to retain information far better through discussion than any other method.

Make the Material Relatable

It is hard for our college students to understand the burden of paying for rent and groceries, so using those as examples for budgeting seemed abstract to them. In contrast, the idea of searching for the best deal hit home when we asked what everyone pays each month for their cell phones. Many students pay for their own phone, think of it as a necessity, and the prices they pay range from thirty dollars to upward of one hundred dollars.

Give out Certificates of Completion

Students who attended five of six sessions earned a certificate of completion. To add levity and encourage pride in this accomplishment, we played "Pomp and Circumstance," called their names, and gave them their award. The students thought it was fun and appreciated the recognition of their efforts. We took a class picture with everyone holding their certificates. This is also a nice reminder for the librarians of why we have taken on this extra work.

FUTURE PLANS

MoneyFitness was highly successful in its first semester, graduating 2 percent of the student body. We plan on expanding the program to increase the number of students reached and the manner in which we reach them. Our financial literacy program will consist of three divisions:

1. MoneyFitness workshop
2. Outreach programming
3. Online education

It will be structured with six positions: four peer mentors, who are managed by an intern, all of whom are going to be supervised by the librarian.

As the library does not have funds to pay students who are not doing library work, we have collaborated with our Center for Social Responsibility, who will fund an "Economic Justice through Financial Literacy" internship. The intern and peer tutors will be trained in personal finance, counseling, and teaching methodology. The intern will teach MoneyFitness, organize and present money management programming to various student groups, and manage the peer tutors. Peer tutors will not be paid positions. They will work with other students on a one-on-one basis for anyone who wants to learn about managing their money and serve as teaching assistants during MoneyFitness. The intern will also implement CashCourse, a free online, customizable money management tutorial from the National Endowment for Financial Education, for students who want to learn more but do not want to attend MoneyFitness or work with a peer tutor. We have applied for a grant to get trainers for the intern and peer mentors and pay for food for MoneyFitness participants.

REFERENCES

Chopra, Rohit. 2013. "Student Debt Swells, Federal Loans Now Top a Trillion." *Consumer Protection Financial Bureau Blog*, July 17. http://www.consumerfinance.gov/newsroom/student-debt-swells-federal-loans-now-top-a-trillion/.

Inceptia. 2013. "First-Year College Students Score Poorly in Basic Financial Literacy, Inceptia Survey Reports." Press Release, January 22. https://www.inceptia.org/resource-center/news/jan-22-2013/.

Roggenkamp, John. 2014. "Financial Literacy and Community Colleges: How Can Libraries Get Involved." *College & Research Library News* 75 (3): 142–43.

Chapter Twenty-Eight

Money Smart Week Activities for Any Library

Joanne Kuster and Maryann Mori

Each April, Money Smart Week is conducted nationally. The American Library Association is a national partner of Money Smart Week (MSW) and encourages libraries to participate in activities and to promote their financial literacy resources during MSW. According to the American Library Association (ALA), "in 2014, 700 plus public, academic, school, and even prison libraries in 48 states participated" in MSW (ALA 2015). Often it is easier for libraries to participate in activities that are sponsored or coordinated by a local or statewide MSW committee, which is the case for librarians in Iowa, where a strong MSW planning team exists statewide along with several regional MSW committees.

However, the absence of a state or regional MSW committee should not deter librarians from getting involved in financial literacy events or from participating in MSW activities. Librarians may want to consider leading the way to develop MSW ideas that can be shared among neighboring libraries, or they may want to serve on a local, regional, or statewide MSW planning committee (if one exists) in order to help the committee realize the value of libraries in the promotion of financial literacy. It is possible that a local librarian will be the impetus for a larger circle of financial literacy activities as a result of this enthusiasm! In fact, the now-retired director at Dubuque Public Library, Michelle Helmer, wanted to be involved in MSW before Iowa had a planning team in that area. She was very involved in financial literacy education and always did a lot of library programming for MSW. Because of Michelle's initial efforts in her area, Iowa now has an extremely active local MSW planning team in Dubuque.

There are many activities libraries can do to observe MSW, but the Money Smart Week Iowa committee has developed numerous creative ideas almost any type of library anywhere can implement. The following are twelve financial literacy event ideas that can be replicated exactly or with variations by any kind of library. These ideas were created especially for Money Smart Week but could be conducted at any time of the year in order to promote financial literacy information. Per Money Smart Week stipulations, all events should be offered free of charge to participants and without any kind of sales pitch or profit motive.

MONEY SMART WEEK READ

The Money Smart Week READ or "MSW READ" is an event for kids and parents or grandparents. It is not a typical preschool story time. Rather, it involves older children and their adult caregiver, who together explore concepts of a book, complete an activity, and receive a copy of the designated book to further discuss the topic at home. In 2014, MSW Iowa piloted a program that provided public libraries with books that focused on the themes of saving and investing. Two different books were selected for the READ, based on availability, topic, and quantity pricing. The first title, designated for students in grades two through four, was *Rock, Brock, and the Savings Shock* by Sheila Bair. The book features a rhyming story about two brothers—one a spendthrift and the other a saver. The second title, designated for older students in grades seven and eight, was *Stock Market Pie: Grandma Helps Emily Make a Million* by J. M. Seymour. This book covers more advanced ideas of saving and investing, including concepts of investing in the stock market. Participating libraries received a copy of each book for the library's collection and up to twenty-five copies of each title to give away at the library-sponsored READ events. Iowa AARP sponsored the program, sponsored the cost of about six hundred books for the READ programs, and encouraged libraries to target grandparents with grandchildren.

The pilot program was so successful that it was repeated again in 2015 with books that focused on entrepreneurship. Longtime MSW partner the Iowa Credit Union Foundation requested to be the READ sponsor for 2015 and provided about nine hundred books. The goal was to connect kids with their parents in discussions about summer jobs, being an entrepreneur, and creating products. The 2015 READ featured *Isabel's Carwash* by Sheila Bair (for students in grades three and four) and *Entrepreneur Extraordinaire: Grandpa Helps Emily Build a Business* by J. M. Seymour (for students in grades five and above). Grade levels were tweaked after the 2014 program and based on recommendations and comments from participating librarians. As previously mentioned, the READ program differs from traditional children's story-time programs; instead of actually reading the book, librarians (or local entrepreneurs) conduct a short discussion about the general topic, perhaps tie in another read-aloud book that brings home the topic, considers a craft or activity tie-in, and highlights portions of the featured READ book. As an example for the 2015 theme of entrepreneurship, librarians and program attendees could have a short discussion about some famous (or local) entrepreneurs and also discuss how kids might start a business to make money in the summer (think lawn mowing, babysitting, gardening). Perhaps a local business owner could address the attendees and discuss (on a child's level) the process of starting and maintaining the business.

A successful READ program was conducted at the Muscatine Public Library in Iowa in 2014. The programming librarian, Betty Collins, wrote in a message to the MSW Iowa chair these comments and descriptions of her program:

> I wanted to let you know that we held our Money Smart Week event on Thursday . . . at 6 p.m. We had a healthy snack (fruit, veggies, cheese slices, milk, and juice) and channeled this program into our regular Thursday evening family literacy session called Sparkplugs. We had advertised via our Facebook page, our website, in-house flyers, and flyers sent out to all local second and third grade students by way of the public schools. . . . We began with the snack, then invited kids to sit down in the front of the room where they met a historic Muscatine businessman, Oscar Grossheim, famous local photographer from the early 1900s. He was portrayed by one of our reference librarians/local history specialists. He spoke about how he had needed to save money in order to establish a successful photography business in town and encouraged the audience to be wise with their money as well. He then sat down with the kids to listen to me read *Rock, Brock, and the Savings Shock*. After the book was done, we gave the kids a demonstration of how to make themselves a "piggy bank" out of recyclable materials such as a macaroni box, a yogurt container, or other free, easy-to-find materials. (Collins 2014)

After the program, those participants who had preregistered for the program received a free copy of the book, provided by the AARP sponsors.

Libraries participating in the READ program are provided with promotional posters that feature Ben Franklin in a library (Ben was an entrepreneur and is a leading "mascot" figure for MSW Iowa) and suggestions for actively promoting their READ in their community. Suggestions to librarians for promotion of the READ include these ideas:

- Send the provided press release to local media.
- Use the Ben Franklin posters to display the library's event date and time.
- Put the READ event on local community calendars.
- Add the event to the library's calendar of events.
- Invite homeschoolers, scout groups, 4-Hers, and the like.

- Send invitations to upper elementary teachers (TAG teachers are particularly interested in entrepreneurship).
- Connect with local financial groups such as Junior Achievement, Chamber of Commerce, SCORE, or the Small Business Administration.
- Set up a display of library books about entrepreneurs and businesses.
- Consider real stories of entrepreneurs that would appeal to children (think Walt Disney and Bill Gates) and kids' books (like *The Toothpaste Millionaire* by Jean Merrill).

DASH FOR THE STASH

Iowa's DASH for the STASH contest is an easy way to participate in Money Smart Week and gives library patrons an educational financial literacy opportunity along with a chance to win a thousand-dollar individual retirement account. Library patrons do not have to know about the stock market, financial planning, or investing in order to participate, so librarians and patrons alike can learn a bit. Librarians only have to hang four posters during Money Smart Week (display one per day or keep four up for the week). The contest mechanics are handled by the Money Smart Week Iowa team. Players use their smartphones (or public computers) to play a quiz game; each poster has a QR code that can be scanned for a quiz question. Answers to the question are available by reading the DASH posters. (The questions can be accessed by typing a URL into a browser as well.) Librarians are eligible to play too! Each poster features a different investing topic: f inding good financial advisors, understanding investment fees, avoiding investor fraud, and building a nest egg. The sponsor of the statewide prize (one-thousand-dollar IRA) is the Iowa Insurance Division and the Investor Protection Institute (IPI). An additional prize of one hundred dollars is presented to the Iowa library with the most players, and more than eighty Iowa libraries played in 2014. For 2015, Iowa opened up its DASH contest for workplaces as well. In addition, the Iowa Insurance Division arranged for librarians to receive investor education materials for patrons, including IPI resources produced by Kiplingers.

A press release, promotional poster, and table tent are provided so librarians can advertise the DASH at their library. There is also a video tutorial to answer FAQs. Libraries are encouraged to display books about investing and introduce all the financial literacy resources the library offers (including those in the reference and periodical sections). They are also encouraged to consider hosting a speaker or two to discuss investing topics and to share information about the event with investment clubs and others who may use the library's meeting rooms regularly (such as Kiwanis, Rotary, or Lions).

SHRED DAYS

Shred events are among the most popular activities for Money Smart Week (and also a good time to highlight Earth Day in April). Money Smart Week Iowa has partnered with a shredding company willing to work with libraries to provide free or reduced-cost shredding. Companies vary in what they will shred, but all shred documents, while some also shred computers and other hardware. Libraries must have ample parking space in order to park the shred trucks and accommodate increased traffic. Shred events are carefully coordinated by the Money Smart Week Iowa committee in conjunction with the sponsoring shredding company.

KITE FEST

The kite fest Set to Soar is the newest Money Smart Week Iowa event, and one thousand kite kits are expected to be completed during the inaugural 2015 event. Set to Soar is being sponsored by Wells Fargo and focuses on concepts of savings. Wells Fargo is encouraging its bankers and financial planners to assist librarians with this program.

Basically, Set to Soar is a two-part event: first, participants assemble a kite with librarian guidance (and using a kite kit), and then participants gather outdoors to fly the kites. Librarians are encouraged to find a local sponsor to donate a small prize (merchandise or gift certificate) for the highest-flying kite. Local kite clubs have proven extremely valuable in running this type of event and are usually eager to be involved, so librarians are encouraged to enlist their help.

The program is geared to older elementary students and could make a good tween program. The kite-making program can be complemented with a story about Benjamin Franklin, who is famous not only for his kite-flying adventures but also for his money wisdom and entrepreneurial activities. Teens may also have fun with this kind of program, and trivia games about Ben Franklin's life and his famous money sayings could be played with this age group.

PIGGY BANK PAGEANT

MSW Iowa's Great Piggy Bank Pageant is on Pinterest this year. In partnership with the Iowa Saves initiative, the program provides cardboard piggy banks (which fold to form a four-by-eight-inch box with a pig design on it) that students decorate. Libraries (and other MSW partners hosting events) can receive up to twenty-five of these banks; nearly three thousand banks were distributed in 2014. The program is ideal as an after-school activity at the library, and previous years' piggy bank programs have proven that it is not just young children who enjoy making banks; even some colleges have had students design banks from recyclable materials! Libraries provide the decorating materials (stickers, markers, paint, yarn, colored paper, etc.). The banks can serve as a craft project for a more traditional story time that includes books about money, savings, and even pigs in general. Participants can then display their banks at the library or a local bank, or photos of the banks can be posted on the Money Smart Week Pinterest site as part of a "piggy bank parade." Prizes are awarded for the best piggies on Pinterest.

The website EveryoneCanSave.org is sponsored by United Way of Central Iowa and includes a variety of support materials that librarians and parents can access to complement a piggy bank program, including a lesson about saving.

TELE-TOWN HALL MEETING

The first MSW Tele-Town Hall Meeting is set to be sponsored by the Iowa AARP in 2015 and will provide financial information of relevance to retirees and pre-retirees. This hour-long event will reach consumers by telephone in their homes. However, a taped session is also expected to be distributed to librarians who want to host a session in their library's meeting room. There is no charge for libraries to participate. Local financial information experts can expand on the AARP topics to make a longer, more personal program for libraries to host.

PERSONAL FINANCE SEMINARS

Libraries are encouraged to host seminars on a variety of personal finance topics during Money Smart Week. Thanks to the Financial Planning Association of Iowa, MSW Iowa is able to provide some experts for librarians looking for a speaker for a library-sponsored event.

Money Smart Week Iowa publicizes these events to librarians throughout the state via a Listserv sponsored by Iowa Library Services. A library consultant from Iowa Library Services serves on the MSW Iowa committee and oversees publicity of any MSW information via the Listserv. Notices about the events are posted in late December or early January with a deadline of January 30 to notify the MSW Iowa committee of a library's intent to participate. Materials for any of the above-mentioned programs are distributed in March to the participating libraries via the Iowa Library Services liaison, who gets the materials from the MSW Iowa committee chair and distributes them to other consultants with Iowa Library Services who are located in various districts of the state. Librarians can then coordinate with their district consultant for pickup of the materials at the district offices of Iowa Library Services.

According to the Federal Reserve's rules for Money Smart Week, all events at the library during Money Smart Week must be free, educational only (no sales), and open to the public. In addition, library events need to be posted on the Money Smart Week website by early February for inclusion as a partner activity.

Joanne Kuster, MSW Iowa chair, has developed several tips for hosting a creative, successful MSW event. Some of her tips were developed with the aid of other librarians. Together, they compiled this list:

- Create a display to complement the program (investing to go with the DASH for the STASH or entrepreneurship for the READ or savings for the Kite Fest).
- Bring in a local entrepreneur, small business owner, or financial expert to speak. Consider speakers not just for adults, but also ones that could be good for teens or children. These speakers do not have to be polished PowerPoint professionals; consider a coin collector or a banker who can bring in counterfeit bills (and the tools to look for counterfeits).
- Have a "be an informed librarian" morning when DASH for the STASH posters are displayed and library staff plays. Everyone, including library staff, is eligible to play, and it is a great way to anticipate patrons' questions about the program.
- Enlist the help of a teen advisory board and have a workshop to make the piggy banks or kites with a younger audience.
- Promote the library's MSW events not just on the library's calendar or bulletin board but also in the local newspaper and at local banks, schools, grocery stores, coffee shops, hair salons, and the like.

BEN FRANKLIN VISITS

The Money Smart Week Iowa committee has several Ben Franklin costumes, as well as a few regular volunteers willing to play the part. "Ben" is willing to visit libraries as part of special MSW programs. Marion Public Library hosted Ben Franklin as part of a special library-sponsored program for home-school kids. Ben was a big hit, and the students liked having him sign their comic book (*Be Money Smart*) and getting their picture taken with him. Ben has also posed on some of the MSW Iowa publicity posters. Ideally, the person volunteering to dress like Ben should have some good biographical insights into Mr. Franklin's life—particularly, his life as an entrepreneur and saver. These additional insights will allow the volunteer to really play the part and interact with audiences in order to complement library programming that may choose to focus on Franklin's life or aspects thereof. The Money Smart Week Iowa team provides volunteer with a script and some talking points so Ben stays on target with the message "Save Your Money."

SCOUT NIGHTS

These events are often held in library meeting rooms, with libraries serving as the sponsor of the event. Events can also be held at schools or community centers. Each community or library determines the age of scouts (girls and/or boys) to invite. For the evening event, the room is set up with multiple "stations" or tables, each featuring a different financial literacy topic for scouts. MSW partners (volunteers) staff these stations and teach about assigned topics such as making change, learning the magic of compounding interest, or comparing costs before buying. Scouts move to a new table every fifteen to twenty minutes.

Templates for setup and financial literacy topics are provided to the hosting organization, all prepared by members of the MSW Iowa team. Special MSW scout badges are provided to leaders to award to scouts later, courtesy of the Iowa Insurance Division. The scout badges and accompanying paper certificate were designed by the MSW Iowa chair Joanne Kuster and are custom made. The badges are especially popular with scouts, but printed certificates or ribbons could also be awarded to participants. Attendance at past events ranged from twenty to 250 people (mostly children with a few scout leaders). Scout Night events are good ways for libraries to open their doors to people who may not have previously visited the library, to display items from the children's collection that promote financial literacy, and to partner with various financial institutions who may serve as the station leaders.

GEOCACHE FOR COLLEGE CASH

This contest is ideal for academic libraries. The MSW Iowa team first unveiled this event in 2013 and based it on the popular geocache concept (a scavenger-hunt type of game). The idea developed because the MSW Iowa team had been seeking a way to reach eighteen- to twenty-four-year-olds since people in that age group typically do not attend MSW events but are still in desperate need of financial knowledge. The MSW Iowa committee determined that this age demographic typically is interested in geocache events, likes to use mobile technology, and could be engaged on college campuses throughout Iowa. Since the committee strives to find highly visible, fun events and programs that can be easily replicated using few resources and a small time commitment from MSW partners, the geocache event seemed like a good idea. It has proven popular with college students and has grown in participation every year; approximately one thousand students across twelve different Iowa college campuses played the GeoCache for College Cash game in 2014. In 2015, even more colleges and students participated.

By playing the game, students earn chances to win one thousand dollars in college tuition, provided by Iowa Jump$tart!, "a nonprofit organization comprised of over 30 individuals and organizations representing business, government, and education that have joined together to improve the personal financial literacy of all Iowans" (Iowa Jump$tart! 2015). Iowa Jump$tart! is "an affiliate of the national Jump$tart Coalition for Personal Financial Literacy" (Iowa Jump$tart! 2015).

Traditional geocaching is a national game that involves "the activity of hiding a geocache container from public view for the challenge of participants using a global positioning system (GPS) device and internet-published coordinates to then locate. Once [the geocache is] located, the participants typically take an item from the geocache, replacing it with one that they contribute" (Iowa Department of Natural Resources 2015). In the MSW version, participants leave proof that they visited by answering a question.

To play GeoCache for College Cash, students found and read seven different posters, each discussing one personal finance topic: car loans, college loans, cyber security, credit scores, paychecks, debit cards, and budgeting to save. Using their mobile devices to scan QR codes, students left answers to seven quiz questions that every young adult should understand. While the GeoCache for College Cash events were most often overseen by college admissions or financial aid offices, college libraries were also encouraged to serve as hosting locations.

POSTER CONTEST

The MSW poster contest is designed for students in grades two through six. The statewide prize is sponsored by Community Bankers of Iowa, which selects a state winner from all entries (about 2,200 in 2014) after the entries are displayed during Money Smart Week. Posters hang in each community during Money Smart Week in locations such as banks, business, and school or public libraries. This is an important part of the contest: the posters hang *during* MSW, and the state winner is named *after* MSW. Local planning teams may also select a local winner (and offer a small prize) prior to MSW.

Posters should be designed on a financial literacy theme, which changes every year. The 2014 theme was "There's a lot to know about money. What should you know now?" The 2015 theme was "Why is it important to know about money?" The first-place prize is a certificate of deposit for five hundred dollars, while second- and third-place prizes are two-hundred-dollar certificates of deposit. Not only do school and public libraries serve as designated places to display the poster entries, but the libraries often strongly promote the contest.

ESSAY CONTEST

The MSW essay contest has existed in Iowa since 2007, thanks to the Iowa Bankers Association. It is for students in grades seven through eleven. Students write an essay (three hundred words or fewer) based on a given question or theme. The 2015 question had two parts: What is the biggest obstacle to saving your money? And what technological or banking solutions might help you and your friends begin to save? Essays are judged by a team of volunteers (note: librarians often make excellent essay judges!). The winning essay writer receives a one-thousand-dollar prize (for college) donated by the Iowa Bankers Association. Essay finalists are announced just prior to Money Smart Week, and the final winner reads his or her essay at one or more events during MSW. Libraries often promote this event but could certainly sponsor it by partnering with their Friends of the Library group or a local bank or similar organization as the prize giver.

CONCLUSION

In summary, librarians who put on their thinking caps can adapt any of these ideas for their community. Partnerships with local financial institutions can often be a viable way to develop these kinds of programs. Money Smart Week is fun, doable, and highly rewarding. In Iowa, the MSW planning team's goal is to find unique, fun, scalable, and easy-to-execute programs that librarians will take and run with, adding their own spin. The librarians have come through every year with new success stories!

REFERENCES

ALA. 2015. "Money Smart Week." http://www.ala.org/offices/money-smart-week.

Collins, Betty. 2014. Email from Collins to Joanne Kuster.

Iowa Department of Natural Resources. 2015. "Geocaching." http://www.iowadnr.gov/Recreation/CampingFacilityRentals/RulesRegulations/Geocaching.aspx.

Iowa Jump$tart! 2015. "Who We Are." http://iowajumpstart.org/whoweare/.

United Way of Central Iowa. 2012. "Great Piggy Bank Downloads." http://www.everyonecansave.org/page54/downloads-2/bank.html.

Chapter Twenty-Nine

Presenting Financial Literacy in Conferences to Public Librarians

Melissa Jeter

The grant specialist librarian and I were researching information on financial literacy in public libraries. We had convinced ourselves that we should implement financial literacy programming in our library. The business technology manager of the main library suggested we present our findings at chapter conferences of the Ohio Library Council. We agreed and gave a lot of thought to how we could present financial literacy to our fellow public librarians.

Presenting financial literacy information to public librarians can be an engaging process if the information is conveyed in a way consistent with how the brain processes information. Knowing how the brain works and how people learn is beneficial when discussing an intimidating topic like financial literacy. This article discusses how people learn, the strategies we used to present information about financial literacy to librarians, and some of the information presented.

HOW PEOPLE LEARN

Information is presented effectively when it is conceptualized in an engaging process of teaching and learning. Consequently, it is helpful to have some basic understanding of how the brain processes information. With this in mind, we understood that an effective presentation on financial literacy to librarians would deliver information so that their brains were receptive. For librarians, issues of privacy and the accuracy of information are central to reference interviews. Being asked a computer question is something a librarian is ready to handle; however, being asked to look at and evaluate sensitive information on a credit report can cause some librarians to have heart palpitations. In order to present information about financial literacy in public libraries—specifically, the reasons to seek information and how to handle questions from patrons—we needed to decrease some of that anxiety.

Theories on how the brain processes information suggest there are strategies that facilitate learning and hinder learning. Maximizing the strategies that facilitate learning was key to teaching librarians about financial literacy in the public library.

Facilitating Learning

According to theories on how the brain processes information, novelty keeps the brain focused and engaged (McGinty, Radin, and Kaminski 2013). Additionally, it is important to build on information people already have. Establishing credibility is also important (Hill 2014). One way to establish credibility is to be transparent. Transparency can come from making information accessible—for example, making the information we present accessible to librarians who may have questions. This is where the compilation of financial literacy information on a wiki came in handy. The environment in which learning is to take place is also a factor. Creating a learning environment includes showing concern for the people learning. Accordingly, theories suggest that learning is better facilitated by knowledgeable people who are good listeners, appear positive, and have a sense of humor (McGinty, Radin, and Kaminski 2013; Hill 2014).

Hindrances to Learning

Learning is hindered when the brain is under stress. The emotional parts of the brain—in fact, the entire limbic system—can take over the rational and cognitive parts of the brain and cause people to be more emotional in their decision making (Garfinkel and Critchley 2014). Hindrances that cause the emotional brain to take over include anything that is perceived as a threat (McGinty, Radin, and Kaminski 2013). According to a survey of librarians in the public library where I work, most were concerned that they might lack the right knowledge, provide inaccurate or old information, be unable to help patrons make informed decisions, or fail to protect private information, especially when using public computers. While they may seem minor, these kinds of threats can override rational thinking. Our presentation would need to avoid this kind of stress on the brain and hindrance to learning.

PRESENTING FINANCIAL LITERACY INFORMATION TO LIBRARIANS

Knowing a little about learning theory is beneficial to librarians presenting information to their colleagues, who in this case are adult learners. There is an entire discipline, called instructional design, that examines learning processes and the strategies used to teach. This discipline provides a variety of theories and strategies steeped in a long history of research on learning and the brain. Having touched on this discipline in information literacy course work in library school, I found that even the rudiments of these learning theories and strategies for teaching were helpful in designing a presentation on financial literacy. The role of a librarian is to teach people "when information is needed, how to locate, evaluate and effectively use information" to solve a problem. This is called information literacy. Consequently, as public librarians who in their own library recognized the need for more information literacy on personal finance and learned how to locate and evaluate personal finance information sources, we were in a unique position to teach colleagues about financial literacy in public libraries. Our purpose was to teach our fellow librarians to recognize patrons' need for financial literacy services and programming in their library.

In presenting information to librarians about financial literacy, using strategies that facilitate learning and lessen the hindrances was important. In alignment with these theories, our presentation was designed to use strategies that would build on the experiences of librarians. The presentation would engage the librarians in order to build a relationship with the presenters and prepare for the overall conveyance of information.

An agenda is a tool that can aid effective presentation. Our agenda included measurable learning objectives. Measurable learning objectives are what the teacher, or presenter in this case, wants people to learn. For example, in presenting about financial literacy to public librarians, our objectives were to get public librarians to know more financial information, feel less apprehensive about reference questions, and consider conducting financial literacy programs in their respective public libraries. In addition, we hoped the librarians would come away with at least three actions that they could take when they received financial questions. Those actions could include intentions to research information on financial literacy. Moreover, it was also important to implement these learning objectives in an interesting, fun way that eased the concerns librarians might have about reference questions and programming about financial literacy.

FINANCIAL LITERACY INFORMATION PRESENTED TO LIBRARIANS

Initially, to engage the librarians in the presentation, we asked them for their thoughts and experiences with financial literacy in their respective public libraries. Asking the librarians what they knew about financial literacy gave everyone an opportunity to demonstrate that they already knew something about the topic, but also to release the concerns they may have about financial literacy questions. Recognizing that the librarians had some knowledge about financial literacy allowed us to build on what they already knew. In addition, as librarians listening to fellow librarians, we were able to build a nonthreatening environment that reduced stress and allowed people to be receptive to learning about financial literacy in public libraries.

In keeping with theories on how the brain processes information, we aimed to maintain novelty and grab their attention. Thus, the presentation included a variety of techniques to deliver the information. The information was be delivered via wiki, PowerPoint with live Internet links, role play, and questions, with incentives for participation.

While it seems like this is a lot of activity for even two presenters to handle, using a well-thought-out agenda with learning objectives allowed for focus and continuity throughout the presentation. One of the basic ideas in learning theory is telling learners what will happen. Stress is reduced when people in a learning environment know what is expected of them. Consequently, we told the librarians what was going to happen in the fifty-minute presentation and what the presentation objectives were, and at the end of the presentation we told them what we had presented to them.

One way to let librarians attending the presentation know what would happen was to share an agenda. The agenda used in the presentations at the Ohio Library Council workshops included objectives as well as a time-specific notes. This agenda was presented on a wiki that was projected on a screen. We referred to this agenda throughout the presentation as links to PowerPoint slides as well as specific Internet sites were shared. The following is the agenda that was used in the presentation:

*5 minutes: Welcome and introductions (*Linda Koss, librarian grant specialist, and Melissa Jeter, adult services librarian, *Toledo Lucas County Public Library)*

Introduce program content: presentation objectives. We will have four parts to our presentation that will be presented in different ways. The informational section will be a PowerPoint, the reference part will include role play where we will ask you to be the patron who has questions (so please think of some questions for that part). The third part of the presentation will be on programming, and the fourth part will be on partnerships. Our goal is to get you comfortable with all these areas of financial literacy, and hopefully you will come away with at least three actions you can take when you receive financial questions.

40 minutes: Present the program content
Informational (informationpresent.pptx)
Reference
Programming
How to make the presentation
Role play—interactive, providing the information that it is a good idea
Librarian to administrators or bosses and administrators to librarians
Partnerships (Partners[1].pptx)
Financially literate
5 minutes: Review program content
List three things you can do to make your community more financially literate
Contact information: Give out link to wiki
Thank them
Survey? Prize raffle?

After the welcome and introductions, we divided the topic of financial literacy into four parts: informational, reference, programming, and partnerships. Print and online sources of information are familiar to librarians. Discussing print and online sources first built on what librarians already do. Of course, books "provide in-depth material on how to save, budget, invest, borrow, and how to anticipate money needs like college, retirement, raising children, and more. For people new to financial literacy ideas, they can explain ideas and provide a roadmap for achieving fiscal soundness. Information can be on many levels, for people new to money management all the way up to sophisticated investors."

Other print sources included pamphlets and booklets. These may come from government or nonprofit agencies, such as the Federal Trade Commission, the Educator's Advisory Board, or the Financial Industry Regulatory Authority (FINRA), all of which have resources librarians can order online. In addition, Consumer.gov has lower-literacy sheets and pamphlets that librarians can order. With links embedded in this part of the presentation, including specific PowerPoint slides, we were able to show librarians the online location of those sources. Therefore, the section on online sources of information on borrowing, investments, and other information was accessible and able to be shown on a projection screen:

> Now, there are online actuarial sources that can give interest rate and payment tables. A fact not well known by many patrons is that there is only one website, www.annualcreditreport.com, where you can truly get your credit

> report for free and many other sites require you to sign up for a subscription to a credit report update. You can also look up your own federal student debt on http://www.nslds.ed.gov/nslds_SA/.
>
> Many other interactive sites can calculate payments, help create budgets, and help with financial planning. Glossaries can tell patrons about words and concepts in finance and investment. Others are created to give people information to help with decisions at particular points in their lives: financing an education, retirement, home purchase, raising children, and so on. For people who want comparative information on financial tools like credit cards and their rates, see www.cardratings.com or www.lowcards.com, or, for information on CD rates, mortgages, and insurance as well as credit cards, see www.bankrate.com. Included in online resources are calculators and budget software, such as http://www.mymoney.gov/tools/Pages/tools.aspx. Other sites have similar tools that can help people figure out both the overall and monthly costs of borrowing money, or how much is needed to retire, glossaries of financial terms, and financial how-tos. You can use these for reference work, but also use them on your library's web page for direct patron access.

The next source of information was fun, interactive online sources. Once again this information was delivered dynamically, as it could be accessed, and showed to librarians how this information teaches children and teenagers the basics of money management and helps them formulate good decisions on money management.

In the informational part of the presentation, contact information for local groups and agencies that assist people with financial education and avoiding predatory lending were suggested for patrons with such questions. Such local groups and agencies include the following:

- National Foundation for Credit Counseling consumer credit counseling services: https://www.nfcc.org/our-services/credit-debt-counseling/
- Local HUD-certified housing agencies: http://www.hud.gov/offices/hsg/sfh/hcc/hcs.cfm
- 2-1-1 call centers: http://www.211ohio.net/approved.htm
- Ohio Save the Dream website: http://www.savethedream.ohio.gov

In addition, we presented federal and state agencies, such as the Ohio Attorney General, the Federal Trade Commission, the Better Business Bureau, and the Ohio Office of the Treasurer.

The reference part of the presentation began by building on the familiar foundation of the reference interview. We asked the librarians about the financial questions that they received. In case a librarian did not receive such questions, we came prepared with cards that listed financial questions. These questions were derived from the survey of librarians at our library. We passed the cards out to the librarians and began a game called "Stump the Librarian." Thus, the librarians were engaged in the learning process. By answering the questions, we were modeling behaviors of a librarian who could conduct a basic reference interview but with financial questions. To encourage as well as reward participation, we handed out chocolate. After the short game, the librarians were given the opportunity to ask questions about the simulated reference interviews. For example, one question involved pulling credit reports and privacy and security issues with public computers. With information from the IT department of our library, we were able to confidently answer that it is necessary to shut down the computer to clear information before another patron can use it. In summarizing this section of the presentation, we referred the librarians to the Business Reference and Services section of the Reference Users Services Association of the American Library Association for online information in the "Public Libraries Briefcase," where various sources are listed that librarians can use to answer patron questions.

In the programming section of the presentation, we gently challenged the librarians. Having presented information about where to locate financial information, it was time to ask the librarians if they thought about doing financial literacy programming in their public libraries. With the aforementioned resources and recognition that there were increasing numbers of reference questions about personal finance, library services could add value by starting financial literacy programming. Creating financial literacy programming, however, could be structured to demonstrate that patrons in attendance at such programs were actually learning and being helped. Similar to how we developed the presentation, we strongly suggested that programming should have outcomes that could be used as evidence that the community has a need for this kind of information. When planning programming for financial literacy, it is important to know the audience to address their financial information needs. If at all possible, find out what they need by asking people in a survey. Public libraries are conventionally seen as a trusted source of information in the community. Asking for information in a survey about patrons' financial information needs lets people know that the library is a place where they can be connected to a variety of sources on financial information.

Programming, however, does not have to be done alone. Programming can be created with partners. The partnership part of the program included information that might be new to librarians. Partners in programming can include financial institutions as well as credit counseling services, community-based organizations and or faith-based organizations, state attorney general offices, departments of commerce that assist people with finances or housing, and state extension services. State organizations and local agencies like the Better Business Bureau may come to speak about a program for free as part of their services to the community. Some organizations may want to work with the public library because it is a trusted resource in the community.

Working with partners adds a knowledge base to your work. They publicize the financial literacy services and programs that are at the public library and are willing to offer their own programming in the library. Many financial institutions and nonprofits already do financial counseling and literacy programs and know their subject and the issues. This is beneficial because many of these organizations may already have programs and are eager to have a wider audience. Partners such as these can add financial information in the form of promotional materials and speakers.

Some organizations may want to work with the library because the public library is a trusted resource in the community. In addition, partnerships are great when considering grant funding for financial literacy services and programs in the public library. Grantors strongly support collaboration efforts between agencies in a community.

The discussion about partnerships brought the presentation to a close. We asked the librarians what three ideas they could take back to their public libraries. The discussion of these three things served as a review of the presentation. There were a variety of responses in this last part of the presentation, including librarians who said that they might create a program at their library, as well as those who said that they felt they had more tools that they could use when addressing questions patrons had about personal finances.

EVALUATION

Librarians at Ohio Library Council workshops were receptive to the financial literacy presentations. Giving thought to how people learn and the role of the librarian in helping adults become information literate was a great benefit. Just looking at the evaluations from the Northwest Ohio Library Chapter, most of the librarians indicated that we met or exceeded their expectations, while most indicated that the content exceeded their expectations. The following are some of the comments from librarians who attended the presentation:

"Many great ideas to assist patrons"
"Sources relevant and easy to access"
"Question prompts helpful because they were real questions; we often forget what to ask when we get here"
"Candy"
"Covered information for teens and kids; too much info for one hour"
"Great at engaging audience"
"Speaker hard to follow"
"Good overview on resources, tactics, strategies, for patrons, staff partners"

The grant specialist and I still research information on financial literacy. There is more and new information that comes out all the time. In addition, financial literacy programs and services have been building in our library system since 2008, when small programs were started. Now, with the financial literacy programs in our library system, people in our community are "living better and spending smarter" (see http://lbss.toledolibrary.org/).

REFERENCES

Garfinkel, Sarah N., and Hugu D. Critchley. 2014. "Neural Correlates of Fear: Insights from Neuroimaging." *Neuroscience and Neuroeconomics* 3:111–25.

Hill, Lilian H. 2014. "Graduate Students' Perspectives on Effective Teaching." *Adult Learning* 25 (2): 57–65.

ICLES. 2015. "Robert Gagne's Five Categories of Learning Outcomes and the Nine Events of Instruction." http://www.icels-educators-for-learning.ca/index.php?option=com_content&view=article&id=54&Itemid=73.

McGinty, Jacqueline, Jean Radin, and Karen Kaminski. 2013. "Brain-Friendly Teaching Supports Learning Transfer." *New Directions for Adult Continuing Education* (137): 49–59. doi:10.1002/ace.20044.

Professional Safety. 2013. "Developing Training to Involve the Audience." 58 (1): 55.

Chapter Thirty

Start Here @ the San Diego Public Library

Cindy Mediavilla

California is home to more military service people and veterans than any other state in the nation. A great majority of these folks reside in San Diego County. According to the U.S. Department of Defense's (2013) most recent "Demographics Profile of the Military Community," more than 204,000 active military personnel and their dependents live in the San Diego area. The U.S. Department of Veterans Affairs (2014) also reports that nearly 232,000 veterans call San Diego County home.

In 2013, the San Diego Public Library (SDPL) received a Smart investing@your library grant to provide a yearlong series of financial and investment services to active-duty military, their families, and veterans. The program, called "Start Here: Your Road to Smart and Savvy Finance," proved to be very popular, especially with participants who attended financial literacy workshops offered at several SDPL branches. The real strength of the program, however, was the various partnerships the library was able to leverage to provide the required services. A nonprofit organization called Home Start and the military's Fleet and Family Support Services were major collaborators, as was Point Loma High School, whose film students created three excellent videos to promote the library's financial resources to military personnel. This chapter examines the library's success in working with community agencies to provide much needed financial literacy services to San Diego residents.

IDENTIFYING NEED

Since 2007, the Financial Industry Regulatory Authority (FINRA) Investor Education Foundation and the American Library Association (ALA) have partnered to offer Smart investing@your library, a grant program that helps libraries provide effective, unbiased educational resources about personal finance and investing. In recent years, over one million dollars in grant money has been awarded annually through a competitive application process. Each year's awardees, representing a mix of public libraries, community college libraries, and library networks, meet together at the ALA midwinter conference to receive training before their grant projects begin. The Smart investing@your library website is also filled with toolkits and other resources to help grant recipients, as well as nonawardees, deliver the best financial literacy services possible. Based on a belief that libraries are uniquely positioned to assist community members with their financial information needs, the FINRA Foundation and ALA partnership hopes to make unbiased resources available to everyone regardless of age or economic circumstance.

In 2012, the FINRA Foundation conducted a National Financial Capability Study to measure how U.S. adults manage their money and make financial decisions. A separate survey of military personnel was undertaken, showing mixed results. While a majority of respondents indicated that they have no trouble paying their bills and, in fact, have "rainy day" funds set aside in case of emergency, nearly half said they engage in risky financial behaviors, like paying credit card minimums, paying late fees, or getting cash advances from their credit cards. Over a third also reported using nonbank, alternative-borrowing methods, such as payday loans, advances on tax refunds, or pawnshops. Moreover, though four out of five military respondents considered themselves financially literate, only 15 percent were able to answer all five financial "quiz" questions correctly on the survey (FINRA Investor Education Foundation 2013).

Although nationwide in scope, the findings of the FINRA Foundation report motivated SDPL to investigate and begin planning financial literacy programs for military families in San Diego. Library staff were asked for feedback on financial education programs they had offered in the past, including number of attendees. This information was then used to identify which financial and investment programs best addressed the needs of San Diego's various communities. A multibranch program was developed and a Smart investing@your library grant proposal submitted.

PARTNERS

The library enlisted several partner agencies when pulling together its Start Here program. The first was Fleet and Family Services, a support center that provides emergency financial and other assistance to military families when needed. With a strong track record of already offering well-received programs at SDPL branches, Fleet and Family Services not only promoted the Start Here program among its constituents, it also hosted its own events in conjunction with the grant project. Five independent, one-day financial literacy workshops for active military were offered at the Logan Heights branch. "Eating Healthy on a Budget" events were also held at both the Logan Heights and Mira Mesa branches. In addition, a financial resources fair was held at Bayview, a military housing complex. Gaining entry into Bayview posed a logistical challenge due to military regulations, but Fleet and Family Services persevered.

Home Start, a 501(c)(3) nonprofit corporation that provides family support services, was another important partner. Through its Financial Opportunity Centers, San Diegans receive employment assistance, financial coaching services, and income support to achieve self-sufficiency. Home Start staff provided extensive content expertise and trained military spouse fellows, who then conducted the grant project's financial literacy workshop series.

The FINRA Foundation was also a major partner, connecting SDPL to its Military Spouse Fellowship program, which supports military spouses as they work toward achieving an accredited financial counselor certificate. Once trained by Home Start, the military spouse fellows then became responsible for conducting the workshops that were so integral to the overall program's success. Without this particular partnership, it would have been extremely difficult to achieve the grant's goals. Military spouse fellows also provided one-on-one financial counseling following the various workshops.

The final piece of the Start Here program was accomplished through the San Diego Unified School District (SDUSD). Unlike new partners Home Start and the military spouse fellows, the library already had a long-standing relationship with the school district. Still, getting permission to work with the school was an arduous process that caused a slight delay in the project time line. An agreement between SDUSD and SDPL had to be approved by the district's legal team as well as the board of education. Ultimately, the project manager was given permission to partner with Point Loma High School, whose film students created three videos promoting the library's financial resources. Students enrolled in the school district's Reserve Officers' Training Corps (ROTC) also helped with outreach to military families.

THE PROGRAM

The library used several methods to introduce financial literacy to its target population. These included community resource fairs, a series of weekly workshops conducted at five branches, collection development, and promotion via brochures, online videos, and local word of mouth. Resource fairs were held in locations close to military housing and installations. Nearly three hundred families attended the first fair, called "Summer Is for Saving," on the lawn outside the Logan Heights library. Teens helped younger children make wallets out of duct tape, and free piggy banks were given away. The library, Home Start, and San Diego Gas and Electric all staffed booths, providing information on how to better manage one's money. A band played music nearby, attracting visitors. In all, more than two thousand people attended a total of five financial resource fairs.

At the heart of the Start Here program were two rounds of weekly financial literacy workshops offered at five SDPL branches. The workshop sites were chosen specifically because of their proximity to military installations: the Mira Mesa and Serra Mesa/Kearney Mesa Libraries, for instance, are adjacent to the Marine Corps Air Station at Miramar, while the Valencia Park/Malcolm X, City Heights/Weingart, and Logan Heights Libraries are all close to the San Diego and Coronado naval bases. These particular branches also have meeting rooms big enough to accommodate large groups of participants and are readily accessible by freeway and public transportation. To support the workshops, Financial Literacy Centers were developed in each of the five branches, making well-stocked collections of financial materials available to all community members.

Subject experts from Home Start developed the workshop series curriculum and corresponding PowerPoint presentations, based on the FINRA Foundation's educational content. All the workshops were aimed at a beginner's level. The hour-long sessions were initially held over six consecutive weeks. But after the first round, the content was combined into four hour-and-a-half-long sessions to attract more participants. Some branches offered the workshops on Saturday mornings; others scheduled them on weeknights. The six- and four-week branch schedules were staggered as much as possible so the trainers would not have to lead more than one session a week.

Each workshop module focused on one or two subjects a week. Topics included the following:

- Credit (e.g., store cards vs. other types of credit cards, how to maintain good credit, and how to check credit reports)
- Budgeting (e.g., expenses, discretionary spending, housing, income, and local support programs)
- Financial goals (e.g., different types of savings plans)

- Banking products (e.g., predatory lending, investing, stocks, bonds, and IRAs)
- Tax rates and responsibilities

All community members were welcome to attend whether or not they registered ahead of time. Participants were asked to sign in each week to track attendance and repeat customers. Some attended almost every session, while others came to only one. A catered buffet, provided at every session, motivated attendees to stay afterward and discuss what they had learned.

Overall, the workshops were very well received. Not only did the presenters make the subject matter easy to understand by interjecting personal stories, they also created a casual, safe environment where everyone was encouraged to share experiences. Several people said they enjoyed the participative nature of the workshops and liked learning from other attendees. Indeed, many participants were happy to relate their experiences with bad credit scores, car leasing, rent-to-own homes, identity theft, and exorbitant loans. Some obviously attended the workshops to address specific issues and so asked very pointed questions, while others were there to gather as much information as possible on all topics. Most people took copious notes on the handouts the trainers provided.

The program was heavily promoted via brochures distributed by the library's partner agencies and by online videos created through a film competition held at Point Loma High School. Thirteen teams of youngsters initially pitched their project ideas before a jury of panelists from SDPL and Fleet and Family Services. Five teams were then invited to create videos that were then judged by another panel, which included a FINRA Foundation representative. In the end, three short films (less than two minutes long) were selected:

- "Smart Investing at Library," featuring two uniformed service members providing commonsense advice about credit and short-term financial planning
- "Draw My Life," warning against overextended credit while encouraging viewers to take advantage of SDPL's financial literacy programs
- "Wants vs. Needs," promoting the library's services to help young military families achieve "a debt-free life"

The videos were posted on the high school's website as well as on SDPL's Smart investing@your library Facebook page. They were also streamed directly to personnel at military installations and on naval ships.

GOALS ACHIEVED

Like most grant-funded projects, an evaluation plan was required as part of the application process. An outside evaluator was hired to measure achievement of the following three project goals:

1. Target audience will be better consumers in regard to spending, budgeting, saving, and investing.
2. Make the library one of the first places people think of when they consider getting information about savings, investments, and loans.
3. Increase awareness of the program and program enrollment.

Because they offered a more controlled group of participants than the community resource fairs, workshops were the program's main evaluation focus. Methods included the following:

- Surveying workshop participants to gauge an increase in financial knowledge
- Attending at least one session of every financial literacy workshop series to observe audience engagement and overall content effectiveness
- Conducting a longitudinal survey to assess the long-range impact of the workshops
- Collecting and reviewing sign-up sheets for all workshop sessions

To measure how well the Start Here program accomplished its first goal of helping the target audience become better consumers, pre- and post-test surveys were administered before and after a sample number of workshops. As the survey responses revealed, many participants gained financial knowledge and even changed some of their spending behaviors as a result of the workshops. "I can buy a house," one person enthused after realizing, for the first time, that the "American dream" was within reach. Another said the training "opened up a conversation with [my] spouse to initiate more conversations on money topics. This is BIG for us!" In particular, those who took the credit workshop indicated increased knowledge on "why credit is important," "how to build good credit," "what a credit score is," and the "difference between 'store cards' and 'credit cards.'" Those who attended the session on budgeting said they now knew how to recognize the warning signs of financial trouble.

In hopes of capturing longitudinal changes in attendees' financial behaviors, an online questionnaire was also conducted several months after the workshop series ended. The questionnaire was sent directly to participants, who had voluntarily provided their email addresses when signing into each training session. Unfortunately, not many people responded to the online survey request. Still, the handful of participants who did respond overwhelmingly indicated that the training had helped them better manage their finances. One person said they were now "able to check credit reports," and another claimed the workshops "helped fix my credit." A third respondent admitted, "I've become more aware of my spending habits."

In addition to surveying the workshop participants, feedback was solicited from the Point Loma teenagers who had created the online videos. The project manager and consultant met with the students to see what they had learned from the process. Certainly, they now know how to use cameras, tripods, storyboards, appropriate lighting, and professional editing software, as well as how to find copyright-free music. But they also gained practical financial experience, creating budgets for their video projects and developing partnerships with the various businesses and agencies featured in their films. Taking the message of their projects to heart, they learned that it is best to invest money at a steady pace and that it is never too late to seek advice. As one student said, "Thanks to the library, you're never alone."

Although it is difficult to measure whether people indeed think of the library first when seeking financial information (i.e., the program's second goal), the student videos did an effective job of emphasizing the availability of reliable, free resources at the San Diego Public Library. The trainers at each workshop also reminded attendees of the various financial materials available for checkout at SDPL. However, since 59 percent of attendees said they learned about the workshops through their local library, it is possible that many if not most project participants were already library users.

More than five hundred people attended the forty workshop sessions offered during the yearlong Start Here program. Of these, roughly half were unique visitors, with 51 percent attending two or more sessions. Obviously, the modules were deemed valuable enough to spend more than just one evening or Saturday at the library learning about personal finance. Most of the sessions attracted an ethnically diverse mix of African Americans, Latinos/Latinas, Asians, and Caucasians. Participants were older—maybe even retired—though younger people did attend, sometimes with a parent in tow. Adult men and women were equally represented. The attendees interacted well and were engaged with the subject matter. In fact, the Mira Mesa participants bonded so well they took group photographs and even held a potluck at their last meeting. In accomplishing its third goal (i.e., increasing awareness of the program), positive word of mouth may have been the library's best marketing plan.

ELEMENTS OF SUCCESS

According to San Diego Public Library director Misty Jones, "Start Here was instrumental in continuing our community partnerships with Fleet and Family Services, Home Start, and the San Diego Unified School District. These financial workshops at our neighborhood libraries connected many participants to the knowledge they need to be smart and savvy about their finances for a lifetime." Indeed, the Start Here program was a huge success. Thousands of people attended the library's community resource fairs, and both rounds of the financial literacy workshops were extremely popular. What made this program so successful?

The workshop participants clearly welcomed the opportunity to learn about topics that relate directly to their lives. "These complimentary workshops are a blessing to have within one public library!" one attendee commented. Another explained, "I found it all very educational and appreciate all the time and effort put into these workshops." When asked why they decided to attend the sessions, many participants said they needed help with their credit or wanted to learn how to better manage their money. In fact, the need for financial literacy training was so urgent that the audience far exceeded the program's original target population, attracting nonmilitary folks as well as veterans, active-duty service members, and their families. Not surprisingly, programs dealing with money management have wide appeal. As San Diego librarians learned, the workshops were so well received that participants wanted more: more sessions, more in-depth information on an array of financial subjects, and more real-life case studies. "I would love to attend more workshops like these to help others with financial planning and goal setting," an attendee offered at the end of one of the series.

Although a majority of participants attended more than one session, attendance was better sustained when the content was combined and offered over a shorter period. In fact, the number of per session participants increased by 45 percent when the series was reduced from six weeks to four. Most people have busy lives and can only make a short-term commitment to voluntary training, even when the topic is as relevant as personal finance. Workshops need to be as convenient as possible to draw the greatest number of participants.

Of course, without SDPL's partners, there would not even be a Start Here program. The success of the project was based largely on the library's ability to make the most of its partnerships. Without Home Start and the military spouse fellows, for instance, there would have been no financial literacy workshops. Not only did Home Start create the workshop curriculum, they also trained the military spouses to present the content in a way that was accessible to a broad cross section of attendees. Participants had high praise for the trainers, describing them as "knowledgeable," "courteous," and "professional." But even more important, the presenters made personal finance easier to understand by sharing their own real-life experiences. Audience members related to their stories and were even encouraged to share stories of their own. The workshops were relevant and engaging, in no small part, because they were led by real people who were sincerely interested in helping improve others' lives.

Credit must also be given to Sheila Burnett, the supervising librarian in charge Start Here. A former navy wife herself, Burnett understands military culture and knows firsthand the challenges faced by military families. Her empathy toward the target population was invaluable in helping shape the program. As with any library service, the best formula for success is good partnerships and staff members who have a strong connection to the community.

EPILOGUE

The Start Here program so impressed the FINRA Foundation and ALA that a second grant was awarded in 2015 to expand the program. Partnerships continue with Home Start and Fleet and Family Services, while new relationships are being cultivated with groups that serve seniors and homeless youth—two new audiences being targeted by the expanded program. Workshops will be offered in Spanish as well as English and credit counseling will be provided. A total of ten branches will participate. The road to smart and savvy personal finance truly does start at the San Diego Public Library.

REFERENCES

FINRA Investor Education Foundation. 2013. "Financial Capability in the United States: 2012 Report of Military Findings." December. http://www.usfinancialcapability.org/downloads/NFCS_2012_Report_Military_Findings.pdf.

U.S. Department of Defense. 2013. "2013 Demographics Profile of the Military Community." http://www.militaryonesource.mil/12038/MOS/Reports/2013-Demographics-Report.pdf.

U.S. Department of Veteran Affairs. 2014. "Veteran Population." http://www.va.gov/vetdata/veteran_population.asp.

Chapter Thirty-One

Volunteer Tax Assistance in Libraries

Wayne Finley and Janene R. Finley

Keeping an ample stock of basic federal and state tax forms was once an annual ritual for many libraries. However, with fewer federal and state tax forms being delivered to libraries each year, librarians are changing the way they provide access to these materials. Librarians now often assist patrons by helping them search for and access tax forms online. Yet without a great deal of additional work for library staff, libraries can offer much more to their patrons than access to tax forms. By partnering with nonprofit volunteer tax assistance programs, libraries can provide tax preparation services and tax advice, free of charge, to their patrons. This chapter describes the three most popular volunteer tax preparation services, discusses the benefits of these services to both patrons and libraries, and gives advice on how libraries can implement these services to best meet the needs of their patrons.

FREE TAX PREPARATION SERVICES

The easiest way for libraries to provide tax assistance is to host a volunteer tax assistance program certified by the Internal Revenue Service. The three most prevalent tax assistance programs in the United States are Volunteer Income Tax Assistance (VITA), Tax Counseling for the Elderly (TCE), and the AARP Foundation's Tax-Aide program. Sponsored by the IRS, both VITA and TCE provide free tax preparation for a wide variety of individuals and families. The AARP Foundation operates its Tax-Aide program as part of the IRS's TCE program (IRS 2015).

The main focus of VITA is to serve taxpayers who have income below an amount set by the IRS. Although the IRS set the maximum family income level for the 2014 tax season at $53,000 (IRS 2015), this limit varies based on location. For example, VITA sites operating in Rock Island, Illinois, and Davenport and Bettendorf, Iowa, were authorized to increase the limit to $57,000 (United Way of the Quad Cities Area 2015). VITA also serves people with disabilities, the elderly, and clients who are not proficient with the English language (IRS 2015).

Although sponsorship of the two programs differs, TCE and Tax-Aide share a common purpose. Both programs focus on serving taxpayers sixty years of age and older with no income limit (IRS 2015). Unlike VITA, all volunteers at TCE and Tax-Aide sites are trained to assist older taxpayers. Pertinent topics include Social Security benefits, pensions, and other retirement income (IRA 2015). Although TCE and Tax-Aide sites focus services for older individuals, they also provide tax services for taxpayers of all ages (AARP Foundation 2014; IRA 2015). Table 31.1 indicates the differences among the three tax preparation programs.

Trained volunteers from a wide variety of backgrounds staff all three tax preparation programs. In many cases, working certified public accountants or professional tax preparers volunteer their time to prepare returns and give tax advice. Some sites rely on the service of retired individuals wishing to stay active; while other sites are staffed by accounting students in college looking to gain experience working with clients or earn college credit. Regardless of an individual volunteer's background, all VITA, TCE, and Tax-Aide preparers receive training through the IRS (IRS 2014f). Further, the IRS requires that all sites have a site coordinator who possess additional experience and who has received additional IRS training. The three programs must follow the IRS's standards of conduct, and all sites may use IRS-provided tax preparation software.

OPERATION OF TAX PREPARATION SITES

Although VITA, TCE, and Tax-Aide sites may differ in their intended clientele, all follow similar operating procedures prescribed by the IRS. Libraries and other organizations offering tax preparation services must keep current

Table 31.1. A Comparison of Tax Preparation Programs

	VITA	TCE	AARP Tax-Aide
Client Focus	Lower income	Ages 60 or older	Ages 60 or older
Income Limitation	$53,000, but may vary	None	None
Sponsorship	IRS	IRS	AARP Foundation in conjunction with IRS

with these operating procedures to ensure that their site meets IRS requirements. If a site does not follow the IRS requirements or violates the standards of conduct, the IRS may close the site.

All volunteers that assist at tax preparation sites must complete a minimum amount of training. This rule applies to all level of volunteers, ranging from site coordinators to greeters. The IRS requires that VITA, TCE, and Tax-Aide sites follow certain standards of conduct, including the following:

- Volunteers must follow the quality site requirements established by the IRS.
- No volunteer may receive payment or solicit donations for tax return preparation services.
- No volunteer may solicit business from a taxpayer or use a taxpayer's personal information for personal benefit.
- No volunteer may knowingly prepare false returns.
- No volunteer may engage in criminal conduct or conduct deemed to have a negative effect on the VITA or TCE programs.
- Volunteers must treat taxpayers in a professional, courteous, and respectful manner. (IRS 2014b)

In addition, the tax preparation site or sponsor may not accept payment from taxpayers in exchange for tax preparation services and cannot have tip jars at the tax preparation site to encourage donations from taxpayers (IRS 2014f). To ensure that volunteers follow these standards of conduct, all volunteers must complete an ethics training course and pass an IRS ethics test. This rule also applies to volunteers who do not prepare tax returns. The good news for libraries hosting a tax preparation site is that not all library staff members are required to complete the IRS ethics training. Only staff members who work directly with taxpayers and assist in the tax preparation services must complete the training.

Volunteer tax preparers must complete an IRS training program on tax preparation. Volunteers may choose from several levels of tax preparation and are allowed to complete returns only for their respective level of training. The lowest level of training is basic training. Under basic training, volunteers complete simple returns, which include a limited number of income items such as wages and salaries reported on W-2s, Social Security income, and interest income (IRS 2014e). If a tax preparation site wants volunteers to prepare more complex returns, the site's tax preparers must complete advanced training. In advanced training, volunteers learn how to handle, for example, self-employment income, itemized deductions, and certain pensions and annuities (IRS 2014e). VITA and TCE sites provide tax preparation for basic and advanced returns. However, Tax-Aide sites are required to provide preparation services for clients with advanced tax returns (IRS

2014g). Additional training options are available if any VITA, TCE, or Tax-Aide site wishes to provide specialized services. These options include tax returns for the following:

- Foreign students
- Individuals with health savings accounts
- Taxpayers who are in the military
- U.S. citizens who live overseas (IRS 2014d)

Although tax sites can offer a variety of services, the IRS considers certain types of tax situations out of scope for all VITA, TCE, and Tax-Aide sites and will not provide training for such situations. Examples of these out-of-scope situations include the following:

- Business losses
- Farm income
- Certain types of partnership income
- Income of nonresident aliens who are not students (IRS 2014e)

All VITA, TCE, and Tax-Aide sites follow a similar set of procedures when working with clients. The taxpayer first completes an IRS intake sheet. The intake sheet lists the taxpayer's personal information and the information of all other individuals listed on the tax return (IRS 2014a). The intake sheet is essential because it lists a taxpayer's income and expenses, and the tax preparer uses it to determine if the preparer is qualified to complete the return and whether the return is out of scope for the tax preparation site.

When preparing a tax return, the tax preparer must make sure that the taxpayer has provided all necessary information, including items such as a photo ID, Social Security cards for all individuals listed on the return, and any forms provided by employers, banks, or other parties that report the taxpayer's income. The IRS requires a second volunteer to perform a quality review of the finalized return. The volunteer who performs the quality review must possess the proper level of certification to prepare the return and should have some prior experience in tax preparation services. After the quality review, the final step is to file the return. The tax preparation site may file the return electronically, and the site coordinator usually completes this step. The taxpayer may choose instead to mail the forms to the IRS and state revenue departments.

All VITA, TCE, and Tax-Aide sites must have a site coordinator to oversee operations. The site coordinator completes ethics training, quality review training, and additional site coordinator training (IRS 2014g). If the site coordinator prepares returns, corrects errors, provides tax advice, and performs quality reviews, he or she must also complete IRS tax training based on the type of tax returns completed at the site (IRS 2014g). If the site offers specialized services such as health savings account returns, the site coordinator must receive training in those areas. The site coordinator must also handle unstructured problems that may arise at a site. Two common problems encountered by volunteers are returns that do not qualify for filing with the IRS and taxpayers who are unsatisfied with the amount of their refund or taxes owed.

Although site coordinators cannot accept payment from taxpayers, they may receive compensation for their time and expenses from the organization operating the tax preparation site. If, for example, a librarian employed by the host library serves as the site's coordinator, the librarian is allowed to receive compensation.

It is important for libraries hosting sites to know that during the tax season the IRS may perform a review of the operating procedures at VITA, TCE, and Tax-Aide sites. These reviews may be announced or unannounced. At times the IRS will perform "shopper" visits, where an IRS representative poses as a taxpayer and observes the tax preparation operations at the site (IRS 2014d).

BENEFITS TO PATRONS

The benefits of volunteer tax preparation programs extend beyond simply completing patrons' tax returns and giving them advice. Volunteer tax preparation services save the taxpayer money that would otherwise have to be paid to a for-profit tax preparer or for a self-preparation software program. This is of particular importance to the lower-income individuals served by VITA, many of whom qualify for an earned income credit (EIC), a tax program designed to give money back to low-income taxpayers. If a portion of the taxpayer's EIC is spent on tax preparation, the net effect of the program is reduced.

Patrons also benefit by receiving quality, professional tax preparation services in a nonintimidating environment. This is especially important for patrons who have difficulty speaking English, and many volunteer tax programs either specialize in working with ESL clients or have on-site interpreters to assist in the tax preparation process. The same is true of TCE and Tax-Aide sites, where volunteers are trained to work with older clients.

BENEFITS TO LIBRARIES

Volunteer tax preparation is not only beneficial to the clients receiving tax assistance. The libraries offering these services may benefit in many ways:

- Attracting new patrons
- Cross-promoting library collections and programs
- Increasing the library's visibility in the community
- Relieving the burden on library staff

Beyond the obvious altruistic reasons for offering tax preparation services, libraries can benefit by attracting new patrons. Along with promoting the tax preparation services to their specific clientele, libraries can use the tax preparation site as a venue to sign up new patrons for library cards. At the same time, librarians and library staff can cross-promote both related and unrelated collections and services to these new patrons. For example, librarians at a TCE site could promote related collections and services by constructing displays of retirement planning books and videos near the preparation site and displaying posters of upcoming financial planning programs. At a VITA site focusing on low-income families, librarians could offer children's programing during VITA hours to assist parents in need of childcare. When done correctly, cross-promotion at library volunteer tax preparation sites can help retain new patrons whose original intentions were to come to the library only for tax services.

At a time when both public and academic libraries often compete with other public organizations for resources, increasing a library's visibility among stakeholders can serve as a valuable tool for securing funding. Libraries can use their tax preparation programs as a way to generate publicity through their own press releases and promotions and through news outlets. Libraries can leverage this publicity to demonstrate their value beyond traditional collections and programs to members of the community otherwise not interested in library offerings.

Finally, library staff members benefit by not having to deal with patrons' tax questions. Of course, librarians will still want to assist patrons with basic directional questions about finding tax forms on the Internet. But having a tax preparation site at the library gives staff the easy task of directing tax questions to the volunteer preparers. And, as detailed in the section on site setup, if the tax preparation site is located in an area clearly visible and easily accessible to patrons, librarians may avoid tax questions altogether.

OPTIONS FOR OFFERING A VITA OR TCE SITE

If a library wishes to offer tax preparation services, it may either set up its own VITA or TCE site or partner with an organization that offers VITA or TCE programs. When setting up a VITA or TCE site, the hosting library must follow several IRS requirements. A library-run site also requires a great deal of work from the library staff. The first step in the process is for the library to request approval from the IRS to host the site. If and when the IRS approves a site, it will provide a Site Identification Number and Electronic Filing Identification Number to the library (IRS 2014d).

Second, the library recruits individuals to serve as the site coordinator and tax preparers. The IRS allows the library to compensate the coordinator with a stipend. However, all tax preparers must volunteer their services to reduce their legal liability and to be protected under the Volunteer Protection Act of 1997 (IRS 2014f).

A third requirement is that the library must offer training opportunities to its volunteers. The IRS provides print and online training resources but no individual training classes. It is extremely helpful to both the volunteers and the tax preparation site if there is a knowledgeable individual available to assist volunteers in tax training, especially if volunteers have no formal education in taxation.

Next, the library must provide adequate computer equipment for the tax preparers to complete tax returns. Although the IRS provides funding through VITA and TCE grants to help cover costs of operating tax preparation sites (IRS 2014c, 2014h), libraries may need to cover the costs of equipment and supplies out of pocket.

Finally, the library administration must allow the IRS to review the tax preparation site as described above. If the administration has an ample supply of resources and a pool of willing volunteers, they may decide that organizing a volunteer tax site is the best option for their library. However, other librarians may find that all of these requirements make creating a VITA or TCE site an unfeasible option for their organization.

Many colleges and universities offer VITA sites. In addition, nonprofit organizations such as the United Way operate VITA and TCE sites (United Way of the Quad Cities Area 2015). If a library chooses to partner with an organization that offers VITA or TCE programs instead of organizing its own site, fewer steps are involved. Although the library still has to seek out a partner, this option allows the library to provide a much needed service to the community without taking on the burden of registering with the IRS and training volunteers. In return for the partnering organization providing the work, applying to the IRS to operate the site at the library, obtaining the proper Site Identification Number and Electronic Filing Identification Number, hiring and compensating the site coordinator, recruiting volunteers, and applying for VITA or TCE grants, the library provides space for the program and may help in promoting the services. The library's partner also ensures that the site coordinator is qualified to oversee the site and file returns, is responsible for any issues that come up, and is accountable to the IRS.

A library may also partner with another organization if it prefers to offer tax preparation services on a limited basis. Some organizations operate mobile tax preparation sites. With mobile sites, the partner will bring the site coordinator, volunteers, and equipment to the site for a few days during the tax season. The partner also obtains a Site Identification Number and Electronic Filing Identification Number to be used at all mobile sites rather than obtaining numbers for each site. This option is best for libraries that have patrons who would benefit from free tax preparation services but which are unable to designate space for such services on a regular basis.

KNOW YOUR PATRONS

To provide the best tax services possible, it is important for a library to understand the best options for its patrons. For a patron base consisting mostly of the elderly, a library may choose to offer a TCE or Tax-Aide site. If serving primarily low-income or foreign-language-speaking patrons, the library may prefer to host a VITA site. In addition, libraries must consider whether a tax preparation site may be of any assistance at all to its patrons. For example, as mentioned above, tax returns for nonresident aliens are considered out of scope for all VITA, TCE, and Tax-Aide sites. If the sites are unable to prepare the returns of its patrons, a library may not want to offer such services. If a library serves mostly an upper-income demographic, VITA's services may be of no use. Also, if a library has some patrons who would benefit from VITA or TCE tax preparation services but not enough patrons to warrant a full VITA or TCE site, the library may prefer to offer a mobile site for a few days during the tax season.

SITE SETUP

If a library partners with another organization to offer a VITA or TCE site, it is important to consider the location of the site within the library. Many libraries that partner with organizations to provide tax preparation services only provide space within the library for the site. It is important for a library to separate the site from normal library functions if possible. This is easily accomplished if the library uses an area separate from the main collection, such as a conference room or activity room. Providing the tax preparation services in a separate room will also allow for the privacy required by the IRS.

When providing tax forms to patrons, most libraries post notices that indicate library staff do not provide tax advice. This is especially important for a library that offers tax preparation services. The library should post notices that indicate library staff do not provide tax services and tax advice, and library staff should refer patrons to the partnering organization for tax advice.

SCHEDULING

One option for libraries offering tax preparation services is to have set hours each week. Another option is to offer services on a very limited basis, such as at one or two sessions throughout the entire tax season. A library must determine how often it would like to offer the services to its patrons, if taxpayers must schedule appointments, and whether the site will take walk-in appointments. Although the partner would handle the scheduled or walk-in appointments, the library should indicate its preference to the partner.

CONCLUSION

Regardless of the type of library, patrons, library staff, and the community as a whole have much to gain if a library provides volunteer tax preparation services. With all the IRS requirements, a library staff may find it daunting to create a site on their own. Therefore, libraries that want to offer these services may find that partnering with a college, university, or other nonprofit organization benefits all parties involved. As an added bonus, these collaborations between the library and organizing group may lead to new community partnerships.

REFERENCES

AARP Foundation. 2014. "About AARP Foundation Tax-Aide." http://www.aarp.org/money/taxes/info-2004/about_aarp_taxaide.html.

IRS. 2014a. "Form 13614-C: Intake/Interview & Quality Review Sheet." http://www.irs.gov/pub/irs-pdf/f13614c.pdf.

———. 2014b. "Form 13615: Volunteer Standards of Conduct Agreement—VITA/TCE Programs." http://www.irs.gov/pub/irs-pdf/f13615.pdf.

———. 2014c. "IRS VITA Grant Program." http://www.irs.gov/Individuals/IRS-VITA-Grant-Program.

———. 2014d. "Publication 1084: VITA/TCE IRS Volunteer Site Coordinator Handbook." http://www.irs.gov/pub/irs-pdf/p1084.pdf.

———. 2014e. "Publication 4491: VITA/TCE Training Guide." http://www.irs.gov/pub/irs-pdf/p4491.pdf.

———. 2014f. "Publication 4961: VITA/TCE Volunteer Standards of Conduct—Ethics Training." http://www.irs.gov/pub/irs-pdf/p4961.pdf.

———. 2014g. "Publication 5166: VITA & TCE Quality Site Requirements: Wage & Investment." http://www.irs.gov/pub/irs-pdf/p5166.pdf.

———. 2014h. "Tax Counseling for the Elderly." http://www.irs.gov/Individuals/Tax-Counseling-for-the-Elderly.

———. 2015. "Free Tax Preparation for Qualifying Taxpayers." http://www.irs.gov/Individuals/Free-Tax-Return-Preparation-for-You-by-Volunteers.

United Way of the Quad Cities Area. 2015. "Free Tax Preparation." http://www.unitedwayqc.org/resources/free-tax-preparation.

Index

About the Editor and Contributors

Frans Albarillo, assistant professor, is the librarian for business, economics, accounting, linguistics, and sociology at Brooklyn College, New York. He obtained his MLISc at the University of Hawai'i at Manoa. His professional and research interests include working with immigrant students, diversity, social science librarianship, and research designs used by practicing librarians. His business experience includes working at the career office in the Shidler College of Business at University of Hawai'i at Manoa, helping undergraduate, MBA, and PhD students engaged in internships and job searches to find information on local, national, and international companies.

Roland Barksdale-Hall, library director of the Mercer County Housing Authority's Quinby Street Resource Center Library, Sharon, Pennsylvania, wrote *Farrell* (Arcadia Publishing, 2012) and *African Americans in Mercer County* (Arcadia Publishing, 2009). He's a member of the Black Caucus of the American Library Association (BCALA) Services to Children and Families of African Descent. Roland has a master's in leadership and history from Duquesne University and a library science degree from the University of Pittsburgh. He's a national diversity speaker; faculty member in the Department of Africana Studies at Youngstown State University, Youngstown, Ohio; and recipient of the 2015 BCALA Leadership Award.

Jenny Brewer is the interim director of library services at Helen Hall Library in League City, Texas. She is a native of Houston, Texas, and a graduate of the University of Houston and the University of North Texas. Prior to becoming interim director, Brewer worked as Helen Hall's teen librarian, adult services librarian, and assistant city librarian. Her library career was preceded by ten years in home finance, and she has been surprised how much of her mortgage industry knowledge has remained relevant through the years.

Jeri Weinkrantz Cohen, head of teen and media services at the Patchogue-Medford Library in Patchogue, New York, obtained her MSLIS from the Palmer School of Long Island University. She belongs to the New York Library Association and the Suffolk County Library Association. Her writing has appeared in *VOYA*, *Young Adult Library Services*, and *Bringing the Arts into the Library* (ALA, 2014). She is vice president of the Suffolk County Library Association, was editor of the Suffolk County Library Association newsletter for five years, and served on the American Library Association's Amazing Audiobooks for Teens Committee.

Jacquelyn Daniel is reference librarian at the Atlanta University Center Robert W. Woodruff Library in Atlanta, Georgia. She is an alumna of Spelman College and holds a master's degree in library science from Atlanta University (now Clark Atlanta University). She has made presentations on mentoring (Association of College & Research Libraries) and financial literacy (National Conference of African American Librarians). Her professional interests lie in information literacy, faculty collaboration, and community outreach. Daniel is the president of her neighborhood organization, the West End Coalition Group.

Roslyn Donald is the supervising librarian for adult and teen services at Cupertino Library, part of the Santa Clara County Library District in California. In addition to her public library experience, Donald has worked as an ESL teacher in mainland China and Taiwan and as an analyst for Gale. Donald's achievements include winning a forty-thousand-dollar grant from the Certified Financial Planners Board for financial literacy workshops and starting the JobSeekers volunteer job-hunting assistance center. For more information, see her LinkedIn profile: http://www.linkedin.com/in/roslyndonald.

Marcia Dursi is the information literacy librarian for Marymount University in Arlington, Virginia. She is the liaison librarian to the School of Business Administration's bachelor of business administration programs, with specialties in accounting, business law, finance, hospitality management, international business, management, marketing and sports management, and the economics undergraduate program. Marcia is the liaison librarian to the master's in business administration program, the master's of science in health care management program, and the master's of art in human resource management program. She received her MSLIS from the Catholic University of America and MEd from George Mason University.

Karen Evans, instruction and reference public services librarian at Indiana State University in Terre Haute, Indiana, has a graduate degree in library and information science from Indiana University at Bloomington and a graduate degree in criminology and criminal justice from Indiana State University. Karen's membership includes the American Library Association and Indiana Library Federation. Her publications have appeared in *College & Research Libraries News*, *Indiana Libraries*, *Choice*, *Journal of Consumer Health on the Internet*, and *Reference Reviews*. She is the recipient of two Carnegie-Whitney Grants from the American Library Association.

Ashley E. Faulkner is an assistant professor and business librarian at Texas A&M University's West Campus Library in College Station, Texas. She graduated with both her MLIS and MBA from Kent State University, and her professional goals center around the meeting of these disciplines within the study, support, and instruction of information and financial literacy. She is a member of the American Library Association and therein the Association of College & Research Libraries, the Reference and User Services Association, and the Business Reference and Services Section, where she serves on the Education Committee.

Janene R. Finley, LLM, PhD, JD, CPA, is an associate professor of accounting at Augustana College, Rock Island, Illinois. She teaches taxation, business law, and accounting principles courses. Janene coordinates Augustana College's Volunteer Income Tax Assistance (VITA) program in conjunction with the United Way of the Quad Cities Area. She created the Income Tax Service Learning Community, in which Augustana College students participate in VITA and receive college credit for their work. Her research has appeared in such journals as the *Pittsburgh Tax Review*, *Seton Hall Legislative Journal*, and *Behavioral & Social Sciences Librarian*.

Wayne Finley, MBA, MSLIS, is the business librarian and associate professor at Northern Illinois University Libraries in DeKalb, Illinois. His research interests include the application of marketing and management theory in public and academic libraries. His research has appeared in journals such as *Journal of Business and Finance Librarianship*, *Behavioral & Social Sciences Librarian*, and *Journal of Accounting Education*. He also authored the chapter "The Art of Personal Selling: Techniques for Library Marketing," which appeared in *Marketing Your Library: Tips and Tools That Work* (McFarland, 2012).

Lisa Fraser, services implementation coordinator for the King County Library System in the state of Washington, has taught library courses in marketing and advocacy at the Information School of the University of Washington. She coedited *Time and Project Management Strategies for Librarians* (Scarecrow, 2013) and contributed to *The Frugal Librarian: Thriving in Tough Economic Times* (2011), *Preserving Local Writers, Genealogy, Photographs, Newspapers, and Related Materials* (Scarecrow, 2012), and *Writing After Retirement* (Rowman & Littlefield, 2014). She holds an MLIS from the University of Washington and a master's of international administration from the School for International Training in Vermont.

Shin Freedman has led collection development and acquisition services at Framingham State University (FSU) in Framingham, Massachusetts, since 2004. Freedman received her master's in library and information science from Simmons College in Boston and a master's in business administration from Bentley University in Waltham, Massassachusetts. During her tenure at Framingham State University as an academic librarian, she has taught research and information literacy and financial literacy courses for undergraduate and MBA students. Prior to FSU, she worked at Brown University Sciences and Medical Libraries in Rhode Island.

Joyce Garczynski is the communications and development librarian at Towson University in Towson, Maryland. In this role she teaches communication students about the research process, manages publicity for the library, and writes grants. She chairs the Association of College & Research Libraries' Communication Studies Committee and recently delivered a webinar about the committee's work to align their "Information Literacy Competency Standards for Journalism Students and Professionals" with the "Framework for Information Literacy for Higher Education." Joyce received her MLS from the University of Maryland in 2009 and holds a master's degree in communication research from the University of Pennsylvania.

Shana Gass is a research and instruction librarian and liaison to the College of Business and Economics at Towson University in Towson, Maryland. Previous positions include reference and instruction responsibilities at Wheaton College, Massachusetts, and administrative support at the MIT Libraries. A member of ALA/RUSA's Business Reference and Services Section (BRASS), she received an MSLS from Simmons College and an MS in social science from Towson and has presented on financial literacy programming, business research, and information literacy instruction.

Aliqae Geraci is the ILR research librarian and assessment coordinator at Cornell University in Ithaca, New York, where she provides research support in employment and labor relations. A former public librarian and labor union researcher, Geraci holds BA and MA degrees in labor studies, received her

MSLIS from Long Island University, and is the coauthor of *Grassroots Library Advocacy* (ALA Editions, 2012). She is active in American Library Association's Allied Professional Association's (ALA-APA) Standing Committee on the Salaries and Status of Library Workers as well as several local and national labor organizations.

Tanji N. Gibson is the business and economics librarian at the Atlanta University Center Robert W. Woodruff Library in Atlanta, Georgia. She holds an MLIS from Clark Atlanta University and an EdS from the University of West Georgia. She has made presentations on mentoring (Association of College & Research Libraries) and financial literacy (National Conference of African American Librarians). Gibson's research interests lie in faculty engagement, outreach, and collection assessment. She also has an interest in collaborating with distance learning faculty to increase positive learning outcomes for students in regard to information literacy.

Daniel Hickey is the assistant director of research and learning services for Cornell's Hospitality, Labor, and Management Library in Ithaca, New York. He did his graduate work at the University of Pittsburgh's School of Information Science. Daniel's public service–focused writing has appeared in *Reference and User Service Quarterly*, *Reference Reborn: Breathing New Life into Public Services Librarianship* (Libraries Unlimited, 2011), *Assessing Liaison Librarians: Documenting Impact for Positive Change* (ACRL, 2014), and *Advances in Library Administration & Organization: Staffing for the Future* (Emerald, 2015).

Sonnet Ireland is the head of government information, microforms, and analog media at the University of New Orleans Earl K. Long Library in New Orleans, Louisiana, and is also the liaison librarian for the College of Business Administration. She earned her MLIS from Texas Woman's University in 2008. She is active in the Louisiana Library Association, currently serving as the chair of the Academic Section, and has given numerous presentations on government resources. Ireland is a member of the 2010 class of ALA Emerging Leaders.

Melissa Jeter has been an adult reference librarian at the Heatherdowns Branch of the Toledo-Lucas County Public Library in Toledo, Ohio, since 2007. She holds a master of science degree in LIS from the University of Illinois. She conducts reference and hosts adult financial literacy classes for the library. Jeter was chosen an Emerging Leader by the American Library Association in 2008 and served as coordinator for the Northwest Chapter of the Ohio Library Council in 2012. Before working in libraries, she worked on housing issues at nonprofit agencies in Toledo.

Jennifer Wright Joe currently works at Western Kentucky University's Owensboro Campus, where she is the campus librarian. She received her MLS from Indiana University–Bloomington in 2010 and her MA in sociology from Western Kentucky University in 2011. Her research interests include community outreach, collection development, information literacy, and the integration of technology into libraries and library practices. She has recently been published in *Progressive Trends in Electronic Resource Management* (IGI Global, 2013) and the *Encyclopedia of Information Science and Technology*, 3rd edition (IGI Global, 2014).

Kit Keller is a librarian and consultant who was the project director in charge of developing national guidelines for library-based financial literacy education and for recommended best practices in this content area. She also served as the evaluator for the national Smart investing@your library grant program, administered jointly by the American Library Association and the FINRA Investor Education Foundation. She has a master's of library science and a master's of science in education and over twenty-five years' experience working in public, academic, and special libraries.

Joanne Kuster, an entrepreneur and journalist with expertise in consumer economics and personal finance, develops products and programs, speaks and writes for the Money Godmother blog, and wrote the award-winning *Stock Market Pie* (DynaMinds, 2014) and *Entrepreneur Extraordinaire* (DynaMinds, 2008). Launching her first business at the age of twenty-five, Joanne helps other entrepreneurs. She's a board member for Business Horizons and Iowa Jump$tart, brought Money Smart Week to Iowa, is on the Iowa State University Foundation's board of governors, is active in community organizations, and has been the U.S. Small Business Administration's Midwest Home-Based Business Advocate of the Year.

Kelly LaVoice is a business research librarian for Cornell's Hospitality, Labor, and Management Library in Ithaca, New York. LaVoice primarily serves the top-ranked School of Hotel Administration, providing research support, instruction, and outreach services. She received her MLIS from Rutgers University in 2013. During that time, she worked as an intern at the University of Pennsylvania's Lippincott Library, serving the Wharton School and Rutgers University's Kilmer Library. She is currently pursuing a master's of business administration degree from the Rutgers University School of Business.

Lisa G. Liu is a librarian at Saratoga Library, part of the Santa Clara County Library District (SCCLD) in California. As project manager of SCCLD's

Smart investing@your library grant from 2011 to 2013, Liu helped implement an online course on personal finance reference strategies and resources for SCCLD staff. Most recently, she was part of a design team sponsored by FINRA and ALA to develop self-paced courses on financial literacy resources and reference approaches (http://smartinvesting.ala.org). Liu is interested in the central role libraries have in lifelong learning for all members of a community.

Cindy Mediavilla is a part-time library programs consultant for the California State Library and teaches part-time for the University of California, Los Angeles (UCLA), Department of Information Studies. She's a freelance consultant and has evaluated several grant-funded programs, including Start Here: Your Road to Smart and Savvy Finance for San Diego Public Library and Los Angeles Public Library's Student Zones after-school homework program and Innovation Leadership Program. Cindy's book, *Creating the Full-Service Homework Center in Your Library* (ALA, 2001), is considered the leading work on the topic. Her MLS and PhD are from UCLA.

Kate Moody is access services librarian at Ripon College in Ripon, Wisconsin, where she regularly teaches a variety of library classes, including makerspace, technology, and library instruction classes. She received her MLS from Indiana University and bachelor's degree from Pennsylvania State University. She is a member of the Wisconsin Library Association. She has a strong interest in personal finance and digital technology. She has recently developed and taught MoneyFitness, a workshop she designed to aid undergraduate students in learning personal financial management skills appropriate to their specific needs.

Maryann Mori has presented at several national library conferences and has been published numerous times. Her work has been included in ALA books, *Social Networking Communities and E-Dating Services* (IGI, 2008), *Serving Teen Parents: From Literacy to Life Skills* (Libraries Unlimited, 2011), and *Job Stress and the Librarian* (McFarland, 2014). Her library experience includes reference, children's, and teen services as well as being a director. Mori is currently a consultant for Iowa Library Services and serves on the Money Smart Week committee for Central Iowa. She completed her MSLIS at the University of Illinois in 2006.

Lauren Reiter, a business liaison librarian at Penn State University Libraries, earned her MLIS from the University of Pittsburgh. She is also a faculty advisor for the Student Financial Education Center and coordinator for library financial literacy programming. Lauren's memberships include the Business Reference and Services Section, American Library Association.

Her work has appeared in the *Journal of Business and Finance Librarianship*, and she has made presentations at the Conference for Entrepreneurial Librarians, the Academic Business Library Directors annual meeting, and the Pennsylvania Library Association annual conference.

Mary Jo Ryan is the communications coordinator for the Nebraska Library Commission. She spent the past twenty-eight years coordinating statewide library publicity efforts and marketing campaigns, including communication for a financial education program funded by a Smart investing@your library grant from the FINRA Investor Education Foundation and American Library Association. Combining an undergraduate degree in English and journalism and a master's degree in adult education and public administration with many years of experience in planning, education, and marketing has led to a career of training librarians to approach marketing from a planning and problem-solving perspective.

Carol Smallwood received an MLS from Western Michigan University and an MA in history from Eastern Michigan University. *Librarians as Community Partners: An Outreach Handbook* and *Bringing the Arts into the Library* are two of her ALA anthologies. Other anthologies include *Creative Management of Small Public Libraries in the 21st Century* (Rowman & Littlefield, 2015), *Library Youth Outreach* (coeditor; McFarland, 2014), *Marketing Your Library* (McFarland, 2012), and *Google for Patron Library Use* (Rowman & Littlefield, 2015). Her library experience includes school, public, academic, and special libraries as well as administration and library systems consultation.

Julie Todaro, 2016–2017 president-elect of the American Library Association, is dean of library services at Austin Community College in Austin, Texas. She has over thirty-five years of experience in all types of libraries and is a speaker and consultant in leadership and management. Todaro's been president of the Association of College & Research Libraries and of the Texas Library Association. She's authored many articles as well as *Mentoring A to Z* (ALA, 2015) and *Library Management for the Digital Age: A New Paradigm* (Rowman & Littlefield, 2014). Todaro received her doctorate of library services from Columbia University and master's of library information science from the University of Texas at Austin.

Jennifer Townes is the unit head for information and research services at the Atlanta University Center Robert W. Woodruff Library in Atlanta, Georgia. She holds an MSLS from the University of North Carolina at Chapel Hill. She has presented on robotic telepresence (Association of College and Research Library) and information literacy (North Carolina Library Association). Townes's research interests lie in information literacy, assessment, and faculty collaboration. She developed an interest in community outreach in academic libraries while at the Atlanta University Center and has honed her expertise in the field ever since.

Linda Burkey Wade is an elected trustee of the Brown County Public Library in Mount Sterling, Illinois, and obtained her MLIS from Dominican University. Wade's writing is in *Pre- and Post- Retirement Tips for Librarians* (ALA, 2011), *Jump-Start Your Career as a Digital Librarian* (ALA Neal-Schuman, 2012), and *Time and Project Management Strategies for Librarians* (Scarecrow, 2013) and coedited *Job Stress and the Librarian* (McFarland, 2013). She's the head of digitization at the Western Illinois University Libraries in Macomb, Illinois, and received the 2010 Distinguished Service Award for innovation and dedication and the 2012 Community Service Award.

Made in the USA
San Bernardino, CA
15 February 2017